AF600160

Liberating Revolution

SUNY series in New Political Science

Bradley J. Macdonald, editor

Liberating Revolution

Emancipating Radical Change from the State

NATHAN ECKSTRAND

Published by State University of New York Press, Albany

Printed in the United States of America

For information, contact State University of New York Press, Albany, NY
www.sunypress.edu

Library of Congress Cataloging-in-Publication Data

Name: Eckstrand, Nathan, author.
Title: Liberating revolution : emancipating radical change from the state / Nathan Eckstrand.
Description: Albany : State University of New York Press, [2022] | Series: SUNY series in New Political Science | Includes bibliographical references and index.
Identifiers: ISBN 9781438486772 (hardcover : alk. paper) | ISBN 9781438486789 (ebook)
Further information is available at the Library of Congress.

10 9 8 7 6 5 4 3 2 1

Contents

Acknowledgments

This book began during a walk I took with my family shortly after watching coverage of the Arab Spring. Having recently completed my comprehensive exams, I needed a topic for my dissertation. Reflecting on events halfway around the world and the potential inability of political theories to explain them began the investigation contained in these pages. A decade later, as I survey the outcome of the project, I am humbled by the significant support I received from so many.

First among those I wish to thank are my family and dissertation advisors. I feel honored to have so many insightful, loving individuals I can turn to for help. It was during a conversation over coffee with my mother, Irene Eckstrand, that I first came across systems theory, the philosophy that became integral to my own worldview. She later introduced me to complex systems researchers who helped me to understand how systems theory approaches questions of being, relation, and agency. As my project expanded into the mathematics of systems, I turned to my father, Stephen Eckstrand, a trained physicist whose notes and thoughtful reasoning helped me reconstruct the development of systems theory. My sisters, Kristen and Laurel Eckstrand, have medical training that helped me to see applications of my project in the realms of psychiatry and animal ecosystems. And throughout it all they have been there with sage advice, love, care, and the occasional Jackbox game.

My dissertation advisors embody the academic professionalism I aspire to have. That they would donate so much of their time to my project's growth is much appreciated. In my desire to articulate a novel contribution to the field of radical politics I strayed into unusual territory for a philosopher, but they were supportive of my decisions as long as I maintained the appropriate critical approach that philosophy requires. They each taught me much about how to put philosophies into dialogue with each other, articulate my own position clearly, and keep focused on the larger project even as I delve into the details. To Fred Evans, Daniel Selcer, George Yancy, and James Bernauer, thanks for your feedback and support. Fred deserves special mention, for he not only stewarded this project from the beginning but has followed my activities closely since I defended, providing excellent advice and friendship at every point along the way.

The bulk of this book—or, more specifically, the revisions I made to my dissertation for this book—were written while I was teaching in China. It was a challenging time in my life, and there was one group I could always turn to for support. The Hallraisers (Ben and Nikki Houchen, Olivia Anderson, Tony Chambers, Margarita and Nick Santana, Dana Loewen, Lee and Jon Watts, Erin and Adam Wilson, Jason Fisher, and more) kept me company, helped me stay in shape, and organized amazing trips. If we ever do a KTV night again, expect a round of drinks and a rendition of "We Are the Champions" on me. Others from Sias University—including Jeremy DeLong, Michael Leibold, Ahneka Valdois, Arianna Valdois, Jeffrey Bougeois, Barbara Leiving, Brian Swanson, and Greg Hotrum—deserve thanks also.

From the time I began work on my dissertation until this point, I worked at multiple schools and taught many classes. I wish to thank James Snyder, Tibor Solymosi, David Leichter, Eugene Rice, Carl Miller, and the rest of the philosophy departments at Mercyhurst University in Erie, Pennsylvania, Marian University in Fond Du Lac, Wisconsin, and Fort Hays State University in Hays, Kansas. Even though my project was outside many of your specialties, you always backed my work. My students at these schools also deserve my thanks. Your engagement with philosophy and persistence inspired me to keep teaching and writing.

My work at the *Blog of the APA* has been rewarding throughout the book writing process. Engaging with scholars from throughout the field kept me convinced that I would value the book writing process. I appreciate the support I received from Lewis Powell, Skye Cleary, Sabrina MisirHiralall, David Johnson, Lewis Gordon, Adriel Trott, Jeremy Cushing, Amy Ferrer, Mike Morris, Michaela Maxwell, Emily Rose Ogland, Heidi Schmidt, and Ashley Bohrer.

Other notable individuals and groups who deserve thanks include the extended Eckstrand and Guthrie clans, Gabriel Rockhill and the Critical Theory Workshop, my Ghanaian students, the Lake Lemon group from Earlham College, and Elyse Purcell.

1

Who's Afraid of Revolution?

The State or Revolution: Separating False Friends

Revolution begins trivially yet ends with great consequence. A solitary suicide,[1] perhaps the right word in the right place,[2] wakes the masses from their slumber. Despair is replaced with a hope for a better world characterized by freedom, justice, and equality, and the isolated and depoliticized find a voice among people determined to act rather than be acted upon. A thousand conversations held in a thousand sites converge into a manifesto that inspires a thousand actions. The groundswell of discontent creates the potential for a new and better world, but can degrade into a nightmare. Either way, it produces a shift to which militants, counterrevolutionaries, and bystanders respond. "Join the revolution and fight for your freedom," one side says. "Oppose it for your own safety," says the other. "But consider carefully," say both, "for a wrong decision could be deadly." Revolution is a tantalizing potential for the oppressed, a perpetual danger for the elites, and, save for the brief moments when it captures center stage, it hovers constantly at the margins of society.

Hope for transformation, breaking down the status quo, and building a new society from the ground up are the sentiments at the barricades of revolution. Throughout the 2010s, protestors for radical change in society and politics declared their commitment to "loving engagement,"[3] "solidarity amongst the protesters,"[4] "rebuilding society,"[5] and respecting the "voice of the people."[6] They made militant demands for "freedom,"[7] an end to "dictatorship,"[8] "consent,"[9] and the obstruction of the "one percent."[10] As revolutionary movements appeared across the globe, the institutions and individuals they targeted clung tightly to their traditions, lamenting the injustice of their circumstances and decrying the vitriol of the protestors. Elites condemned the "bad actors"[11] and speculated about what sinister reasons motivated the demonstrators to "vilify . . . success."[12]

Justified or not, these movements raise a question: How does revolution transform the status quo? What transpired in Tarhir, Zucotti, Ferguson, Moscow, Cape Town, Hong Kong,[13] Paris,[14] and more—before our very eyes, yet still unseen—to bring about the greatest protests of a generation? Why did the "shot heard round the world"[15] at Lexington and Concord catalyze a revolution when all the previously fired bullets did not? How is it that the deaths of several hundred protestors in Tehran became more significant to the Iranian people than the thousands killed in the decades leading up to Black Friday?

This book arises from my realization that no theory conceives of revolution without relying on the state, broadly defined as a consistent arrangement of concepts, subjects, objects, and forces. Concepts of revolution have always been centered around concepts of the state, while in political theory the attempt to understand the state has always preceded the attempt to comprehend revolution. Using concepts, subjects, objects, and forces that describe the state to define revolution renders the concept of revolution a product of the state. Until revolution is conceptually freed from that to which it is opposed, our attempts to use it to bring about transformative change will only reproduce the constraints of power under the guise of removing them. My goal is to separate revolution from the state—to study, analyze, and dissect radical change in order to understand its possibilities, its dangers, and its ability to inform our collective struggles.

Theories of revolution provide some guidance, but we do not yet have one that describes all revolutions. For example, the usual theories of revolution cannot satisfactorily explain the events of 2011. The protestors were not traditional proletarians—many could even be classified as bourgeoise—nor did they aspire to seize the means of production. They did not desire a social contract that would lead them out of their natural state and establish a sovereign. Their target was not a repressive regime of signs, concepts, and structures; their goal not the deconstruction of meaning for the freedom of indeterminacy. To this day, most analyses of the events focus on the motivations and strategies of the protestors.

A model that explains the what, why, and how of revolution remains a mystery. For every revolution in which a particular theory has currency there is another revolution that calls that same theory into question. Jeff

Goodwin and Theda Skocpol point out that the conventional causes for the Cuban and Vietnamese revolutions—the suffering produced by imperialism and the capitalist exploitation of resources—fail to explain why other countries experiencing similar or worse conditions did not revolt. They conclude "one need merely raise these questions in order to see that the 'misery breeds revolt' hypothesis does not explain very much."[16] Alexander Anievas and Kerem Nişancıoğlu say that not only have there been few studies theoretically engaging revolutions, but that the field of international relations has "largely bracketed out revolutions from their conceptions of international politics."[17] In his historiography of the French Revolution, François Furet vigorously denies that revolutionary events were primarily motivated by successive attempts to embody the "people's will." Analyzing only how the ruling classes upheld or betrayed the legitimate interests of the common man ignores how revolution itself became its own telos. According to Furet:

> That rationalization of the political dynamic of the French Revolution has one major flaw, for in reifying revolutionary symbolism and in reducing political motivation to social concerns, it makes "normal" and obliterates what calls for explanation: the fact that Revolution placed that symbolic system at the centre of political action. And that it was that system rather than class interest, which, for a time at least, was decisive in the struggle for power.[18]

As Hannah Arendt notes, those reading the American Revolution as the product of social concerns and new technologies ignore the almost exclusive focus of the revolutionaries on the proper form of government.[19] Theories of revolution constantly struggle to find consistency in the number and variety of revolutionary events. They apply concepts developed by early modern political philosophers to communist revolutions, or read gender and racial uprisings through the lens of the dialectic. Their inability to unlock the state and revolution concurrently with a foundation that explains both has resulted in frustration. But as long as we hold that the state and revolution are intrinsically connected, we cannot abandon standard revolutionary theories without forfeiting the corresponding models of the states these theories are drawn from. If we do not want political thought to collapse into contradiction and inconsistency, we must question whether a theory of revolution must rest upon a theory of the state. Perhaps a more fruitful avenue for exploration is to examine revolution from the perspective of revolution, so as to let revolution speak. The point of this project is to explore this possibility, and to see what utility it may offer.

Conventional theories of revolution are grounded in a specific understanding of the state. When the state collapses, revolution arises parasitically, using what it can from the state's framework for its own existence. The state itself disappears, but its cadaver remains, animated by a revolutionary spirit until a new state forms to replace it. The revolutionary model described in Hobbes's *Leviathan* is simply the misuse of the structures with which a proper state is composed. To desire a Grecian or Roman democracy is as "the biting of a mad Dogge" and "wanteth nothing more than a strong monarch . . . [yet who] when they have him, they abhorre,"[20] while opposing the sovereign in an organized fashion is to "set up a *Supremacy* against the *Sovereignty*" that afflicts the commonwealth with inconsistent commands.[21] Hobbes argues any violation of sovereign power—including revolution—is an intolerable appropriation of the state. Likewise, Marx's communist revolution consists of "the violent overthrow of the bourgeoisie"[22] and the "conquest of political power by the proletariat."[23] Reforms of extant institutions like private property, the power of the nation-state, and labor are only possible because the proletariat has acquired a new status as a "ruling class" in control of the same "conditions of production"[24] the bourgeoisie once managed. Marx's communist revolution is, by this account, an exchange of leadership. The recognition of this danger leads Michael Hardt and Antonio Negri to say the use of nationalism by activists is a "perverse trick" that offers up the revolution, "hands and feet bound, to the new bourgeoisie."[25] Foucault also recognizes this danger when, in his debate with Maoists, he states that "the forms of state apparatus which [revolutionaries] inherit from the bourgeois apparatus cannot in any way serve as a model for the new forms of organization," as they carry a danger of repeating "the domination of the bourgeoisie."[26] In sum, revolutions act in political models like surgical operations. The state is broken apart, modified, and sewn back together. The result is an alteration of what was, but every vital part of the model remains.

These conceptions of revolution misrepresent what revolution is capable of. If revolution is drawn from the state, then it has meaning only in reference to the state, and its scope is limited by the state. A government may be overthrown, or a set of laws or policies changed, but a state will persist if fidelity to a certain perspective or set of practices remains. Without a change in its foundation, the state will be reconstituted along similar lines over and over despite uprisings that put different people in control. Howard Zinn's work on the Founding Fathers shows how the American Revolution, successful in defeating the British government, yet maintained the legitimacy of "a government to protect [the rich's] property" in which "rebellions could be controlled."[27] Economic and social arrangements such as agricultural wage labor and slavery were outside the purview of the American Revolution. The Founding Fathers intended for the socioeconomic order of the colonies to persist throughout the revolution.

The co-option of the American Revolution is an example of how concepts, forces, and systems pulled from the state can reproduce oppression through successive governments. Believing that something must persist throughout a revolution—for example, a socioeconomic system or a concept of human nature—hides the creative potential of revolution and replicates the same order. We learn to see the end of a revolution as merely an altered version of the state that was overthrown. The figure of the sovereign reappears (perhaps with a little less power and the crown on another's head), or production resumes with the workers in control. In either case, the oppressive foundation remains. Subjugating revolution to rules, ends, or concepts drawn from a state is to misunderstand the power of revolution, which is to rewrite the state from top to bottom so that nothing necessarily persists. To say otherwise is to see revolution as part of what is universal and eternal, as a function of the conceptual system that determines our world rather than as an opening to radically new possibilities. It is to treat revolution as though it were a tool wielded by an empowered sovereign and not a potential open to the disenfranchised many. It is, in short, to turn revolution into the state.

If we are to understand revolution, we must learn concepts particular to it, not ideas that force it into a predetermined or circumscribed shape. Revolution's radicality, fecundity, and creativity call for a particular thematization. To take the topic of revolutions seriously means articulating a changing, productive, destabilizing force that resists incorporation into any prescriptive framework. The theoretical and social importance of this analysis comes from its ability to comprehend the agency that revolutions impart to the world. This agency is nonsubjectified as it is the product of the forces and processes that arise within revolution, and rather than being pure stems from the particular manner in which each state is organized. A new conception of revolution framed in this way will reveal new potentials for revolutionaries in both theory and practice.

The Dangers of Misusing a Revolution

Revolution, as a potential remedy to systems of exploitation and domination, lends itself to utopian visions of future societies. And yet to treat revolution as panacea is dangerous. It leads to flowery, romantic images of revolutions as festive,[28] omnipresent,[29] superhuman,[30] and immortal[31]—as though revolution is a one-stop shop for a picture-perfect life. Revolution's job is not to produce utopia, for problems and issues will inevitably arise within the new states that revolution creates. The aftermaths of the French and Cuban revolutions show how revolutionary zeal can distract one from the vital work building a new society demands.[32] The Arab Spring's success in overthrowing tyrants and Occupy's victory in casting a harsh light on systems of inequality triggered new struggles against these forces. Utopian visions can manifest themselves through an obsession on previous triumphs and a desire to recreate the spirit of the past rather than act in the here and now—a trait Wendy Brown calls "left melancholy."[33] As Rosalyn Deutsche notes, following the 2003 invasion of Iraq, leftist protestors idolized the anti-war campaigns of the 1960s and 1970s to the point of foreclosing "possibilities of political change in the present."[34] For its message to successfully pass from the streets into the homes and institutions of society, revolution must follow an arduous process of organization, demonstration, and advocacy.

Treating all revolutions as a priori evil is also flawed. By ignoring legitimate grievances and portraying protestors as "growing mobs" engaging in "dangerous . . . class warfare"[35] the empowered can isolate revolutions from people sympathetic with their goals. Those who hate revolution equate it with pandemonium, violence, and destruction, ignoring revolution's ability to address serious issues. States embody order and stability, despite the fact that they are responsible for more pandemonium, violence, and destruction than any revolution has caused. Cuban and Russian revolutionaries garnered much support from their violent attacks upon the state while killing no more than several thousand enemy soldiers, while the nationalist fury of World War I and imperialist hunger of Vietnam together led to the deaths of at least eighteen million and the decimation of the continents hosting them.[36] Revolutions are dangerous, but the violence and destruction associated with them does not necessarily inhibit, and in some cases advances, their positive goals. Viewing revolution as destructive or as a cure-all does not reduce revolutions to the state, but also does not provide it a rigorous philosophical articulation. As panacea or poison, revolution is oversimplified and its powers distorted. Calls for revolution and protestations against it, when poorly formulated, resemble romantic tales devoid of intellectual understanding.

Serious consequences come from circumscribing or oversimplifying the concept of revolution. Establishing a new state that reflects the old stifles revolutionary sentiment and exacerbates hostilities, as happened in the French Revolution when new rulers responded to the revolution's demands with another monarchical system. The numerous smaller rebellions that compose the French Revolution happened because attempts to return to a feudal system failed.[37] Even if revolutionary passion isn't further inflamed, assuming the return of a specific state can generate a brutal program of state formation, as happened in post-revolution Russia. The transition to communism theorized by Lenin begins with armed workers replacing capitalists and bureaucrats, but posits that many of the former state mechanisms should be available to the workers for the purpose of controlling society, labor, and consumption.[38] Taylorism, the study of how management can optimize the productive capacity of a workplace, was imported wholesale from the United States into Lenin's Soviet Union. Using Taylorist maxims of scientific management like "The work of every workman [must be] fully planned out by the management at least one day in advance," "Maximum output, in place of restricted output," and "The development of each man to his greatest efficiency and prosperity,"[39] the Soviets (with Lenin's blessing) organized their factories and workers using the same techniques, practices, and means of production as the capitalists they opposed.[40] Lenin's opposition to Taylorism was conditional; when it was attached to the capitalist system it stood for "man's enslavement by the machine,"[41] but when organized by the Soviets it was "a necessary feature of [the] state."[42] The Soviet appropriation of Taylorism is a prime example of how elements of a prior state remain after a revolution, as Soviets only altered, but did not abolish, the factory.[43] Lenin's theory forms the basis of Stalin's post-revolutionary program, which takes as dogma that the state will only wither away if violence and state power intensify for the purpose of crushing the "dying classes."[44] By using a theory that prescribes vicious actions as necessary to reach the post-revolutionary world, Stalin's mass executions,[45] his brutal Gulag archipelago,[46] and his treatment of traitors and capitalists "with an iron hand"[47] became affirmations of success.

Analyzing revolution as internal to a state has serious implications for philosophy, as it invests revolution with necessity or a shape that restricts what revolution can achieve. Karl Marx's revolution is immanent to a specific material world and because of this follows a path to actualize a communist society. This interpretation is not speculative, but is a *real* movement that "results from the premises now in existence."[48] The new state is drawn from the old; revolution only acts as the intermediary, with its beginning, middle, and end already decided. Hannah Arendt, too, sees revolutions as immanent, but her revolutions are intrinsic to the world formed when people come together in a community. Revolutions result from action that "can be accomplished only by some joint effort"[49] and have as their end "the foundation of freedom."[50] Any revolution that alters the premise of human plurality obliterates the phenomenon that produces it. Revolution's purpose is determined by the world from which it comes. This in turn narrows what counts as a revolution, a fact demonstrated by Arendt's unwillingness to embrace the Haitian Revolution and anti-colonial movements in general. Her revolution requires citizens to forget narratives of violence that cannot be embraced by everyone. Since it is hard to develop a common narrative between slave and master, she ignores harms endured by oppressed minorities. Jennifer Gaffney says a better concept of citizenship "seems to depend on developing a new and more expansive notion of homecoming that makes room in the space of politics, not just for citizens, but also for the ghosts of the past that continue to haunt the modern political arena."[51] For Marx and Arendt, concepts of the state—conceived of here as a definite and immanent world—drive revolution, plotting its course and all the stops along the way. Revolution is only along for the ride.

What is needed in revolutionary theory is a model of exceptionality, inasmuch as revolution should be contrasted with the rule of law sponsored by the state. If the state always indicates an order and circumscribes change, then to theorize what is apart from it requires understanding the chaotic and disordered. Revolution must uncover what happens when the rules of the state cease to function. Understanding change as a difference between two stable forms or as movement governed by laws, forces, or predictable cycles must be replaced by a concept of unconditioned change whereby any limits to change can themselves be changed. Change must be an agent or a motive, not a result of interacting forces and beings. Several fields have formulated models of how change operates when a central buttress of traditional systems is removed. Set theory demonstrates how systems fall into paradox without axioms that define what is part of a set.[52] Chaos theory questions whether systems can predict the future without comprehending the present and studies the vastly different outcomes that can result from minor changes.[53] In other words, the utility of traditional systems is limited by their assumptions and the available data, leading contemporary theorists to study how manipulating assumptions or data alters how a system functions. Yet these new studies do not free change, but only swap one set of laws, forces, and predictable cycles for another. They provide a view of how change operates under specific conditions, not of change as a motive. A study of exceptionality must focus on understanding change without reintroducing limits. In philosophical terms, it is necessary to find the borders of fields like ontology and metaphysics, where states begin and end. This is different from seeking where one ontology replaces another or where one metaphysical system becomes another, as such exchanges happen only within the confines of another state. We must seek the frontier of all states and systems, for only at this point can we contemplate a truly independent revolution.

Modeling Revolution 1: Deviating from the Norm

If we can encounter revolution without the state and without depicting revolution as universally good or evil, what concept of it appears? What are the potential and dangers of revolution? What relation can it have to the state? The answers require a bipartite model that sees revolution from several angles, relating it to the state without reducing it the state. I call this model Dynamic Anarchism: "dynamic" to emphasize that the model does not refer to a constant situation—a status quo—but to movement and creation, and "anarchism" because the model purposefully avoids dependence upon the state.

To separate revolution from the state implies several things:

- Revolution has no definitive arrangement, design, or organization.
- Revolution cannot be anticipated (no one can know of its coming).
- Revolution cannot be determined (it is impossible to chart its path or manufacture its end).

Revolution is an *anomaly* in that it is entirely apart from the state, exempt from the status quo, and a deviation from the natural order. The state's supposed consistency and ubiquity is inapplicable to revolution, for within a revolution the characteristics of the state we reflexively assume in our day-to-day lives move into a state of flux. Even to describe revolutions as pure potentiality, contingency, or creativity is inadequate, as each carries a functional relationship to its opposite—potentiality to actuality, contingency to necessity, creativity to constancy—and in doing so brings with it an element of normalcy. Revolution abstracts itself from the oppositional terms potentiality/actuality, contingency/necessity, and creativity/constancy. To the degree that these characteristics are applicable to revolution, they must have a meaning different than the one they have in relation to the state. The exceptionality of revolution necessitates that even the category of Being cannot be applied to revolution. Since what counts as a Being is determined by the state, inasmuch as revolution escapes the state, its ontology is unknowable. If we are to grasp revolution as more than a function of a political system, we must hold that *no* codes (e.g., revolution reverts back to the state of nature), *no* purposes (e.g., revolution overthrows the elites of the dominant class), and *no* methods (e.g., revolution undermines established meanings) belong to it.

As anomaly, revolution has three primary characteristics. First, because revolution cannot be arranged, it is *incommensurable*—it does not fit with what is around it, temporally, spatially, or otherwise. No common measure exists between it and the state, and the state provides no tools with which to build one. There is no definite where, no exact when, no specific what to revolution, yet its very absence is its where, when, and what. From the perspective of the state, its precise spatial, temporal, and descriptive coordinates are *somewhere*, *somewhen*, and *something*. Its presence is its inarticulability, its incapability of being delineated. The state cannot structure, fix, or organize revolution, and any attempt to do so further inflames revolution or extinguishes it entirely. It is impossible for the state to be the vanguard of revolution, for it is the lack of the state, the indeterminacy of revolution's where, when, and what, that marks it.

Second, because revolution cannot be anticipated, it is *unpredictable*. It follows no determinate path, no causal or dialectical chain, that tells us to expect its arrival or permits us to plot a course to the other side. Because it does not behave according to the laws of the nonrevolutionary world, its appearance is erratic and its effects are unknowable in advance. Conditions that brought about a revolution at one place and time will not necessarily do so again, nor does producing another revolution guarantee the same outcome. Strategies and tactics used to understand or anticipate events in the state are destined to fail in comprehending revolution, for the unpredictability of revolution applies not just to its presentation but to its comprehensibility.

Finally, because revolution cannot be determined, it is *indiscernible*. Our very attempt to chart a path for it is an attempt to control it. Whatever understanding of revolution comes out of this project cannot reduce it to a handful of determinate steps or conceptualize it in such a way that its anomalistic character is erased. Revolution resists all attempts to synthesize it with the world we encounter, so it is impossible to be truly faithful to revolution. Fidelity requires being able to see some essence or promise within revolution that compels one to action. Similarly, developing a program for revolution implies the ability to chart a path between it and the state. Yet within the anomaly of revolution no such path or promise exists. The fidelity that is often claimed by revolutionaries is more accurately a fidelity to the appearance of revolution in the state. Although revolution must be held apart from the state to be truly revolutionary, it must be able to be made manifest for revolution's possibilities to come to fruition.

It is important to note that revolution does not form a binary opposition to the state. This preserves revolution's independence insofar as binaries carry a logic and an order from which revolution must exempt itself. Jacques Derrida describes this well, saying, "An opposition of metaphysical concepts (e.g., speech/writing, presence/absence, etc.) is never the confrontation of two terms, but a hierarchy and order of subordination."[54] Signs, as Derrida demonstrates, do not have intrinsic meaning, nor do they receive it by allusion to an external referent. They gain their meaning through the play of differences between them and the signs surrounding them[55]—especially those with which they share a direct opposition.[56] However, this logic cannot apply to revolution, for unlike the hierarchical oppositions and networks of significations Derrida describes, revolution is not encountered on the same strata as the state. The relationship between revolution and the state is one of exception, not opposition. Revolution is beyond the state, but not necessarily against the state; it is nonstate without being anti-state. Were the latter true, the path of revolution would be easier to chart, because revolution would consist of a contradiction to the state. Revolution's coordinates would be *nowhere*, *nowhen*, and *nothing* rather *somewhere*, *somewhen*, and *something*. If it were anti-state, revolution would be the opposite of what is counted and measured within the state.

To avoid a dualism between the state and revolution, and the host of problems that would accompany such a division, it must be the case that the two do not have a stable, consistent relationship. Revolution cannot be in relationship to the state, even as a negation of the state, because its nature as exception extracts it from any bond; instead, their association is unclear, hazy, and ambiguous. Revolution appears to move away from the state in an endless number of directions, with no one direction being definitive. The purpose of revolution lacks definition, because there are many possible ends without any particular one being more authentic. Because revolution removes itself from the logic of the state, it should be understood as lacking any definitive label or designation. The anomaly of revolution can be seen from the state only obliquely and indirectly.

Modeling Revolution 2: Changing the Changes in the World

The definition of revolution must include a discussion of revolution as it is encountered in the state. How is it that revolution is able to affect the state, causing changes that are rightly celebrated—or justly condemned—from the USA to China? Defining revolution as anomaly captures its separation from the state, but it also appears in the world. In doing so revolution and the state become associated, though the connection is not one of mechanistic causality or teleological determination. Rather, revolution appears in the state as a *catalytic change*, a change that changes the changes within the world. Every variation of the state describes a range of means by which change is introduced in the world. Thomas Hobbes delineates a series of affects that alter both the moods of individuals and the orderliness of states. Michel Foucault describes how alterations in the power relations that create subjects lead to new practices for tracking mental health or discussing sexual behavior. The result of naming such changes is that the state is able to "reestablish ideologies of command and authority"[57] by hiding the possibility for other changes. It sets up a "transcendent power"[58] that colonizes the "plane of immanence."[59]

As a catalytic change, revolution undoes and redoes changes by modifying or removing them and in the process replacing them with others. It speeds up and slows down processes in the state, dissolving the old and producing new mechanisms for change. It restructures not just the things in the state but the state itself. Revolution is not just an intensification of existing forces or the quickening of the rate at which society's possibilities are produced, for the changes of revolution are qualitatively different from the changes of the state. To say otherwise ignores the radical creativity of revolution.

Some of the traits unattributable to revolution (such as establishment of a legitimate sovereign) may appear to be true of revolution when seen from the perspective of the state. In applying itself to extant forces and values, revolution seems to operate with a program. Nevertheless, revolution is not expressing a determinate character when it acts as catalytic change. Rather, it is applying its destruction and creativity to the status quo. One way to conceive of this incursion of revolution into the state is to think of it as undoing the specific "world horizon" that is furnished to us by a state. According to Merleau-Ponty, a world horizon is a context or unity in which novel phenomena appear. This "horizon of all horizons"[60] is open, incomplete, and allows for many different appearances; at the same time, however, it emphasizes convergence instead of radical difference and sees all potential changes as latent possibilities within the horizon itself. Revolution does not operate with a world horizon itself, but is able, from the perspective of the state, to completely rewrite and add on to any extant world horizon. If the rewritten world horizon spreads enough that it becomes widely accepted as the norm, it will ultimately become a new state to replace the old. As catalytic change, revolution associates with the state, is of the state, but is not subjugated to the state. It maintains its independence and irreducible novelty.

This ultimately leads to a possibly contentious claim, but one supported by my analysis, which is that revolution can create ex nihilo. To grasp revolution's potential implies that revolution does not simply rearrange the material within the state or produce new beings using the substance of old ones according to natural laws. It produces what was literally not a possibility prior to it, or what was inconceivable before its advent. This is different from saying that revolutions produce possibilities that were conceivable but not actualizable, or that they can bring about what before was only a dream. It means that they can bring about what was neither a logical possibility nor an actuality, they can create what was neither a dream nor a reality.

Revolution shifts the terrain of existence rather than redrawing its boundaries. In doing so, it creates new impossibilities and new dreams alongside new realities. This is not to say that God-like revolutions create entire worlds down to the smallest detail, but they do create the outlines of worlds out of nothingness that in turn produce people, objects, and forces in fundamentally new ways. Revolution creates states ex nihilo using new methods for the articulation and arrangement of such things in the world, creating beings out of each state's unique framework. My claim is that outside the framework for a particular world there is nothing, or nonbeing, the nature of which we necessarily must grapple with. Beings are conditioned by their state, revolutions yield the particular conditions of a state, and outside of that there is nothingness.

Although it is possible to posit in simple terms the ex nihilo creation of revolution, a bipartite answer is needed to identify that to which ex nihilo creation is applied. One cannot say that revolution operates only on the state without bringing revolution back to the state—this time by limiting revolution to reorganizing what was already there. Yet it is also impossible to say revolution operates on nothing without raising the question of how revolution is able to affect the state. Revolution can connect to the state without limiting it to that domain if we draw a distinction between the operations of revolution qua anomaly and revolution qua catalytic change. As anomaly, revolution is defined by creativity, and not attached to the state in any necessary way. What it operates on is unclear and inexact, and any impact it has on the state is encountered indirectly. But as catalytic change revolution operates directly on the state, and possibly all the changes, forces, and systems within it. It creates ex nihilo, but that creation is only measurable from and in relation to the state it operates on. Revolution manipulates the state, but it also extends into a beyond that from the state's perspective is unclear and indefinite.

Ex nihilo creation also means revising our conception of nothingness. Nothingness is often understood as emptiness or void, but recent discoveries and empirical data undermine this definition. Pure void and emptiness were reasonable understandings of nothing in the past, but science has revealed millions of substances, fields, waves, and more, that are out of sight yet detectable. Even the vacuum of space—perhaps the thing closest to emptiness we know of—is filled with plasmas, radiation, and particles, among other things. When you add in quantum physics' theories of the relationship between energy and mass, holding to our previous understanding of nothingness is problematic at best. A better description appears when we understand nothingness in relation to movement, not substance.

What at first glance seems to be lacking in this model is a place for thoughtful political action. It seems there is little to be done if revolution can rewrite the world from the outside in one, sweeping manner. But withdrawing revolution from the state does not mean radical change is wholly beyond our control. Though such a view is perhaps a necessary consequence of situating revolution outside the state (where nothing can control or dominate it), revolutionaries can play a role in channeling the flow of radical change. The direct control revolutionaries have in other models of revolution is replaced in Dynamic Anarchism with an ability to shape the manner in which revolution occurs (even as they are shaped by it). One must be attentive to participate in revolution effectively, for by ignoring a revolution's currents and holding dogmatically to a prescription for change one becomes blind to the many possibilities revolution offers. This is why specific demands are anathema to revolution, for you cannot demand in advance what you are unaware of, and to create demands using concepts or institutions drawn from the prior state lays the ground for the return of that state after the revolution. The May '68 slogan of "Demand the Impossible!" better captures the openness found in revolution, though even that can be interpreted as a nebulous antipathy toward the state rather than as a call for constant attention, activity, and critique. Demands, if there are to be any, must be open to change without endangering the transformation sought within the state.

Revolutionary action takes place in a world of incomplete and inaccurate information, so while demands can (and often are) given prior to revolution, there is no guarantee that they will be relevant or useful following it. If, on the one hand, revolution cannot be controlled, yet, on the other, we are not destined to be like Hegel's Owl of Minerva, coming "always . . . too late"[61] to do anything but describe what has already been, what can revolutionaries achieve? First, activism and protest spread revolution's message. And although revolution is not tethered to anything in the world nor motivated solely through subjective affectations, rebels play an important role in increasing or augmenting the scope and impact of revolution's catalytic changes. The broad range of tools within a revolutionary's belt affect how the revolution is seen and taken up, and whether revolution will renew itself or taper out. The most effective revolutions are those that cascade from place to place, revitalizing themselves each and every time they reach a new population or area. Revolutions do not need leaders to form their message, but participants to sustain and extend their impact.

Discovering the Outside of Time

The exceptionality of revolutions implies that there is no simple temporal or spatial description of revolution. A complete account of revolutions demands an account of how revolution—both as anomaly and catalytic change—relates to temporality and, to a lesser extent, spatiality. Some theories address this issue by portraying events as instantaneous. Events are not part of a situation but follow a logic of their own, and because they operate as an exception to the norm, they are singular in nature. To characterize events as temporal is to include them within the situation, since temporal language drawn from the situation carries with it an ontology that events resist. But instantaneous events except themselves from a situation's temporality and retain their singular integrity. Events can prescribe a new understanding of time, yet they themselves lack a temporal structure. To avoid presenting events as part of a particular state of affairs, or undermining the deep-seated shift that events supposedly produce, theorists of events avoid describing events in the same terms as situations. Such a concern is entirely warranted, but nevertheless does not necessitate seeing events as instantaneous.

The bipartite model of revolution I propose exempts revolution, in the mode of anomaly, from a situation's temporality, but, in the mode of catalytic change, allows the revolution to be described—though not perfectly captured—using temporal terminology. Revolution's appearance in the world entails that it provisionally acquires a temporality, though there is no guarantee that the temporality will hold. This does not mean that revolutions are eternal, for the same reason that exempting revolutions from the world does not make them nothing. Designating revolutions as eternal implies normativity inasmuch as infinite time is logically opposed to sequential or unfolding time (compelling revolutions to obey the logic that accompanies binary oppositions). To claim events are eternal does not avoid their encapsulation in a world; it just avoids their encapsulation in *our* world by placing them in another. Events should be seen as atemporal in the sense of having no designated temporality and thus being outside of time altogether. The encounter with the temporality of revolution is an encounter with the absence of time inasmuch as time, in such a context, is indeterminate and unnamable. Nevertheless, the encounter of revolution from inside the world takes place within a temporal structure, and as such it is possible to say that the experience of revolution is one that can be designated temporally.

The temporality of revolution as it is experienced has elements of both itself and the world it mixes with, but properly belongs to neither. It results partially from what revolution introduces into the world, and partially from what was already in the world. As anomalies revolutions are atemporal, but seen from within the state they can be instantaneous or seemingly without end. Similarly, revolutions are not localized within the state, but can appear to be so. They do not originate from a specific place, and cannot be reduced to a set of spatial coordinates, as they except themselves from the state's spatiality. Specific settings may play a symbolic role in revolutions, but this does not mean that they limit, cause, or determine anything. Squares, parks, and streets are a vehicle for the expression of revolution. But like temporal designations, locations within the state can change, and any attempt to situate revolutions within the world will not capture them perfectly either. It is only possible to conditionally localize revolutions in terms of their origin and effects on the state.

The Pathway to a New Theory of Revolution

The Dynamic Anarchism model of revolution takes its cue in part from contemporary theorists who have begun the process of thinking through the structure of events. The most salient questions concern the nature of an event—What is its fundamental being, how does it appear, and to what degree can we know or experience it? To answer these questions requires knowing how events relate to the world, and how they exempt themselves from its otherwise smooth functioning.

Before venturing into the contemporary discussion of events, it is necessary to demonstrate the importance of disconnecting revolution from the state by revealing how theories of revolution that fail to do so cannot capture the exceptionality of revolution. To that end, I will begin my investigation by critiquing three approaches to revolution, those that describe revolution as a function of the state, those that provide revolution with a telos or that constrain its movement, and those that use the notion of an event in an imperfect manner. Social contract theory, discussed in chapter 2, is a major example of the former approach. As the first unified school of thought to isolate revolution and treat it separately from war or civil unrest, social contract theory believes that the rational study of politics reveals how to build a government that obeys natural laws and respects individual rights. It sees the role of revolutions as the overthrow of unjust institutions. Social contract theory's strategy of measuring the state against ideals of freedom and justice provides an important tool for critiquing the state's existence. But, with the exception of concepts like sovereignty and the state, as well as John Locke's innovative uses of ideas like "people" and "power," it offers very little for a comprehensive analysis of revolution. Other modern philosophers like Hume and Montesquieu as well as contemporary philosophers like Habermas and Rawls, also use this approach when discussing revolution, and will be incorporated into my critique.

Dialectical theories—Marxism being the most well-known—follow the second approach, discussed in chapter 3. These theories claim that the modern society inevitably develops in due course as the result of working out the contradictions they form, whether ideological or material. According to these theories, revolution is a product of historical forces like poverty, alienation, property, and the desire for wealth. No longer is it just a corrective, for dialectical thinkers say past revolutionary developments have led to negative as well as positive results. Ultimately, revolution will teleologically resolve all the contradictions in society, bringing humans back to their true selves and destroying society's artificial institutions. Dialecticism undermines many of social contract theory's illusions, but does so through the development of a state organized around permanent processes, actions, and needs. While some of the dialectic's errors are fixed by later dialectical thinkers, none fully escapes the subjugation of revolution to a telos or program. I will focus on six variations of dialectical thought: (1) the idealism of Hegel, (2) the absolute idealism of fascists, (3) the materialism of Marx, (4) the communism of Lenin, Trotsky, and Mao, (5) Benjamin and the critical theorists, and (6) postwar French Marxism, which can be subdivided into the structuralism of Althusser and the humanism of Sartre and Merleau-Ponty.

Evental theorists, who are discussed in chapter 4, have a lot to offer theories of revolution. Theorists like Badiou, Kuhn, Foucault, and Deleuze will be examined in light of their additions to both evental and revolutionary theory. Their transposing of transcendental structures into immanent ones helps us think about how states can be rewritten. In addition, they emphasize how figures, subjects, and objects are the result of accidents, presubjective processes, and discursive formations. Particularly anathema to these thinkers are schematic expressions of revolutions that accentuate figures, stages, and agency in an attempt to prescribe a revolutionary formula. Instead, they emphasize differences, productive forces, multitudes, and powers. The resulting focus on newness leads them to examine revolution's creative potentials. Revolution plays an important role throughout the political philosophy of evental theorists, although thus far it has been connected to the methodologies with which these thinkers work. Processes and operations persist through both states and revolutions, shaping the outcomes of movements for radical change. While these thinkers leave meaning and being open, these processes and operations constitute protostates that still tether revolution to an abstract order.

The theory of Dynamic Anarchism is laid out in chapter 5. In addition to referencing evental theory, Dynamic Anarchism will engage with systems theory—and in particular phenomena like emergence, resilience, adaptivity, complexity, and interconnection—in order to make Dynamic Anarchism's case for a new theory of revolution. In addition to discussing the phenomena in systems theory that indicate the need for Dynamic Anarchism, the chapter will spell out the advantages of this theory in comparison with other event ontologies. The previous three sections of this chapter discussed the basic tenets of this theory.

After laying out the theory of Dynamic Anarchism, this investigation will shift from a study of the form of revolution to its practice in order to show the relationship of Dynamic Anarchism to the strategy of revolutionaries. This occurs in chapter 6. I will concern myself primarily with writers who develop tactics and strategies for revolution. Drawing from chapter 5, chapter 6 will provide advice to demonstrate how the theory of Dynamic Anarchism can help revolutions succeed. These pieces of advice are meant to indicate how one can best conduct a revolution amid a state that is a complex and interconnected system composed of many moving parts. Numerous well-known revolutions—such as the American, French, Russian, Cuban, Algerian, and Chinese—will be discussed, and many revolutionary figures—Guevara, Lenin, Mao, Washington, Robespierre—will be cited. Additionally, the chapter will study practical actions and organizing. Chapter 6 will study which tactics are effective by analyzing examples of those that have worked well and those that have not. The theories motivating these revolutions will be discussed as needed to clarify how these previous revolutions and figures operated.

At the end of this investigation, it will be clear that revolutions themselves are in need of a revolution. Great strides have been made by studying how society experiences revolution, developing tactics and strategies to master it, and avoiding the various pitfalls revolutions can fall into. But over time the space set aside for revolution has been strewn with the detritus of other theories and leftovers from fetishists of revolution. To unlock the bonds holding revolution back we must find a new theory. Here in the early part of the twenty-first century, we may be at the beginning of a seismic shift. Signs show that, unless we fix the harms of human civilization, the natural world and the vengeance of the injured of the world will, quite simply, leave us without the ability to fix much of anything. The historically low levels of faith in government reveal how dissatisfied people are with minor reforms and demonstrate the need for a movement that can create a better society from top to bottom. Within that context, I submit this analysis of revolution as a step towards an understanding of the nature of revolution, within the larger path we must follow in the creation of a free and egalitarian world.

2

Regulating Revolution

Nature, the Sovereign, and the Social Contract

The Dawning of Revolution

In the heady days of the French Revolution, just prior to the Reign of Terror, Louis Saint-Just put words to what was becoming a common view at the time: "It is impossible to reign in innocence. The folly of that is all too evident. All Kings are rebels and usurpers."[1] At Louis XVI's trial, the prosecution's words were no less profane when Maximilien Robespierre declared, "Regretfully I speak this fatal truth—Louis must die because the nation must live."[2] And just slightly earlier the American revolutionary Tom Paine penned a similar truth, saying, "Of more worth is one honest man to society, and in the sight of God, than all the crowned ruffians that ever lived."[3] In Europe and the American colonies, a shift had happened. A previously impossible truth was becoming not just feasible, but necessary. The beliefs and methods of the revolutionaries were incompatible with old structures. The world of the divinely endowed monarch was dissolving even as it fought its last battles along the ramparts of its palaces, and in its place the ideas of early modern political philosophy were achieving a foothold among the former subjects of the king, who were taking up the mantle of citizen and autonomous individual. Though there were many battles yet to be fought, many discussions yet to be had, many endeavors yet to be undertaken, ineluctably the passage of time was making more and more certain a new political reality—that no longer could the king be allowed to keep his head.

Early modern political philosophy—which is composed of several overlapping strains of thought, including social contract theory, rationalism, conservatism, and liberalism—separated religion from politics. It had for centuries been taken as a fundamental truth that the sovereign ruler was endowed by God with the authority to rule, and that no other defense of the sovereign's power was needed. The first intervention early modern political theory makes into this ideology is to cast doubt upon that proposition by questioning the validity of justifying one's rule with God, advocating instead a turn to reason.[4] A politics that begins with reason discovers the natural ground of society as well as the appropriate distribution of rights and responsibilities. The right foundation prevents political collapse by indicating laws that regulate the political relationships in society,[5] preventing excess and channeling state resources. Within these laws numerous associations and policies are possible, and early modern political theory remains neutral about them as long as they don't adversely affect individuals' rights or the sovereign's power. If and when revolution enters this world, it enters for the purposes of serving these larger goals, becoming a mechanism within a larger program of society building. It resets the system by bringing a deviant society back to its starting point. Yet because revolution can easily go awry political theorists place it in a world of rules that govern its impact. The appropriate limits of revolution, its function, and its goals, are supposed to be obvious from the dictates that are revealed when reason contemplates nature. But drawing revolution into such a well-regulated world opens the door for a crisis, for revolution inevitably destabilizes these political systems by undermining the structures of the natural world and the state. This crisis compels many changes in the social contract as theorists try to resolve it, yet it is ultimately unsolvable, as the problem comes from the ground of their political systems.

Early modern political theories share several features: an analysis that begins with separate individuals or a focus on what is natural, an emphasis on rationality, a transition to the state that codifies the most important parts of the natural situation, and a description of the possible forms the state can have. They are also subject to many of the same criticisms: the excluding of "nonrational" peoples, ignoring classes, and ignoring social and political forces that privilege some while handicapping others. Finally, they always treat revolution in the same way: as a function of the state. Revolution is operationalized in a way that provides value for purposes of the state, limiting its ability to enact change beyond those purposes. I will demonstrate each of these claims in turn. In addition, I will show

how, despite important modifications made to early modern political frameworks, multiple strains of contemporary political philosophy are still subject to the same criticism. In order to simplify the terminology going forward, I will refer to all philosophies that follow this pattern as *regulationism*, and those who advocate for such a system as *regulationists*, to emphasize how they see revolution as part of the same system of rules as the state. As I will show, social contract theory is the dominant, though not the only, form of regulationist theory

At stake is whether we can rely on any version of regulationism to justify or plan revolutions. If we adhere to regulationism, sovereigns, publics, contracts, and more, take on an eternal quality. Revolutions are rendered incapable of challenging their existence or function. Revolutions become tools for regulationists, limiting what radical change can accomplish.

Capturing our Natural Freedom

The regulationism found in early modern political philosophy is based on the claim that human society is composed of separate individuals. It inverts the traditional relationship that places individual choice and rights subordinate to the genealogical hierarchies and the chains of command found in earlier political systems. If previous political arrangements come in at all, it is to serve the goal of helping people to make rational decisions, not vice versa. The relative equality of all in nature means the traditional classes are often unnecessary. Hobbes says, "Nature hath made men so equall, in the faculties of body, and mind; as that though there bee found one man sometimes manifestly stronger in body, or of quicker mind then another; yet when all is reckoned together, the difference between man, and man, is not so considerable."[6] Rousseau is explicit: "Which people, then, is fit to receive laws? . . . A people without deep-rooted customs or superstitions."[7] Regulationism "[sweeps] away ecclesiastical power and privilege at the same time that it [curbs] sectarianism and religious dissension"[8] and refuses to posit "any particular branch of humanity [that possesses] a special gift or genius to enlighten and instruct others."[9]

Rationality is the primary way political relationships are determined. The nature of the relationships—contractual, regulatory, conventional, or otherwise—are uncovered when reason contemplates nature and human needs. Once found, they provide a normative content to political arrangements and sanction those that deviate. The political systems of Hobbes and Locke are grounded according to the "general rules of reason"[10] or the dictates of "natural reason,"[11] on the one hand, and consensual agreements[12] or mutual transferring of right,[13] on the other. Reason funnels, channels, and puts to good use the affective and irrational elements of society by properly situating them so that they do not interfere with rational governance. It is universally identified with progress and improvement,[14] though thinkers differ as to its ultimate goal. Mary Wollstonecraft believes the ultimate goal of reason—open to anybody—is liberty and progress, while Hobbes argues that rationality's goal of stability is safer when stewarded by an elite few.[15] All believe reason can produce a rationally organized society, though the name and nature of that society differs from thinker to thinker. Burke refers to the "spirit of a gentlemen, and the spirit of religion" as the foundations of civilization,[16] Hume to "family-societies" that we are born into and that expand outward,[17] and Adam Smith to a "civilized society" in which every person must cooperate with "great multitudes."[18]

Regulationism's temporal order is defined by lack of change, for the same dilemmas, possibilities, and choices that confront the state today confronted every prior state. Time is cyclical—as leaders pass and societies come and go, each individual is able to choose again from the same options that previous generations did. Locke believes history confirms this view of time, since by "looking back as far as records give us any account of peopling the world . . . we commonly find the *government* to be in one hand"[19] and that "all peaceful beginnings of *government* have been *laid in the consent of the people.*"[20] Though more open to change than Locke inasmuch as he rejects the idea that any law is eternal,[21] Rousseau sees a natural tendency in all governments to "pass from a greater number to a smaller number, that is, from democracy to aristocracy, or from aristocracy to royal government."[22] For him the "principle of political life"—the sovereign authority expressed through executive and legislative powers—keeps all states functioning.[23] The order dictated by reason is ubiquitous. New adults always confront the question of joining or leaving the state, and new states must deal with the same threats that endangered previous ones. Social context may affect which answer is appropriate (Montesquieu and Rousseau each describe different types of government, saying they have different uses and dangers),[24] but the general outlines of each thinker's political philosophy applies to all humans universally. Paine sees all hereditary systems as bad,[25] Locke proclaims a universal "spiritual" equality,[26] and Spinoza believes that ceding one's "natural right" upon entering society is something that each person must do no matter the circumstances.[27] Time is measured by the repetition of patterns and the need to understand both the dangers and potentials of every alternative.

This pattern is how regulationism traps revolution and excludes numerous sociopolitical interests, though to see why this is we must describe it in more detail. To begin, all regulationism formulates a natural ground out of which the state will arise. All the artificial constructs of the state are pulled away and the essential human form is laid bare. Lacking laws, governmental institutions, and social conventions, humans are found to be in "a state of perfect freedom"[28] that "prohibits nothing but what no one desires or no one can do"[29] and where "the notions of Right and Wrong, Justice and Injustice have . . . no place."[30] The absence of rules in this state of nature may at first seem advantageous, but the license it offers produces conflict and war. Even though regulationists do not all believe that license is absolute—only Hobbes believes everyone has the right to everything,[31] while by contrast Locke believes that men do not have the right to harm others[32] and Rousseau questions slavery[33] and the principle of "might makes right"[34]—they all agree that the lack of a power that can enforce rules is a problem. There are several responses to this challenge. Social contract theorists believe this gives rise to an agreement among all people in the state of nature to forego their natural power, set down laws, and abide by the judgments of a sovereign power. Such a system of justice originates from "the principles that free and rational persons concerned to further their own interests would accept in an initial position of equality"[35] and not from arbitrary or inequitable judgments. Rules of justice are developed to limit one's freedom in return for security and order. Regulationists that do not believe in the social contract argue for some benefit that comes from association. David Hume says that obedience to authority, which likely arose when one person took control following a state of war, provided the benefit of fidelity to laws. Order is "much better maintained by society" while people have a "love of domination" that government satisfies.[36] Montesquieu believes there is a "pleasure one animal feels at the approach of an animal of the same kind" and a "desire to live in society" that encourage association.[37] And while Edmund Burke believes that society can be seen as a contract, he says the contract is not one of exchange but partnership, the difference being that an exchange occurs quickly while the partnership is an ongoing process. Burke claims society's partnership is one that includes citizens of the past and future who, together with those living today, are working together to achieve long-term goals.[38]

But do the limits on freedom only begin with the institution of order, or are they latent within the very description of "natural humans"? People within the state of nature are defined narrowly, using characteristics that obligate specific behaviors. Most regulationists expect people in the state of nature to be governed primarily, if not exclusively, by their rational self-interest. People who engage in war do it for their own defense[39] or gain,[40] only forming alliances for the "advantage of both parties."[41] Even raising children is calculated and lacks altruism, for parents should expect children to return "respect, reverence, support, and compliance" in exchange for their "care, cost, and kindness."[42] Rousseau similarly believes in this motive, but argues that familial interest is another principal motive. Though preserving oneself is both within man's nature and "Man's first law," the care a father has for his children is another driving force preceding any organization of society.[43] Regulationists who deny the primacy of self-interest—such as Hume, Burke, and Montesquieu—do so by arguing that humans obey base instincts and emotions. Hume says humans are naturally frail and perverse,[44] composed of instincts that are "all simple."[45] Burke says the "feeble contrivances of our reason"[46] must be bolstered by tradition to keep emotion from overtaking us,[47] while Montesquieu says in nature people are dominated by feelings of inferiority and desires for nourishment.[48] Regulationists also argue that one who is "free" within nature will inevitably want to form a society. Hobbes says men "naturally love Liberty, and Dominion over others," and so their "finall Cause" is "the forsight of their own preservation, and of a more contented life"[49] in civil society. One may initially desire to live alone, but obstacles will build up until, according to Rousseau, "the human race will perish if it doesn't change its mode of existence."[50] Simple passions like desire, love, and grief lead to felicity, misery, and war,[51] just as a desire to "live in a . . . more agreeable Manner"[52] leads to seizing property and, ultimately, to society. While Hume follows the pattern of describing nature and a desire to form society, he is unique in arguing that what is natural (other than our bodies) is only emotions and instincts. Individuals are around others from the moment of birth, so society is a constant presence throughout one's life. Nature provides one with desires like those for preservation, glory, and wealth; our reason, culture, or emotions inevitably draw us into association.

The world is also restricted in the state of nature. The descriptions of nature provided by social contract theorists delineate a limited number of operations the world has and forms the world can take. Arranging the world through disparate spatiality and cyclical time, and animating it through rationality and particular interactions, gives the world an eternal order it cannot surpass. This order is consonant with the defining characteristics of individuals found in the state of nature.

Humankind's natural self-interest and desires are explicitly attached to the limits of the world. Rousseau says that man must "watch over his own preservation" and that "as soon as he reaches the age of reason . . . he becomes his own master."[53] Spinoza connects men's self-interest with their nature, saying, "It is a universal law of human nature that no one neglects anything that they deem good unless they hope for a greater good or fear a greater loss, and no one puts up with anything bad except to avoid something worse or because he hope for something better."[54] Spinoza concludes that "no one will promise without deception to give up his right to all things, and absolutely no one will keep his promises except from fear of a greater ill or hope of a greater good."[55] For those who see the contract as a basic form of interaction, its character, which has force when it is in one's interest and becomes void when it is not,[56] comes directly out of natural law. Grotius's legitimate causes of war require a clash of interests between disparate individuals, such as when "Securities are demanded against a Person that has threatened an Injury" or "Punishment [must be] inflicted."[57] Other forms of rudimentary interaction have similar origins. Edmund Burke sees respect for authority and tradition as part of human nature,[58] while Wollstonecraft, in response, says the cultivation of reason is just as natural and many times more valuable.[59] The world produces an individuals' natural environment and possible choices, while the actions of natural individuals maintain the features of the world. The two sides work synchronously to produce and regulate the entire state of nature. Everything that does not conform is marginalized or goes uncounted. The presentation of the state of nature as a space of freedom and impulse takes place within a grid that carefully screens what characteristics a free person can express and controls how the natural world appears. For the natural world to seem free, it must confine everything that is in it.

Regulationism has multiple opinions regarding what is natural and where society begins, all of which tend to fall on a spectrum between two extremes. One extreme argues that the individual self, or parts of it, comprise the natural, and the move to society begins when one comes into association with others. The other extreme argues for natural relationships that carry natural obligations. What is likely, what is possible, and what is justifiable within nature depend upon the degree to which some sort of natural organization of individuals can be posited. Hume,

Grotius, Hobbes, and Spinoza are closer to the former extreme—which I call the *isolate* perspective—that sees nature as lacking any concept of justice or virtue, where one acts primarily according to one's self-interest. Locke, Rousseau, Burke, Wollstonecraft, and Paine are closer to the latter—which I call the *relational* perspective—where there is a more natural organization to human society that conditions more generous actions and a normative framework. Montesquieu is roughly halfway between the two extremes, and puts forth elements of both.

Adopting a more "isolate" perspective often means believing that nature lacks any necessary human relationships, and that the dominant mode of relating to one another is through one's rational self-interest. Hume is closest to this pole, as for him nature is composed of instincts, aptitudes, and capabilities. There is no "state" that is completely natural, for elements of society (i.e., parental relationships) exist from the moment every human exists.[60] What is natural are human capacities, which in general are frail and perverse.[61] Because of this arrangement there is no natural law and no rules regarding right and wrong. In a sense, one does not even act according to one's self-interest, but from one's urges, needs, and desires, which precede the development of rational self-interest. Law develops as a way of keeping order, and is not based on nature but on the value that comes from obedience to authority.[62] What is natural are individual passions, anxieties, and similar urges; the social begins upon any human association.

On the isolate side of the spectrum, those who posit a social contract have a more robust concept of nature, since the contract's provisions arise from the natural. They provide natural humans with a more developed sense of self. Hugo Grotius says natural law comes out of the rational investigation of a thing's essence and is enforced by God.[63] Natural law is infinite, eternal, unchanging, immanent within the world, and evident to reasonable people with common sense.[64] It reveals that "man is by nature a mild creature,"[65] though the unsociable have "grown so by addicting themselves to Vice, contrary to the Rules of Nature."[66] Instincts[67] and a predilection to protect one's property ineluctably lead to war, which nature allows for the preservation of one's belongings and natural condition. Warring over property is just inasmuch as property is a right of ownership[68] and war a dispute by force that repels violations of rights.[69] A state develops once free and autonomous individuals come together "to enjoy peaceably their Rights, and for their common Benefit."[70] It establishes the legal framework that ensures the protection of one's rights and limits one's actions to protect others. A sovereign, unaccountable to any human, acts as lawmaker, magistrate, and judge in regard to "the making and repealing of Laws"[71] and affairs concerning "the publick Good."[72]

Hobbes's state of nature is more unpleasant, for in it men live a "nasty, brutish, and short" life where people are constantly propelled into quarrel because of competition, diffidence, and glory.[73] Because there is no concept of justice, one has the right to do whatever is in one's power,[74] resulting in a constant drift toward war (which is bolstered by humankind's inadequate reasoning powers[75] and the lack of any concept of property or privacy within the natural world[76]). Reason recognizes this natural situation is untenable and forms natural laws that dictate the proper organization of society—laws compelling individuals to seek peace, renounce their claim to everyone and everything, and set up a sovereign who will ensure compliance.[77] Both Grotius and Hobbes emphasize the close proximity of nature to war and that protecting what one views as one's own is a major cause of war. They disagree about which considerations give rise to natural law. Grotius believes it comes from investigating the nature of things (or acts), while Hobbes believes it comes from the contemplating what is needed to preserve human life.[78] For both, the proper function of an object is given by the relations it forms with the rest of the world and how reason summons us to respond.

Spinoza does not start out far from Hobbes, for he puts forth an account of how in nature right and power are equal. As "natural right" is equal to God's power (and because God is all-powerful), in nature one has the right to do whatever is in one's power.[79] Reason plays no necessary role in determining action or behavior at this point. This existence is tenuous, for one is in danger of losing one's property, family, or life. Reason enters Spinoza's considerations upon the formation of society, as reason naturally leads individuals to choose the protection of society over the "hostility, hatred, anger, and deceit"[80] of individual living. Spinoza is distinguished from Hobbes by his treatment of the problem given to reason in the state of nature. It is not only a matter of seeking peace by renouncing the power one possesses but also of preserving one's right to express one's reason and thought freely. The purpose of the state is "to allow [peoples'] minds and bodies to develop in their own ways in security and enjoy the free use of reason, and not to participate in conflicts based on hatred, anger, or deceit."[81] Instead of focusing on the war and misery of the natural state, Spinoza conceives of nature as a germ of enlightened discourse and reasonability that blossoms into a wholly different civil society than the ones Hobbes and Grotius envisioned.

The thinkers that fall on the isolate side of the spectrum (Hume being the most extreme, Grotius and Hobbes the next most, and Spinoza the least) argue for a nature composed of individuals' interests, power, and passions more than reason. For Hume, reason doesn't begin until one is in society, while Hobbes, Grotius, and Spinoza say that reason is the beginning of society. These thinkers similarly adopt varying views on the role of rights and the protection of property, as the further one moves away from the isolate pole, the greater a role they play in the beginning of society. This indicates that the further one moves away from the isolate pole, the stronger a sense of natural value (which can be recognized by the individual) one finds. Yet value from association or that arises from relationships is still foreign to the natural world in the isolate perspective.

Montesquieu is roughly halfway between the isolate and relational. This is because he sees a role for relationships in nature, but they are relationships that are very basic and come without any obligations. Humans start out with basic urges—the premise of isolate philosophers—but unlike the thinkers discussed above, Montesquieu says the most basic urges are those of one's inferiority and the need for nourishment. In nature, one will overcome one's reticence at association upon seeing others having similar reactions, and over time bonds will form. The pleasure of association will increase the desire to associate more.[82] As associations grow, society forms (the tipping point being when associations become complex enough that government is necessary). There is little role for reason here, other than the partial role reason plays in overcoming anxiety and urging association. These relationships are natural, not the product of society, yet they do not carry a set of natural laws that influence society. For this reason, Montesquieu's account of nature is midway between the two extremes.

"Relational" thinkers like Rousseau and Locke associate nature with the familial, arguing for a natural organization characterized by impartiality and cooperation that leaves one without a vehicle to express one's thought publicly and an effective means of protection. Locke insists that reason requires the establishment of a commons by compact, since food, drink, and other necessities for subsistence were given to all of mankind. It is only because of this commons that property, which originates by "taking any part of what is in common, and removing it out of the state nature leaves it in,"[83] can be manufactured. Rousseau claims there is a "natural bond" between parents and children that becomes an association of choice later.[84] Because war is "not a passionate and hasty, but a sedate settled design upon another man's life,"[85] it will not happen for minor reasons.

Locke epitomizes nature as a state of equality, where "all creatures of the same species and rank . . . should also be equal,"[86] but says there are various mechanisms that put individuals into unequal relationships. Paternal power or skill are natural forms of inequality,[87] while the election of a sovereign power is artificial (though it refers back to paternal rule).[88] Rousseau's state of nature is articulated in much the same way. Everyone starts life tied to her or his father, lacking an immediate state of equality but with an equal potential for liberty. Equality is gained when children no longer need their parents for their preservation, at which point the bond is replaced with reciprocal freedom and equality.[89] In civil society everyone begins free and equal. They surrender their freedom when it is to their advantage so as to give the sovereign a paternal position.[90] There is some natural disparity, but those able to depend upon themselves are free and equal with respect to one another, entering into civil society by choice in order to benefit from its protection. Rousseau claims the family is the basis for the original social covenant,[91] and that civil society is natural inasmuch as it follows the family, but artificial when it moves beyond that. Locke sees a stronger difference between the two, for while both have a compact at their heart, it is only political society that wields the legislative power of life and death.[92] Thus while the first society was between a man and woman, new powers needed to be found to produce political society. Both believe reason advocates the development of civil society for comfort, safety, longevity, and peaceable living.[93]

Both Burke and Wollstonecraft expand on this account of relational nature, though in doing so they reach notably different conclusions (as I will discuss later). Burke argues for a kinship between present members of our group and those of the past, which is why he argues that traditions and customs should not be thrown off lightly. We owe a debt to the past, as we are carrying on their project of building a sustainable civilization. The subordination of our interests to theirs is natural.[94] Political society is to be based upon this relationship rather than, as Locke and Rousseau would have it, the familial one. By contrast, Mary Wollstonecraft theorizes a natural relationship to authority that demands we challenge it. We must eventually confront all authority, whether it is that of Locke and Rousseau (the family) or that of Burke (the past). Once our reason is developed, it is the only thing to which we should subordinate ourselves. While we can recognize that our relationships (like friendship or ownership) to others will, at times, come with obligations, no relationships have a natural, permanent authority.[95] Too much parenting, like too much subservience to authority, produces weak individuals. So while both Burke and Wollstonecraft recognize more relationships of authority than both Locke and Rousseau, Burke subordinates our reason and decision-making to those relationships while Wollstonecraft privileges the former over the latter.

Tom Paine argues that humans are created equal,[96] that special kinships are shared,[97] and that reason leads to forming societies that supply one's "natural wants" and satisfy one's "social affections."[98] Paine is unique among "relational" theorists for attributing kinship to the entirety of mankind. A natural community precedes and grounds the formation of civil society. Like all social contract theorists, Rousseau, Locke, and Paine point to reason as the origin of the rules structuring the natural world, but they each disagree about the degree to which individuals can be relied upon to reason correctly. Locke and Rousseau argue that structural bulwarks must act as safeguards against natural biases and inclinations that pervert reason.[99] Paine argues that reason, wielded publicly by a democratic government, is by far the finest way of protecting society from its possible ills.[100]

All the philosophers on this spectrum, from isolate to relational, arrange the state of nature to contain embryonic states in the form of natural urges, rational individuals, paternally controlled families, inheritances from the past, or natural communities. The social contract thinkers on the spectrum generally have more clearly defined relationships and operations occurring in nature, since it is from these that their natural laws—and thus the dictates of the social contract—are drawn. Yet, social contract theorist or not, these entities or groups are the same ones that wield the force of revolution and condition revolution's very existence after society forms. The power controlling revolution becomes the same power expressed in the state, as the state and revolution are formed by the same authority. The manner of control differs depending on how each theorist depicts nature. The isolate perspective discounts any relationship not defined by mutual exchange on the basis of self-interest, including natural groups (Hobbes holds that when it comes to the social contract familial relationships are irrelevant until after the institution of the commonwealth),[101] and sometimes discounts any relationship whatsoever (Hume says that human sentiments, not natural relationships, decide government).[102] The relational perspective disallows the development of unnatural groups, which vary based on what groups they think occupy nature. For Grotius and Hobbes, a subject who wants to disagree with the sovereign must have standing, which comes from having suffered a direct slight at the sovereign's hands.

Hobbes's possible slights involve issues of "Debt, or of right of possession of lands or goods, or concerning any service required at [the sovereign's] hands, or concerning any penalty corporall, or pecuniary, grounded on a precedent Law."[103] Slights Locke recognizes include those accepted by Hobbes, but also a sovereign's violation of a society's right to property[104] or to provide for itself.[105] In these latter cases one's standing comes from mankind's inalienable rights, which a sovereign must respect. In other words, when thinking about the propriety of opposing the sovereign, one's reflections should stop at the limits of one's personal interest—for Hume, Grotius, Hobbes, and Spinoza—or one's communal interest—for Locke, Rousseau, Burke, Wollstonecraft and Paine (Montesquieu only recognizes those slights that corrupt the authenticity of natural human associations).

It is almost impossible to justify a revolution using isolate theory since only individual grievances can be brought before the sovereign. Spinoza differs from Hobbes and Grotius in that he does allow for free speech in his state provided one does not advocate rebellion, meaning subjects can disagree with a sovereign's policies even without having been slighted by them. Similarly, Hume does advocate for principles of common good that arise from their utility in producing such.[106] However, Spinoza does not ground this freedom of speech in the rights of mankind, or in public welfare. It is an isolated individual who deserves this right by virtue of being a free-thinking individual, not by being part of a larger community.[107] Similarly, Hume grounds his principles in the individual's desires for stability and order, which predispose humans against revolution and countenance against radical change.[108] The shared discontent that frequently provokes revolution is recognized by the relational perspective, but only when it stems from a natural group like a family, commonwealth, or community. Both perspectives give no consideration to dissent originating from racial, gender, or class-based offenses. Referencing the interests of people with a common ancestry is disallowed, which is why modern thinkers like Samuel Coleridge, Benjamin Constant, and Alexis de Tocqueville reject the social contract tradition.[109] Even sympathy with the plight of the suffering is excluded. Acting with reference to these alternative interests makes one irrational and incapable of forming contracts, someone whose very presence is excluded even from the state of nature.

Regulationists arguably qualify revolution to prevent it from becoming a destabilizing force that can be used by the self-centered or irrational to attack legitimate sovereigns. Humans should follow the political forms nature indicates. Overturning those forms rejects nature, which in turn rejects God. "Liberating" revolution means appropriating unnatural powers, which threatens to topple the carefully constructed societies regulationists describe. Given this, why should we seek a liberated revolution?

Regulationists aptly state revolution's risks. History shows that radical change can go awry. The mistake regulationism makes is thinking that the state must limit revolution. Revolutions should be unlimited in concept, but in practice particular revolutions will operate with limits. For example, seeking representational government means limiting your revolution to what is likely to bring about that goal. Many of revolution's excesses come from radicals who equate any attack on a despised authority as a step towards change, but history shows this strategy to be bad. Effective revolutionaries develop strategies that connect their individual actions together as part of a larger plan to bring about their desired goal. These limits can do the same work as regulationism's statist limits, the difference being that revolution as such is not limited by any particular limitations. Individual revolutions will limit themselves while leaving the concept of revolution free from any state. As long as revolutionaries don't seek complete disarray—which has never been a goal of any major historical revolution—then the dangers regulationists worry about are unlikely. Moreover, sovereigns can misuse authority just as revolutions can, and more deaths have been caused by oppressive sovereigns than revolutions. Limits don't guarantee society's health. Instead of focusing on the "right" limits, we should ask if the problem of disorder doesn't stem from regulationism's antipathy towards development and adaptation. Both sovereigns and revolutionaries deal with difficult situations where the rules of regulationism fall short. For this reason, we should not circumscribe revolution but use it as a tool to change society when our current system no longer works.

For regulationism, any revolution that refers to an alternate logic besides that of rational self-interest, exchange, natural association, disparate individuality, or cyclical temporality is prima facie indefensible.

The Covenant that Binds

The state of nature never lasts. Humans are drawn into association for many reasons, and regulationism believes people need organization to facilitate their interactions. The best practices for beginning those associations can provide clues for how to develop the state over time. This, in turn, has implications for the practice of revolution as described by regulationism.

Leaving nature behind is depicted as a major transformation, either for the individual or society. With the exception of Rousseau, for whom the covenant is a regretful necessity, regulationists portray the founding of society as a significant accomplishment. It is the point where a new lifestyle, a new way of interacting, is created—one that will be sustainable and productive. Locke describes this event as coming "out of a state of nature"[110] to "make one body politic under one government, put [oneself] under an obligation, to every one of that society, to submit to the determination of the majority."[111] Hobbes calls it a transference of one's natural right[112] through a contract that is enforced by the establishment of a common power other than nature.[113] Even with his ambivalence, Rousseau admits that the creation of the social contract amounts to a new "mode of existence."[114] This focus on the momentousness of leaving nature hides how, despite these descriptions, one never leaves it. Passing into society does not erase nature, nor are the many feelings, desires, and interests of nature left behind. Rather, nature is channeled by society for the purposes of building an ordered world. Society attempts to make nature useful by identifying what within nature is applicable for the purpose of building a lasting state. Society does not pull humans out of nature—it authorizes a part of nature, both in the sense of legitimating it and reproducing it. Nature thus pervades and surrounds the state, and the state does not efface nature but consolidates it. Together, the state and nature produce a more comfortable place than nature alone.

Regulationism can be divided into three different schools when it comes to the state—radicalism, liberalism, and conservatism. The oldest of these three perspectives is conservativism, which proposes a hegemonic sovereign that leaves little room for engagement with the multitudes of people composing society. Liberal thinkers take much from conservatism, but differ because they view humans as more accommodating and less in need of the sovereign's protection. The liberal tradition depicts a society where the multitude has a greater role in governance and where the people are more independent of the sovereign. The closest one gets to a society of indispensable freedom is radicalism. It argues for sweeping reform, fundamental liberty and equality, limits to sovereign power, and a naturalism that sees humans as parts of an organic whole rather than solitary stewards within the world.

It is interesting to note how each thinker's society influences the school they fall into. Grotius and Hobbes lived in societies threatened by civil conflict, as Hobbes's England was torn apart by a civil war where it is estimated that hundreds of thousands died, while Grotius's Dutch Republic (which was at the time controlled by the Holy Roman Empire and France) was torn apart by the Thirty Years War. In both societies, there were many powerful advocates for an absolute monarchy and not much in the way of empirical evidence about how a constitutional system would function. In addition, Hobbes's England was defined by religious upheaval, which Jeffrey Collins says had an enormous impact on Hobbes's scholarship. Hobbes's desire for the sovereign to control ecclesiastical matters was an attempt to end such problems.[115] Burke, too, lived in an era of upheaval (the American and French Revolutions occurred during his lifetime), though not one nearly as bloody as those of Hobbes and Grotius. Thus while I categorize Burke as conservative, he is on the liberal side of that type. By contrast, Rousseau, Locke, Hume, Montesquieu, and Wollstonecraft each lived when there was less civil strife, for even though the Glorious Revolution took place during Montesquieu's and Locke's lifetimes there were comparatively few casualties (it is sometimes referred to as the bloodless revolution). In addition, constitutional governance had taken root in both of their societies to a limited extent, and so both had some direct experience with what it was like and how it worked. The difference is that Hume's, Wollstonecraft's, and Locke's English government was more hospitable to Enlightenment ideas than Montesquieu's and Rousseau's France. It was the schools and intellectual societies in France that cultivated new ideas and scientific study in that country. Finally, both Spinoza and Paine lived in relatively free societies. At the time of Spinoza's life the Netherlands was a republic, while during Paine's lifetime the colonies became a representative democracy. While there were elites in both societies (mainly as a result of wealthy merchants or traders), politics was free from the restrictions that defined most early modern European nations. There was a lot of experimentation, exploration, and creativity to be found. As how much the sovereign of each thinkers' society intrudes upon daily life roughly maps onto the type of government he or she proposed, all three schools of thought can be seen as responses to the types of events, issues, and ideas at work during his or her lifetime.

Conservative thinkers emphasize a centralized power system, dominating structures that allow only for limited change, and a preference for monarchy or aristocracy. Grotius's discussion of sovereignty's nature emphasizes how important it is that sovereign power—the power to legislate, judge, and execute law—be unified, most plausibly under one man.[116] The implication that the sovereign could be anything other than one person is not found in Grotius at all, while Hobbes reluctantly allows that the sovereign could be a group of people as long as, within that group, sovereign power is still unified.[117] Any other form of government is subject to fracturing and eventual collapse.[118] The sovereign is above the rest of society to such a degree that it cannot be punished by society—only by God.[119] The authoritarianism of the sovereign in Grotius and Hobbes is best explained by the relatively small role of reason in nature, for while reason exists and drives individuals towards the social contract, the affectivity found within nature—the fear of attack, the stress of providing everything for oneself—often overwhelms it. The actions of irrational individuals, and their prominence in nature, indicate that no true unity of purpose can exist prior to the establishment of the sovereign, so for this reason the contract Grotius and Hobbes describe is not a pact with a society but a pact between individuals from which the sovereign emerges.[120] The unity that exists between people is subsumed into the will and judgment of the sovereign, which becomes the actor for every individual in the commonwealth. Government works best when the monarch acts with the community's interests in mind, and any social reform must take place under the guidelines laid out by the sovereign, for it is always wrong to try to place society—or any common good—above the sovereign. To reference a power over the established monarch as a justification for one's actions is a recipe for chaos and the inevitable collapse of society.

Burke employs many of the same ideas as Grotius and Hobbes, but with notable differences. His contract is between all individuals from which a sovereign emerges, but that contract is not an exchange; it is a partnership. And the sovereign is not one individual, but all of society, past, present, and future. Individual states are only clauses in this ongoing, perpetual contract formed necessarily by the nature of society.[121] While the sovereign in Burke is more than one person, present-day society is still subordinate to it, and the authority of the sovereign is unified. Moreover, Burke is similarly cautious regarding the irrational elements of society. He does not trust the reasoning abilities of humans, as he argues emotion and instinct play a bigger role than we often recognize.[122] Finally, he does provide the king a role to play, saying that while he is not sovereign, neither is he simply a servant. We follow the dictates of the king, while no one follows the dictates of a servant.[123] Kings are stewards of and spokespersons for the sovereign mentioned above. Burke sees value in constitutional governance, but only when subservient to the conservative forces people like Hobbes and Grotius describe.

Liberalism argues for a freer and more representative society, undergirded by a moderate amount of restraints to prevent slipping back into the state of nature or war. Freedom and equality are tempered by artificial structures that mediate human excess. Because democracy assumes an equality between humans that cannot ever exist,[124] Rousseau's just society requires that the general will be mediated and properly enacted by a legislator. As long as the government follows this will, the specific form of government can be determined by the people governed in view of their society's context.[125] Locke mitigates the democratic elements of his philosophy with references to the need for a legislative authority separate from the people. He is skeptical about locating power entirely in society's hands, for there needs to be some sort of distance between the people and the ruler, and a sense of permanence to notions like justice and authority. Hume references "mutual trust" and the "general interest of mankind,"[126] Wollstonecraft the "common principles of humanity,"[127] and Montesquieu the role of the people[128]; nevertheless, they all incorporate processes to differentiate lawmaking from those preferences.[129]

All this is not to say that liberal thinkers express the same philosophy in different language. The first point of difference comes from who legislates. Rousseau has faith in the deliberations of educated citizens to reach the public good and believes that the actual laws of a state must be measured up against this general will. By contrast, Locke measures laws against their ability to protect natural rights like property, and defines the common good as the protection of these rights.[130] While Hume has magistrates take up the act of ruling, the ultimate decider of right and wrong in law is social utility, which legislators are required to follow.[131] For Wollstonecraft it is reason, which is common to all and, when exercised properly, will reach the same conclusion about which laws are best.[132] Finally, for Montesquieu, the governing power differs depending on one's government. In monarchies the primary principle to legislate is honor; in democracies, virtue; in despotisms, fear.[133] In all cases of liberal philosophy, there are specific legislators, but the justice of what is being legislated must be measured against certain rights, values, or desires. Second, because the governments of liberal philosophers follow ideals like the general will (for Rousseau), reason (for Wollstonecraft), or utility (for Hume) without their actions being dictated solely by it, there is a more egalitarian distribution of power than in conservatism while still maintaining a rational and normative structure. Locke provides the people a role in governance,[134] but requires that they use the channels of legislating and governing designated by reason. He says, "This legislative is not only the supreme power of the common-wealth, but sacred and unalterable in the hands where the community have once placed it."[135] Rousseau's typology of the various forms of governance exemplify normativity, for "the government under which . . . citizens increase and multiply most, is infallibly the best government,"[136] implying that there is a happy medium between the authoritarianism of monarchies and the strife characteristic of democracies.[137] Hume argues for a government that balances liberty and authority, checks the individual desires of perverse minds, and allows for change as needed.[138] Montesquieu provides a typology of three different types of government, describing rules for how to make each function well.[139] And while Wollstonecraft doesn't give much in the way of normative laws, she does argue that different governments serve society differently, and that the needs of society should dictate which government is enacted.[140]

Finally, radicalism argues for a society organized not by legal buttresses against mob rule, but by the free expression of thought and the protection of man's natural rights. Sovereign power begins when individuals transfer their rights and powers to society, and it is only by doing this that they are able to prevent the alienation of their natural rights.[141] The sovereign is obligated to work for the public interest, as reason dictates that the purpose of combining power is the collective welfare of the individuals comprising society. Because the sovereign forms by giving one's rights and power to society, democracy is the ordinary form of government. It is the unmediated form of the commonwealth, a "united gathering of people which collectively has the sovereign right to do all that it has the power to do,"[142] and "society governing itself without the aid of secondary means."[143] Every government must maintain fidelity to this fundamental equality or it violates the rational directives of nature. Spinoza says sovereign power may be exercised by one person or many, but needs to be grounded in democracy and free expression.[144] As William Large says, this is a direct outcome of Spinoza's rejection of transcendent philosophies. The only way to effectively maintain the plurality of nature is with a government that recognizes plurality.[145] Paine agrees with grounding society in these values, but contra Spinoza claims that monarchy and aristocracy degenerate into ignorance and confusion, and only representation can adapt itself to the different ideas in society.[146] Radicalism frames freedom as total and separate from any possible remnants of tradition or history. Spinoza believes, "It is impossible to deprive men of the liberty of saying what they think,"[147] while Paine says, "Men are born and always continue free, and equal in respect of their rights."[148] Even those who exercise sovereign power are not raised to a higher class, for their status comes with the responsibility to act in the public interest (which for Spinoza's means administering the state using reason,[149] and for Paine aligning the government's policies with the interests of the people[150]). There is less a ruler can do unilaterally, and a greater capacity for participation in governance, in radical thought. Because Spinoza and Paine think citizens can be trusted to act rationally, they make reason indispensable for the continued success of the commonwealth.[151]

Authorizing Control

Revolution's role is directly correlated with these accounts of authority. Each tradition describes revolutionaries in relation to the ruler since revolutions use the ruler's power. Revolutions connect to nature just like rulers. Radical change is woven into the regulationist's world.

The differences between the conservative, liberal, and radical traditions in regulationism come from the part of nature that each chooses to authorize and expand to the whole of society. The conservative tradition maintains that a strong sovereign creates the best chance for an ordered community, and for Hobbes and Grotius this means a monarchical system of governance. Any division or opposition within the sovereign is liable to create civil unrest, and so the sovereign must be completely united.[152] The place of unity within the state of nature described by Grotius and Hobbes is the autonomous individual, who is the only being able to make decisions and enter agreements. The sovereign in their philosophy is an authorization of the natural, rational human; it is the individual writ large. Burke, by contrast, authorizes the historical community. Though Burke means to include the future along with the present and the past, it is the past that has authority. The reason for bringing in other generations is to instill respect for tradition as that "which works." As we cannot follow traditions of the future, Burke is asking us to think of the past. And notably, Burke's historical community is not composed of a plurality of viewpoints and projects, as for him we are all pursuing the same thing. This is where his unity comes from: not the individual as such, but the common purpose of society (which in practice is the purpose of prior elites, now imposed on the present).

Revolution is disliked by conservatives because it implies an unnatural equality between the interests of the sovereign and the people in the state when the peoples' interests should be subordinated to the sovereign (similar to how the autonomous individual may have numerous desires, but those desires are supposed to be subordinated to the rational self-interest of the individual; or how the imperfect individual must defer to the aggregated wisdom of the past). Though Grotius and Hobbes barely treat revolution, their brief mentions of it demonstrate how they believe it to be among the most inexcusable forms of insolence, and rebels themselves are but "insolent rebellious Slave[s]"[153] or irrational romantics[154] who deserve swift retribution. To the extent that Hobbes does discuss revolution, he refers to it as a process of synthesis and analysis where revolutionary sentiment builds among citizens being governed by a ruler who is not following the laws of nature (synthesis). This is followed by an attempt at usurpation, after which the rulers analyze what happened to prevent its reoccurrence.[155] The closest Hobbes and Grotius get to accepting revolutionary sentiment is their listing of legitimate grievances that subjects may bring to the sovereign for redress.[156] Burke, of course, treats revolution at length, but condemns "reformation by subversion," saying the state should be approached with "pious awe and trembling solicitude."[157] Grandiose claims of rights and freedoms must be tempered with reverence for tradition and prejudice.

The philosophers of the liberal tradition recognize a larger collection of interests but remain bound to a hierarchical social organization. Natural order stems from arrangements where people are generally equal but maintain different levels of power. Montesquieu, Locke, Hume, Wollstonecraft, and Rousseau all mention families as a natural hierarchy that contributes to political power (though Hume would argue the family is not a *natural* hierarchy so much as an *inevitable* hierarchy more accurately categorized as form of society). Mankind is composed of individuals with different skills and strengths, who grow up in different circumstances, all of which contribute to natural inequalities.[158] These natural differences are vital for the preservation of the state, and are the part of nature the liberal tradition authorizes. Some people are better at ruling, some at judging, and some at legislating; expertise should be recognized and empowered, but not at the expense of individuals having a say in governance. The relative equality of all men is tempered by natural human hierarchies to produce a state that is neither authoritarian nor disordered. Important to liberalism's thought is the recognition that, while hierarchy itself is permanent, the particular ordering of individuals within hierarchies is not. Children outgrow their parents' authority, and the unskilled can become more skilled with practice. Hierarchy remains, but who is dominant or submissive changes; because of this, liberals see within the state a natural tendency toward change and renewal.

Liberals accommodate revolution more than conservatives, because there is nothing inherently unnatural or indefensible about overturning a particular order as long as the overall organization of the state remains. Revolution is not just another form of conquest, Locke says, because revolution ends the government from within rather than through outside forces,[159] and unlike conquest it can be a healthy expression of the people's discontent.[160] Locke explicitly justifies revolution by specifying which governments are legitimate under the social contract, for a legitimate government that becomes illegitimate loses the consent of the people and can be overthrown. As Elizabeth Frazer and Kimberly Hutchings say, Locke believes "revolution is about the restoration of legitimate political order, in which the originary moment of the polity is replayed in overcoming the state of war into which the state of nature is prone to degenerate."[161] The peoples' voice is not heard only at the founding of the social contract; it is a continual presence that the government must take into account.[162] Rousseau, like Locke, believes revolutions carry both good and bad possibilities; they are not to be universally inveighed against, but neither should they be completely welcomed. Revolutions carry a potential for great violence to which people react in horror,[163] but they can also return the state of things to its natural order.[164] Because states have a tendency to degrade, forestalling the dangers of revolution requires constant affirmation of civil society in order to prevent corruption,[165] though if this fails to happen revolution may be the best option. One must be attentive to ensure revolution is approached constructively, not destructively.[166] Similarly, Wollstonecraft argues that revolution provides a valuable tool for moving to rational laws, and that corruption in government (i.e., making laws using ambition, usurping reason for one's own ends) legitimates such radical action. When rights are violated, revolt is justified,[167] though she recognizes that revolutions can go awry and must be handled properly.[168] Hume gives a smaller role to revolution than Locke and Rousseau, as he sees significant danger in popular rule. It is the sentiments of people, and not their reason, that decides whether governments survive. Hume claims that people are inclined to prefer existing government rather than usurpation,[169] but also that all governments are destined to end.[170] One must proceed carefully by weighing the various factors conditioning radical change. Finally, Montesquieu speaks of revolution in broad terms, and in so doing reinforces the liberal principles of revolution without clarifying precisely what role he would have it play.[171] He does indicate an ambivalence toward popular insurrection when positing that confederate governments can help to put them down.[172]

Finally, the radical school of thought sees order located in the free interaction of the whole society. An individual is only autonomous in the context of other autonomous individuals, and hierarchies are a danger if not properly regulated by people who can critique the excesses of the rulers. What is natural are interactions between individuals in society who are motivated by diverse interests, purposes, and desires. It is this part of nature that the state authorizes by recognizing the inherent value of protecting the right to express oneself freely. Despite particular hierarchies, nature's best quality comes from preventing anyone's power from becoming too great, so a state that wants to preserve the interactions of a community must rein in the sovereign's influence by countering it with that of the numerous individuals who compose society.[173] The state, like nature, must develop laws and mechanisms to share power and prevent tyranny. There is a fundamental recognition of an individuals' ability to question the sovereign and its policies enshrined in Spinoza's and Paine's systems. Spinoza is reluctant to validate any calls to abolish the state,[174] yet Paine claims that revolution is justified if it is necessary to preserve the free expression of rational thought.[175] They both allow citizens to question the sovereign unconditionally, but while Spinoza is ambiguous about the possibility of revolution (he is silent on how the people should respond when the leaders fail to uphold their side of the contract, implying that only in such instances may it be justifiable for others to seize control),[176] Paine argues that when such measures do not produce change in accord with universal principles of justice, then revolution is allowable.[177]

These three ways of organizing the state each lead to a different relationship to revolution, but the similar assumptions they begin with ultimately produce the same two paradoxes for all of them. The first paradox occurs at the moment when the state has deviated so far from its professed goal that a revolution becomes necessary. Ostensibly, when a revolution overthrows a sovereign, it does so for the purpose of undoing a state that has deviated from proper norms. Revolution finishes this task by returning everyone to where they were prior to the state, allowing them to begin anew. Locke says that revolutions "*introduce a state of war*, which is that of force without authority,"[178] where there is no social contract and some individuals have designs upon the lives of others. Rousseau says that revolutions return things to their natural order.[179] Yet as revolutions undo the state, they end up reinforcing the very power structure that the state rests upon. When a sovereign becomes corrupt, revolution's role is not just to undo the sovereign, but also to return people back to the natural framework that will produce a proper state. Revolution is the expression of a peoples' right to question the legitimacy of a government that has either broken the social contract or become unnatural.[180] Once this happens, the people in the state are returned to nature, and, from there, speak through revolution to call forth a state that can protect the peoples' rights, property, and liberties.[181] To complete its task, revolution becomes an expression of the state as it should be, one that is not opposed to nature. Revolution ends up in tension, for while it is meant to herald the downfall of the state, it ends up actually becoming the voice of the state. It must support state power even as it opposes it, and is never able to speak with an independent voice. In regulationism, revolution is always already captured by the voice of the state.

Another paradox that forms when revolution is put into a necessarily reciprocal relationship with the state (while also being grounded in a natural world) is that the ostensible beginning and end of the state are put in tension with one another. Upon adding revolution to the world, the state is no longer absolute. The state is the result of the people and—for social contract theorists—the contract they form, but at the same time the state acts upon the people through the laws and rules that it puts in place. The citizen of the regulationist state is both the author of and subject to the state—she or he plays a dual role of both standing in judgment of, while also showing fealty to, the state.[182] These two roles are always in tension with one another, for the citizen must place oneself within the state to act according to rules, yet beyond the state's control to legitimately assume the ability to critique it. In addition, as a subject of the state, the citizen is prohibited from violating certain rights and liberties that of necessity are inalienable parts of each individual. However, it is the citizen, as author of the state and through his or her reflection on nature, that designates the rights and liberties that are off limits, as well as how the state oversees the protection of them.[183] The specifics of policy are decided and implemented by individuals representing the commonwealth,[184] who aim such laws at citizens,[185] yet the authority of any legislative power inevitably rests with the citizens who originally constituted the body politic.[186] Citizens holds dual roles of subject and author that forbid them from altering, yet put them in control of, how rights and liberties are handled by the state. They must be able to undo everything they are forbidden from in order for both of their roles to be actualized, yet the impossibility of this puts citizens in the delicate position of navigating their dual roles as judiciously as possible, and never being able to reconcile them. In sum, the foundation of the state is divided against itself inasmuch as the state is meant to affect the very thing that creates it. This paradox is the result of withdrawing the attribute of infallibility from the state and thereby creating the possibility for individuals to question, modify, and, in certain cases, overthrow the sovereign.

These paradoxes are not completely unrecognized by regulationists. At times they mention the inconsistency of saying that individuals create the sovereign but can have only a small effect upon its policies, and the futility of a revolution that only sets up another restrictive government of the type that was overthrown. Yet they place the origin of these paradoxes in the idea that nature has not yet been properly described, or that the origins of the state are inadequately understood.[187] The history of regulationism shows a continued attempt to redescribe these topics in such a way that gives revolution more leeway without overturning the world of regulationism. By the end of the French Revolution, regulationist theories give the people much more control over governance, and the criteria that must be met to legitimize a revolution has diminished substantially. Rationales justifying revolution are much stronger than at any previous point. Nevertheless, revolution is always limited to the role of speaking for the regulationist world, as the state and revolution are in every instance tied together through their joint origin in a fixed nature. Revolution is always prohibited by regulationist theorists when it is seen to transgress the boundary between order and chaos, in the process becoming a disruptive presence that unsettles the sustainability society works to produce.[188] This can be seen as part of the larger Enlightenment task of eliminating difference and irrationality by binding experiences together into one consistent system.[189] Fred Evans, in *The Multivoiced Body*, mentions this, saying that the West has traditionally adopted a "fearful . . . attitude towards chaos."[190] Nature and revolution are not independent of one another; rather, nature always limits revolution, and because of this, the paradoxes of regulationism remain.

Regulationists might respond by acknowledging these paradoxes but saying they beg the question of what grounds the state, revolution, and order if not nature. We are biological beings intertwined with a world that seems to obey basic laws. Given the problems of looking to God for rules, where else to uncover political principles? My critique doesn't reject studying nature for clues about the state and revolution, but does deny that we find laws there. Nature, to the extent it can be separated from society, is complex and doesn't provide absolute rules (I will expand on this point in chapter 5). Regulationists give a selective account of nature to avoid this problem, as is shown by their handling of issues of race and gender. To uncover absolute rules, regulationism simplifies nature by excluding what it considers irrelevant or circumstantial. This account is also problematic because it assumes that nature is static. Nature, including the relationships and entities within, changes. For example, unimportant relationships (two unconnected species) can become vital (a symbiotic relationship) and vice versa. Regulationism cannot ground the state in nature because nature is not a stable ground. It is too complex and too dynamic. Finally, the one-way relationship between nature and the state found in regulationism doesn't reflect how the state and nature can affect each other. The state is one of the things that influences nature to change (e.g., the effects of climate change are radically changing species, environments, and relationships). Nature is conditioned by the state, which problematizes the possibility of grounding the political in it. The real question we must ask is not "What other than nature can ground the state?" but "Does revolution need grounding?" Though my argument does not come until chapter 5, I believe the answer is no. The practice of grounding politics, such as regulationism's practice, is only useful when seeking order, not radical change.

The Voice from Outside the Social Contract

Though revolution can lead to moments of chaos as one sovereign is replaced by another, ultimately it speaks for order. As framed by regulationism, it is produced by the same natural context that leads to the state. The idea of regulationism was developed in response to a series of political crises in the Western world for the purposes of answering the questions of when and how rule is justified. But in developing this idea and those that accompany it, were other important ideas forgotten? Who or what is outside of social contract theory? The answers to these questions require analysis of the details of regulationist theories, which purposefully eliminate references to groups, temporalities, relationships, rationalities, and juridical frameworks that do not properly legitimize the sovereign.

In their haste to eradicate the stratification of society prevalent in medieval political theory, regulationist theorists push to the margins categories of individuals who are counted as nonpeople, beasts, or property. The supposedly nonstratified world of regulationism becomes, in practice, a highly stratified world in its process of othering what cannot fit into the meticulously spaced zones of individuality that define citizenship. Such biases manifest clearly within the state of nature, where (with the exception of Hobbes, for whom the distinction between man and animal comes from the way matter combines itself to form different motions in humans than in animals)[191] every thinker articulates a clear ontological line that separates humans from beasts and material objects—or that which is worthy of consideration from that which is not. Since by definition it is impossible to have a contract with that which is incapable of rational thought, establishing ontological norms is a necessary part of the regulationist world. Speaking about the social contract, Charles Mills reveals how a historical and epistemological racial contract sets up spaces that exclude nonwhites, saying:

> The supposedly abstract but actually white social contract characterizes (European) space basically as presociopolitical ("the state of nature") and postsociopolitical (the locus of "civil society"). . . . This space is *our* space, a space in which we (we white people) are at home, a cozy domestic space. . . . By contrast, in the social contract's application to non-Europe, where it becomes the Racial Contract, both space and its inhabitants are alien.[192]

The homologous spaces that found the social contract, and the natural world in which those zones are first related one to the other, form an exclusionary world; a world that, by making reason the price of admission, turn the ability to create contracts into a racial privilege. While Mills speaks about the social contract, his criticisms of it—along with the critiques I mention below—are applicable to other forms of regulationism. The difference is that the other types of regulationist philosophy refer to natural spaces, laws, or attributes that exclude, and that form the basis of the state. Though no compact occurs, the natural does the same work of exclusion that the contract would otherwise accomplish.

Nonwhites are not the only ones excluded from the social contract. In Carole Pateman's examination of contract theory and sexuality, she notes that

> the original pact is a sexual as well as a social contract; it is sexual in the sense of patriarchal—that is, the contract establishes men's political right over women—and also sexual in the sense of establishing orderly access by men to women's bodies. The original contract creates what I shall call, following Adrienne Rich, "the law of male sex-right." Contract is far from being opposed to patriarchy; contract is the means through which modern patriarchy is constituted.[193]

Mills and Pateman point out that excluding groups that don't fit the criteria of people is a danger internal to social contract theory. It is a reflexive function of founding a world on disparate and homologous individualities, and this is why both Mills and Pateman emphasize the coextensive nature of the social contract with the racial and sexual contracts.[194] Though Mills is writing an account of a contract that is a historical actuality while Pateman is trying to map out the internal dynamic of an implied contract,[195] this aspect of the social contract holds for both. Yet exclusion from the social contract is not simply the result of drawing lines that categorize—it comes from deeply isolating certain groups by predetermining them to not meet the criteria for consideration, as social contract theorists have done to blacks, Native Americans, and women. Blacks are systematically portrayed as incapable of engaging in the rational exchanges demanded by the social contract as a result of their race.[196] Native Americans are forever caught in the "brutish" state of nature by both Hobbes and Locke, their culture insufficiently developed to be classified a civil society.[197] Women, by virtue of their differences from the ideal citizen, are marked as unable to even make the leap from nature to society while retaining their sovereignty.[198] Social contract theorists describe marriage as a situation where "the rule . . . naturally falls to the man's share,"[199] and men as natural rulers, since "the head of state bears the image of the father."[200] The social contract does not just bring together the community of the "free" and the "equal," it segregates at the margins of society the "nonsocial" to prevent the contamination of the social contract world by the irrational, infantile, and dangerous. For these unfortunate individuals, the social contract becomes the hegemony, the commonwealth the despised elites, and the ontological line an invisible barricade that can never be crossed.

The cyclical temporality of regulationism only reinforces this divide. Because the same choices present themselves over and over, it becomes necessary to reproduce the exclusions of regulationism continuously. There is no possibility for change in the vital structures that compose the world, which is why, as Pateman points out, "Locke takes it for granted that a woman will, through the marriage contract, always agree to place herself in subordination to her husband."[201] While the passing of time may bring new struggles for democratic liberalism, Pateman points out that for contract theorists such struggles will always exclude women's liberation, since "the subordination of wives to their husbands [is] seen as natural."[202] (Hobbes again must be excepted from this generalization. He sees no good reason for the subordination of women to man, saying, "Whereas some have attributed the Dominion to the Men only, as being of the more excellent Sex; they misreckon in it,"[203] claiming that historical contingencies have been the primary reason why men are dominant over women.) The repetition of exclusions is vital to the survival and perpetuation of society, so the social contract must constantly maintain its exclusionary measures. Depending on the level of the threat and the means at one's disposal, certain measures may at times be preferred over others, but the existence of such measures is a constant. Mills claims "the police, the penal system, the army," are necessary to "maintain the racial order and detect and destroy challenges to it," concluding that "one has to recognize [the long bloody history of brutality against blacks] not as excesses by individual racists but as an organic part of this political enterprise."[204] Similarly, Pateman argues that the systematic subordination of women to men indicates that "the past and present *content* of the marriage contract reveals the underlying assumption that women are *not* free and equal."[205] The passing of time presents only limited possibilities for change, as the essential components of politics always remain.

Rationality works with the spatiality and temporality of regulationism to exclude. Those outside society are assumed to be resistant to traditional logic. Attempts to engage them rationally are doomed to fail, as the semiotics produced by regulationist theory are incomprehensible to those incapable of being categorized as a disparate and rational individuality. Beyond the social contract, Mills says, one is not simply different, but subject to "a basic *in*equality . . . in the capacity of different human groups to know and to detect natural law,"[206] "lacking in essential rationality,"[207] "[excluded] from the original pact,"[208] and "[excluded] from the status of 'individual' in the natural condition."[209] Once barred from reason, contracts, and individuality—and thus unintelligible to the social contract—one can be legitimately attacked or enslaved. Those incapable of rationality are by definition absurd, and thus foolish, evil, or (inasmuch as their interests are always at odds with the public's) rebellious. The rational response to such "barbarity" is ownership, destruction, or enslavement—acts that represent taming or incorporation of marginalized people into the social contract world. Slavery is not an alternate contract, but the employment of the excluded. A slave is a captive kept in chains,[210] left in a perpetual state of war,[211] who is not governed by any covenant. When slavery doesn't work or is found to be unjustified,[212] the only alternative is the destruction of all potential enemies to civil society.[213] Carole Pateman analyzes the logic of enslavement, saying:

> Slavery came about because an example of subordination and "otherness" had already developed. . . . Men must have observed that women easily became socially marginal if they were deprived of the protection of their kinsmen or were no longer required for sexual use, and so men "learned that differences can be used to separate and divide one group of humans from another."[214]

The sexual contract contains within it an implicit recognition that women are different enough from men that the social contract does not apply to them, demanding the enslavement (primarily) of women. Regulationism, and social contract theory as a variety of that, constantly attempts to mobilize the marginalized as they spread their doctrine of universal equality and freedom. When an entity is not rational enough to be incorporable as a citizen, it gets incorporated as property, as a slave, or as an enemy, and forever barred from participation in society.

Pateman's analysis of women and slavery within the social contract is exemplary, but she fails to take into account that, when it comes to women who are hostile to civil society, the sexual contract treats such women as enemies and seeks to destroy rather than enslave them. Such treatment is only an exacerbation of the traditional attitude, as in both there is a mutual feeling of enmity, and both are employed as needed by the sovereign. Emma Goldman is an example of this. Her antagonistic relationship to the US government and the male establishment led to her condemnation as "dangerous" and a person of "undue harm."[215] Instead of being enslaved, she was ostracized, imprisoned, and deported.

While the crucible set up by the rationality of regulationism justifies the oppression and subjugation of women and minorities, regulationism governs the relationships made with such supposedly "nonhumans" after the creation of the civil state. Even though women and minorities are not conceived of as autonomous individuals, and thus are unable join society, regulationist theory governs the relationships formed with them. Members of civil society uphold its dictates by developing strategies that protect them from ostracized groups like blacks or women. If the group being discriminated against is portrayed as a threat, then the sovereign can deploy the power of war or slavery, while if the group being discriminated against is portrayed as infantile, the sovereign can deploy Locke's paternal power, among others. Civil society, or more specifically, its form and practices as dictated by reason, is a vehicle for the systematic and methodical victimization of groups of individuals within society. It relies on the justification of rationality but operates independently, as unlike rationality it deals with the actual exchange of goods or services and the production of actions. Multiple actions are legitimated and encouraged, everything from the reasoned and mutually beneficial relationships that organize the arrangement of property in Locke to dictatorial relationships governing how and in what manner the sovereign can enslave or kill others. For blacks, laws encourage enslavement and violence, ostensibly for purposes of justice and harmony but in actuality for the purpose of regulating their place within the larger civil society. Charles Mills says, violent "acts have to be seen not as arbitrary, not as the product of individual sadism . . . but as the appropriate moral and political response—prescribed by the racial contract—to a threat to a system predicated on nonwhite subpersonhood."[216] The systematic program of discrimination against blacks is conditioned by a contract or laws that legitimate coercion for the defense of society. It is an agreement between citizens to form institutions such as the police, prisons, and army that guard against and use as needed the black population (in the case of war-making power or enslavement), or alternatively to care for them given their inability to care for themselves (in the case of paternal power).

In many ways the sexual contract is similar, in that the marriage contract has traditionally aimed to encourage a type of fidelity and slavery from women,[217] though the forms of domination expressed in the sexual contract are more about exclusion and cultural manipulation than overt violence. Contracts are for the most part unchangeable, as they are based on reason's reflection on the status of individuals, groups, and objects, and are not alterable through the predilections and peccadilloes of others. Pateman's discussion of marriage emphasizes this:

> A married couple cannot contract to change the "essentials" of marriage, which are seen as "the husband's duty to support his wife, and the wife's duty to serve her husband." The relation of protection and obedience cannot be legally altered, so that, for example, a married couple cannot contract for the wife to be paid by her husband for her work as a housewife.[218]

Contracts or natural roles articulate what is necessary for a reliable and well-balanced society. Change is only allowed in those situations in which it does not disrupt the fabric of society. For those too irrational, foolish, or emotional to be autonomous individuals, a systematic hierarchy must be established over or against them—not because they agreed to such treatment, but because such treatment is implied by their very being.

The outside of regulationism's civil society is irreconcilably opposed to the inside, and the measures that exclude one from the other are wholly a part of the system rather than incidental additions. The tension produced by regulationism creates a world that must maintain its egalitarian and ordered character by denying equality and order to whatever does not fit. And, just as the paradoxes inside the civil society produce attempts at reform, so too does this outside call for change. The voice of the excluded and marginalized can become a voice for revolution—one that questions the legitimacy of regulationism. The revolution recognized by regulationism does not capture the entire potential of revolution; outside the boundaries of that contract, the anarchic revolution that regulationism fears still waits.

Regulationist Patterns of Contemporary Thought

The work of Mills, Pateman, and others shows the limits of regulationism, especially the social contract. Numerous contemporary thinkers attempt to overcome these limits by reframing the contract or political regulations in nondiscriminatory terms. While they achieve this goal in important ways, the issue of revolution must be treated separately.

Despite the many alterations made since the modern era, much political thought retains the essence of regulationism and falls prey to the same problems. Specifically, it often begins with a concept of the natural—understood broadly here as an unchangeable situation out of which much of society emerges—and authorizes its most important part to form the state. In doing so regulationism restricts revolution such that revolution must now reproduce the same state. To illustrate this point, I will summarize the philosophy of four contemporary political thinkers from different schools of thought whose work contains this problem: John Rawls, Ronald Dworkin, Robert Nozick, and Jurgen Habermas.

Rawls's original position contains many of the same aspects as the state of nature. It excludes anyone who is envious or affectionate,[219] incapable of acting according to agreed upon principles,[220] interested in another's interests,[221] or possessed of "irrational" biases involving "pointless or arbitrary" traits like skin color or gender.[222] Only "general facts about human society"—political affairs, economic theory, psychological laws, and so on[223]—should be known when deciding what rules to follow, meaning that an appeal to solidarity based upon "arbitrary" or nongeneric aspects of humanity is unacceptable. The state comes out of the reasonable standards of justice uncovered while contemplating this generic picture of humanity in the original position.[224] Rawls develops this concept of reasonableness in contrast to the idea of rational self-interest. Rationality concerns individuals calculating what is to their advantage and acting based on that determination. Reasonableness calls for individuals to act based upon fair rules for exchange—sometimes sacrificing what is to their direct advantage—as delineated by the considerations that take place within the original position.[225] After the state forms, the concept of reasonableness leads Rawls to the idea of reflective equilibrium that, as the consideration of the "shared fund of . . . basic ideas and principles," provides the foundation for a comprehensive theory of justice.[226] Accompanying the institution of a sovereign power is the creation of an inviolable concept of justice that, rather than allowing that "the sacrifices imposed on a few are outweighed by the larger sum of advantages enjoyed by many," only institutes an injustice to "avoid an even greater injustice."[227] Pluralism is "a permanent feature of the public culture of democracy,"[228] though anyone part of a democratic plurality must possess "common human reason" and "similar powers of thought and judgment."[229] Rawls excludes from the public sphere anyone incapable of thinking in conformity with the rationality he recognizes as belonging to all persons, such as those who make judgments based on irrational characteristics like class, race, or gender. Revolution is only justified in reference to this concept of rationality, meaning that anyone exercising it must already believe in the principles of justice Rawls believes to be fair; other states are a priori wrong.

Dworkin, like Rawls, advocates for a legal and political system based on principles,[230] and while he does not promote natural principles, he does say that justice requires the principles be equally distributed among all members of society.[231] The principles we follow, and the rights and goals based on them, come from the political theory that society uses as its foundation. Our political theory provides aims for society that become rights when individuated, and goals when collectivized.[232] While Dworkin doesn't explicitly invoke a concept of nature, his examples of rights and goals continually reference human needs and desires as the source of law. For example, Dworkin argues that rights like freedom of speech can be limited by collective welfare, while property may be distributed in part by need.[233] For Dworkin, the natural motivates political theory and it is generally comprised of human desires and needs. The state is the authorization of those desires and needs in the form of rights and goals, and it must authorize them in a form that serves all equally by enshrining the needs and desires as ones that are consistent, equally distributed, and based in principles held by all. This system necessitates a fidelity to the law that only allows for minor deviation. In his essay on civil disobedience, Dworkin argues that disobedience should only be exercised to bring challenges before the law.[234] Because the law is changeable there are times disobedience should be allowed, but ultimately the law has final say over right and wrong.[235] Revolution, to the extent that it is the same as disobedience, speaks for Dworkin's vision of law as based in principle, and only operates to challenge the institution of a particular principle, not the idea that law must be based in principle. Revolution is also prohibited from disrupting the equal distribution of rights, and can only mount challenges that are conceivable under the law as it currently stands.

Robert Nozick explicitly embraces the concept of a state of nature, though he changes it in notable ways. Nozick follows Locke in studying what rights and relationships exist in the state of nature, concluding that in nature the most common relationship will be protective associations in which people promise to protect each other's rights and property.[236] These associations will institute rules about how to act and resolve disputes so members won't feel ostracized or abused, and the association will continue.[237] As different associations grow and come into conflict, they add new members or merge with others in order to guard against bigger protective associations. This will happen until each protective association takes on the form of the state: it obtains a monopoly on power and protects everyone in its domain.[238] Nozick calls this the "invisible hand" explanation for the state, as it shows how states form through natural processes and inclinations, not an exchange.[239] Nozick's description of the state is clearly connected to nature, as it is the continuation of the same form of association that existed in his state of Nature. Nozick emphasizes that even when the state forms, people within it still retain the same rights they had in protective associations in nature, while dominant protective associations (another term for the state) have the same responsibilities as protective associations in nature.[240] While Nozick doesn't discuss revolution explicitly, he argues that the state is prohibited from doing anything that individuals don't authorize it to do.[241] As Nozick brings all state power back to the individual, it is clear that revolution would have the same restriction. Revolution is limited by what the individual authorizes, which, like regulationists who advocate individualism in the state of nature, prevents revolutions from advocating for social concerns or changing individual rights.

Finally, Habermas presents a regulationist theory that is notably different from all others we've discussed in this chapter. The primary difference is that Habermas excludes norms from his equivalent of the state of nature, called the lifeworld. Norms come from the lifeworld's interactions with the subjective, social, and objective. Additionally, the lifeworld is not independent of others, as for Habermas interdependence is embedded in our most basic forms of existence. The lifeworld is composed of many agents and their communicative utterances, which reference the subjective, social, and objective worlds. Through our utterances we build a collaborative world comprised in part of norms about behavior as well as truths.[242] By speaking, we "test" utterances for their truth-value,[243] though at all times the lifeworld remains in the background, as it can never be the reference for a statement.[244] Despite the differences between Habermas and the other regulationists, he still follows the pattern identified by this chapter. If the lifeworld is his "nature," the state is the authorization of that. In *Beyond Facts and Norms*, Habermas holds that law comes from the legitimating process of will-formation in which all individuals freely participate.[245] Law is the authorization by the state of the communication Habermas describes in the lifeworld and the process of normalization found there. While Habermas does treat the topic of revolution, he claims it is the outcome of same processes that produce laws and the state.[246] Revolution is a product of political world-building and only occurs when normal legal remedies aren't possible. Thus revolution advocates for deliberative democracy, for it comes from the same process as deliberative democracy.

The same objections mentioned above (unconditioned revolution is dangerous, what grounds revolution if not nature) are also applicable here. Rawls, Dworkin, Nozick, and Habermas clearly resist giving radical change free reign so as to ensure the integrity of their state. My arguments against previous forms of regulationism—briefly, that they give an exclusionary version of nature and paradoxical account of change—are also relevant to contemporary regulationism, but one point remains. In conditioning radical change, contemporary regulationist theories display a tension with diversity and openness. They accept it on their own terms only. They don't reject the concepts—thus their advocacy for liberalism, democracy, and individualism—but filter them through their state. Perhaps necessary when state-building, this practice becomes dangerous when applied to revolution. Revolution has historically served as a solution for states that exclude diversity, of which there have been many. When problems were realized (e.g., the omission of nonwhites and women), regulationism tried to redraw boundaries to embrace people who were excluded. Yet this process has been necessary many times, and to this day political movements argue that this work is not done. Perhaps the best argument for Dynamic Anarchism is not that it is more consistent with the concept of a liberated revolution—though I do say this—but that it can help regulationism achieve its long-held, highly elusive goal of an inclusive society.

Spilling over the Edges of the World: Why Revolution and Nature Cannot Be Regulated

Regulationism's spatial, temporal, and relational boundaries regulate the world, but they cannot contain the destructive force of revolution. While necessitated by regulationism's innovations, revolution is always at odds with the regulationist system. Because sovereigns are no longer the origin of reason, public goodness, and nature, they do not found, but rather exemplify, justice and order. This means that citizens can petition the sovereign for redress of grievances where it has failed to meet the standard of fairness reason demands. In extreme cases, the sovereign can be overthrown. Hugo Grotius, as early as 1625, says kings are liable for damages if they do "not use such Means, as they may and ought, to prevent Robberies and Piracy"[247]; and, as late as 1776, Tom Paine tells the British colonies that "a government of our own is our natural right."[248] The sovereign can embody reason, but cannot be reason; there is always a potential for a gap between the dictates of reason found in nature and its instantiation by the state. Because the goal of regulationism is a state that approximates the optimal framework discovered in studying nature, it is necessary to renew the connection between the sovereign and nature when they diverge. Sometimes the renewal comes from the sovereign, which may set up systems that monitor whether it has deviated from natural law, but it is not able—and often is not willing—to address every deviation. Revolution enters the regulationist world as a force that can reestablish the sovereign's embodiment of rationality on those occasions when the sovereign has failed to carry out the duties nature prescribes.

Regulationism's engagement with revolution ultimately fails, but it is not without value. As it includes some of the first political traditions to take revolution seriously as a possibility, it grapples with what revolution is and how it can be justified. It does not take the established order of society for granted, thereby opening a new space to think about how people can engage one another beyond the confines of sovereign power and creating the possibility of a two-way relationship between sovereign and subject. The separation of the people from the state brings forth revolution, which requires new concepts (e.g., limits on sovereign power to justifications for dissent) to deal with the potentials and dangers that follow. Regulationism provides the basis of a particular theory of revolution.

The failure of regulationism with regard to revolution comes from its attempt to regulate what is incapable of being regulated. Revolution is situated alongside, but opposed to, the state. Both are drawn from nature, which limits revolution while creating paradoxes in the state. These paradoxes lead to more calls for change and further attempts to separate the state from revolution. At the same time, revolution can originate from outside civil society, meaning that the limited place provided for revolution within civil society fails to fully exhaust the capacity of revolution. Revolution destabilizes the regulationist world from within while undermining it from without. Regulationism fails to anticipate that regulation of revolution and nature is doomed to fail. It tries to capture the essence of nature, of humans, and of the state while allowing for degrees of variation, but it does not account for the possibility of radical change.

Nature develops and shifts beyond the limits of regulationism's natural laws, and when it does so people, the world, and society change as well. Regulationism describes only one possible world, and its regulations are easily rendered irrelevant upon the alteration of human relationships, the development of new technologies, or any one of a whole host of other potential changes. When it comes to regulations, revolution is just as easily an expression of nature's ability to surpass these regulations as it is of citizens' discontent with the sovereign. Regulationism is premised upon an untenable assumption that nature has static processes or laws. Placing revolution in this world inevitably leads regulationism's theory of revolution into a dead end. The attempt to regulate nature grounds one form of power to the exclusion of all others, and revolution becomes just another expression of the same power found in the state. Revolution is irrevocably bound to the state, with the voice of the people yet to be heard.

To solve this problem, philosophy must develop a new treatment of revolution. This treatment must not regulate nature, but recognize its ability to change and develop. Revolution is an expression of this change and development, and the natural world must be seen as a part of a larger system. This is where dialectical theories of revolution enter, providing an alternative articulation of revolutions that responds, in part, to the lacuna found within social contract theory. Dialectics provides a more sustained engagement with revolutions, including them directly within the process by which governments form, rather than as a stopgap when governments go awry. From this point on, while regulationism loses its monopoly on theories of revolution, some of its concepts are incorporated into other projects. It is an ironic legacy of regulationism that, while its theorists were most concerned with legitimating sovereign rule, one of its most enduring contributions is beginning the discussion on how that rule can be put to an end.

Seeing regulationism's problems developing a unified political framework, many thinkers take a different approach by developing a political trajectory. Society evolves over time in response to challenges, and in doing so comes closer to a healthy society. Revolution plays a role in helping society develop. Definite figures like the sovereign come and go in the "trajectory view," but does this mean revolution is extricated from the state? Determining this requires a closer look at these theories, which I will do in the next chapter.

3

The Trajectory of the Dialectic

Guiding the Process of State Formation

The Appearance of the Dialectic

Following the attempts at state-creation in the early modern era, which purposefully limited the tasks of revolution, a new epistemology took hold. Having its roots in ancient Greek philosophy, it was given a specific role in Kant's transcendental system before becoming the defining feature of Hegel's. Called the dialectic, it has been given many forms and roles in the generations since its first delineation, including in the creation of the state. The dialectic becomes a strong tool for those advocating revolution, as it rejects the idea that knowledge is found in a purely objective form, relatively static and unbiased. Knowledge is a process, ongoing and incompletable. To the extent that the state is the product of such knowledge, it too is subject to constant revision and requires constant creation. Revolution, then, is not the product of the state, but one of many processes of state-creation. It is not to be held at a distance and closely monitored, but advocated as a way society can perfect itself as it wrestles with the legacies of the past or desires for the future. While the primary school of revolutionary thought that uses the dialectic is Marxism, fascism incorporates it too. The difference is that Marxism associates the dialectic more with revolution, Fascism more with the state. I will call dialectical methods of conceiving of revolution *visionary* ones, and the process of doing so *visualizing*, given their attempts to use the dialectic to see either the state's proper development or the best methods to use when developing the state. The chapter will begin with an analysis of Hegel's dialectic, proceed into a study of the dialecticism that produced fascism, and discuss Marxist thought at length, before finally demonstrating why dialectics ultimately fails as a theory of revolution. While the dialectic frees revolution from the restrictions placed on it by *regulationism*, it does not liberate revolution in the sense that it deserves to be. Revolution, rather, is harnessed and, at times, reified for the purpose of producing harmony both with and in the state. Revolution is given a telos and an operational plane that ascribe to it characteristics of the state, while occasionally allowing the hard work of revolution to be ignored.

Hegel's dialectic begins with the idea that one must include both the subject and substance to have a full picture of existence.[1] As Hegel puts it, "The True is the whole. But the whole is nothing other than the essence consummating itself through its development."[2] The challenge with this is that any understanding requires one to present the external world as independent of oneself as knower, but in doing so one misses how the thing being known is actually part of oneself (and vice versa). Thus the dialectic is a process of understanding whereby reason posits a subject and a substance—the knower and the known, respectively—as independent of each other, and then overcomes that bifurcation by uncovering their interconnectedness. Additionally, this process is one that admits of change, for once one has a new understanding enabled by the dialectic, one sees one's initial understanding of subject and substance was inadequate. The subject and the substance form a new entity ready to be explored using the same method as before. This ongoing process is the nature of reason, which is a purposive activity that reaches actuality in unfolded becoming (as opposed to pure immediacy).[3] Over time, reason elaborates a whole system of being and tracks its ongoing development; only in this way does the whole become a science and reason find completion. One must constantly use the dialectic to posit objects for study before ultimately returning them to the living substance in a never-ending dialectical process.[4]

With this basic understanding of the dialectic, we can now see the place revolution has in Hegel's thought. For him, the French Revolution began because the government was not able to make actual the abstract idea of freedom individuals had in their heads. The will of individuals for independence sought expression in the actual, and revolution was the best vehicle for it at the time. The path of the dialectic is mirrored inasmuch as there is a similar positing, extending outward, and returning. Seeking principles of justice, the French posited those principles as independent of them, and sought them in the objective world. As the revolution unfolds the events are measured against peoples' images of right and wrong with the goal of finding harmony between the two. After each attempt, the ideas of people and the political formations change in response, adapting to each other until a holistic arrangement is achieved. Revolution is part of the process of finding the reasonable political order, as Hegel indicates when discussing the French Revolution. He argues that the revolution was a way of bringing the French state into accordance with principles of right,[5] which in turn arose from the wills of individuals and developed in the context of feudal and monarchic society. Revolution, then, serves as the enactment of a just state. It follows subjective principles of right in an attempt to create them objectively through the state. Ultimately, the state itself must serve as the vehicle for producing the freedom and rights that people desire, and revolution is just a process along the way toward that goal.[6] While Hegel is most interested in demonstrating the relationship between ideas and the state as objective enactment of those ideas—showing how they evolve in relation to one another—he does indicate in several places that a constitutional monarchy may be the best form of government for how it allows for effective implementation of law in a way that still encourages freedom.[7]

There is clearly a visionary element to Hegel's theory of revolution, as it uses ideals like right and freedom to project an image of a new and better world in contrast to what exists before trying to bring about this world's actuality. One must be able to visualize something not yet in existence in order for revolution to occur.

Fascism

Before transitioning to the main focus of the chapter, Marxism, I need to discuss the other prominent political theory that uses the dialectic: fascism. As will be shown, fascism's engagement with revolution is minimal, as for them change must be undertaken by the state itself. The state is supposed to develop, so the very things revolution is supposed to bring for other *visionary* thinkers are brought by the state. Revolution is anathema to the proper political operations of the dialectic, and must be resisted as both unnecessary and irrelevant.

The rationale for this begins with the reframing of the dialectic given by Italian thinkers like Benedetto Croce and Giovanni Gentile. Both identify as dialecticians, but argue for an "absolute idealism" that relegates the empirical world to a function of thought. Dialectics, for them, occurs only in the conceptual, not in the world of things.[8] This is because things themselves are inert and disparate, while thought is dynamic. Thought is an act and a process; it brings unity to concepts that in turn provide understanding.[9] For example, history is not an external thing, nor is it an encounter between the historian and the outside world. History is a creation of the historian's mind, and the dialectic the process by which it is created. The same principle holds for all understanding.[10] To say otherwise reduces thought to a thing, not a process. Plato does this in focusing on the content of thought rather than its action. Similarly, Hegel treats the dialectic as an abstraction by applying it to both things and thought, rather than to the operations of thought. To the extent we can see movement and development, we do so through thought. Thought underlies, supports, and creates reality as we encounter it. Reality, in short, is thought in act.[11] Beyond that is nothing knowable, and attempts at understanding that do not begin with the operations of thought are inevitably fruitless.

Fascism fits into this theory by arguing that politics begins with acts of thought and will that attempt to understand themselves.[12] Fascism looks for the conditions giving rise to thoughts, and attempts to create a state that disciplines thought for all within. In doing so, the state forms people as austere, moral, and serious. As people develop, so too must the state, and like thought it obeys dialectical logic (inasmuch as the state itself is the outgrowth of thought, and thought underlies its existence). Indeed, the purpose of the state is to create a conscious and collective human will, one which is unified and ordered. People in a fascist society should not live lives of ease, but take on the hard work of forming society according to principles of self-overcoming along the lines of dialectical transformation. Thus do fascists see the state as a living, ethical entity and a spiritual force that brings value to the spiritual lives of its citizens. Any organizations that challenge the order of the state—like unions, which cut society into classes—do harm to the ability of the state to modify itself as citizens require. Thus these impure presences need to be challenged and overcome for the collective harmony of society, and the state's role in creating it. Revolution cannot play a role in fascist politics because it is always an impure presence that wrests control of political development away from the state. A fascist politics that condones revolution in any way posits a dialectical process of will formation independent of the state, which in turn inhibits collective will formation by creating different groups. The only way in which revolution could be a part of fascism is in the process of bringing a fascist government into being. But once that's finished, there is no room left for revolution.

The visionary dimension in Hegel's dialectic of understanding is transferred to the state as that which both takes control of development and which undergoes development itself. The state, including the people within it, goes through a process of creation that includes both identifying an ideal and working to bring it into being. Fascism utilizes the visionary model of the dialectical revolution, but where Hegel placed it within the process of understanding, fascist thinkers place it within an all-encompassing state responsible for developing everything in society in accordance with its vision.

Of course, giving the dialectic to the state is only one possibility, and a poor one at that. Political theory contains many other ideas of how the dialectic could affect social development. Marxism looks to laborers or other oppressed groups to initiate dialectical movements.

The Assimilation of Revolution

The *visionary* theory of Marxism treats revolution differently. Revolution is inevitable and necessary to create the communist society to come. It is jarring, visceral, and always looming until the moment it breaks. Because the repressive "institutions, mores, and traditions" of European countries are so entrenched, "the lever of [the worker's] revolution" must not be nonviolence, but "force."[13] There is an urgency to Marxism that stems from its calls to create meaningful progress through concrete praxis and constant engagement. A better society must be collectively built, not entrusted to abstract philosophical reflection.

Marx worked for the liberation of the working class by studying the material realm. He sought to use his discoveries to undermine capitalism's harsh conditions. The ideals of justice and equality alone are incapable of bringing about this end, because it is one's actual conditions that truly stimulate change. A real account of politics must return to the material world and study the conditions that gave rise to each age of humankind. Authenticity is found in the concrete relations expressed within one's material situation (e.g., classes, needs, abilities, and means of production), not formal identities (e.g., nationality or religion).[14] Ideological concepts such as those found in social contract theory or capitalist economics reproduce oppressive systems despite their ostensible devotion to principles of freedom and justice. Recognizing this fact reveals strategies for overturning such oppressive systems. The magnitude of this realization presents the world anew as fundamentally inequitable, and as the fantasies dissolve in front of us it becomes clear that only radical change will set everything right again. Only revolution has the capacity to overthrow the ruling class and its supporting ideologies, and only revolution will bring humanity to its next stage of development. When freed from its ideological bonds, revolution can go beyond just fixing the problems with the state; it can move the world forward along its inevitable trajectory. Marx sees each stage of existence as part of a sequence, and no government or economic system is fully intelligible until viewed as part of a larger, historically unfolding progression.[15] Failed social orders did not simply lack the right prescription—they needed to fail for us to evolve. As a vehicle for numerous historical changes, revolution must play a central role in this theory. Whereas the social contract keeps revolution at the margins as a potential, Marx presents revolution as an integral part of human development.[16] A sovereign cannot prevent radical change by keeping to the social contract, for it is sovereignty itself—and the fixed system it heads—that attracts the potency of revolution.

Marxism has a specific target in the creation of an egalitarian world and describes a definite path to get there. It is primarily because society is not organized in a manner that allows for the full expression of our nature that previous social systems led to oppression, poverty, and suffering. Revolution's goal is the overthrow of the pernicious capitalist order and the institution of a society that both recognizes the material needs of every human and provides for their fulfillment. "From each according to his ability, to each according to his needs"[17]—that is the maxim a liberated society must follow. Where social contract theory portrays revolution as a fix to a system in crisis, Marxism wholly absorbs revolution into its workings. Revolution is given a more prominent and active role, but at the same time it is overwhelmed with the meanings the Marxist project prescribes. The attempt to salvage revolution by giving it a more prominent role only further draws it into the state, for the revolution Marx describes speaks for Marx's ontology and metaphysics. Ultimately, Marx's revolution confirms the trajectory of his world, and proves that the relationship between the material and the ideological is exactly as he described. Even the different interpretations of Marx's thought, with all the innovations they bring, cling to the basic outlines of the Marxist world and the trajectory it entails. While revolution remains incorporated into Marxism, it is incapable of speaking with its own voice.

As many individuals have noted,[18] defining Marxism has grown more difficult over time as it is constantly reinterpreted. This chapter does not seek to solve this problem, but as I want to be clear what is at stake at different parts of the chapter, I will use the following terminology: "Marxism" will be used to refer to the set of Marx-inspired philosophies genealogically related to one another (such as those I will be dealing with later in the chapter), "classical Marxism" will be used to refer to Marx's own philosophy, and "historical Marxism" will be used to refer to the political ideology of Marxism and its specific history.

Making Politics Friendly to Revolution

Marx undermines the social contract by framing his theory around a concept of nature that is sensuous, nonideological, and objective.[19] Nature is not static, but an external world that affects humankind just as humankind affects it. Because no natural essence grounds living creatures, Marx's discussion of nature begins at the first concrete encounter between humans and nature, neither having been theorized in advance.[20] Humans are not formulaically free and equal individuals[21] who can be conceived apart from nature[22] as simple abstractions;[23] rather, understanding them requires understanding the physical reality in which they live.[24] Humans are defined by "the totality of the actions whereby they reproduce their own material existence."[25] Starting in the most primitive human societies, the differences between men and women grow, "by virtue of natural predisposition (e.g., physical strength), needs, accidents, etc.," into a division of labor.[26] This first division becomes the blueprint for other divisions, and as new tasks are apportioned to segments of the populace a hierarchical class system forms.[27] Marx views space as highly stratified, for human civilization throughout its history has been composed of conflicting groups in dominant-submissive relationships. "The history of all hitherto existing society is the history of class struggles,"[28] Marx and Engels notoriously proclaim. Human consciousness has yet to reflect upon a world not riven by the clashes of hostile groups.

The groups that compose society are the products of material conditions. When material conditions change, old classes pass away as new ones take their place. No particular division of humans is permanent, for the factors producing social groups constantly change. The causes motivating change vary, but are always rooted in objective and nonideological conditions. The influx of colonial resources into European countries during the seventeenth century, combined with increased demand for new products, created the industrial era's division of labor (boss vs. factory worker) as well as new tools like looms, ships, and levers.[29] Massive amounts of natural resources and industrial machinery erased national identities, religions, and traditional moralities in order to create "everywhere the same relations between the classes of society."[30] Changes in geographic location, technology, and availability of material wealth, produced the capitalist classes of bourgeoisie and proletarian that replaced the feudal divisions of lords, vassals, knights, plebeians, and slaves.[31] The capitalist doctrine and modern concept of human were developed to justify these transformations of society, just as new ideologies are developed in response to every significant change in the material world. Such ideologies present the world as a given, not as a product of industry, society, and the activity of previous generations.[32] Ideologies disguise the world by developing artificial concepts, hiding the forces that developed the predominant worldview, and presenting themselves as irrefutable truths. As Peter Osborne says, "Ideologies are systems of ideas that misrepresent society. . . . For Marx at this time, German philosophy was the German ideology because it was the primary means through which German culture (mis)represented the world to itself."[33] Each new ordering of human society is accompanied by new ideas as humans continually try to come to terms with the actuality of nature and the human condition. Ideologies motivate human actions that, in turn, produce the world (e.g., estrangement from our nature erases animal needs and produces a need for work),[34] but they also result from the material world. The dialogical relationship between ideology and the material means it operates in constant connection with physical objects, not apart from them. It is a grave error to see ideological changes as unrelated to social organization; the two fields are intrinsically linked.

Marx rejects definitions of humanity that see individuals as "*egoistic*" and "in [their] *true* nature only in the form of the *abstract citizen*."[35] Humans must be conceived of materially as "*corporeal*, living, real, sensuous objective being[s] full of natural vigour."[36] Marx's materialism focuses on concrete subjective action through a study of the context that provides the actions with their meaning or significance. Marx examines actions within their social situation, looking at how human activities and human relationships reciprocally form each other. *Capital* shows that human labor—and the commodities it produces—are only valuable inasmuch as they are appreciated by society,[37] yet only through the process of producing commodities for exchange is society put in a position to apply value to them.[38] Such trends are identifiable because they occur on a massive scale, and as a result constitute a predictable process. As Eric Fromm puts it, "Change is due to the contradiction between the productive forces (and other objectively given conditions) and the existing social organization. When a mode of production or social organization hampers, rather than furthers, the given productive forces, a society, if it is not to collapse, will choose such forms of production as fit the new set of productive forces and develop them."[39] Historical trends can be anticipated by studying the contradictions between production and society, then extrapolating what will be needed to solve them. The material realm is a realm of actions and relationships. As their product, thought is generated by this realm and represents a relationship one takes toward oneself or society.[40] These actions and relationships produce the world and its contents. They act as homogenizing forces, for each set of actions and relationships dictates a different arrangement of society, and when a new set is developed a new dictation is dispersed throughout. Productive forces, technologies, and practices carry a compulsion to conform, which occurs both on an individual and societal level. The development of industrial machines transformed workers into machines themselves, nurturing their "helpless dependence upon the factory as a whole"[41] and transforming society from one characterized by manufacture to one characterized by industry.[42]

New homogenizing forces, like those that produced the factory, create bonds and rifts between individuals. Marx's accounts describe both the contradictions and the similarities that develop in each era. In every situation, the relationships that exist are classifiable in terms either of association or of antagonism. The modern bourgeoisie are supported by the "executive of the modern State" in their fight against the proletariat, yet in the past the bourgeoisie shared with the serfs a common enemy in the nobility.[43] Peasants in the industrial world are not identifiable with the proletariat, yet their interests are the same and in the future the two will unite against the capitalist.[44] Such associations are overshadowed by the larger contradictions produced by conflicting classes, such as those between the lord and serf, guild-master and journeyman, or capitalist and proletariat.[45] It is by understanding relations of association and antagonism that Marx predicts times of radical change. In nonrevolutionary times, the relations are dynamic and flexible, and the conflicting groups have not yet been able to recognize their common interests in order to form a political program. Revolutions occur when the interests of competing classes become so divergent that sustainability is no longer possible even in the short term. At this point, the relations of antagonism and the relations of association both catalyze the revolution, as the former push each class toward militancy, while the latter encourage solidarity.

The ongoing alterations of the world reveal that, for Marx, temporality is the succession of systems. Individual systems often have their own unique means for measuring time stemming from material conditions, but the principal way of tracking the passage of time in classical Marxism is through the replacement of one system by another. Particular arrangements of society do not present time objectively. The ways time is measured for the purposes of paying wages in capitalism did not exist in feudal societies,[46] while Newtonian mechanics is connected with capitalism as a theoretical precondition for it.[47] Engels sees Kantian and Newtonian systems—including their concepts of time—as stages within a Hegelian-like system that privileges process.[48] Social systems measure time for their own interests, and each time one is overthrown a new standard for time develops. The only persistent concept of time Marx leaves us with presents time as a movement leading from one arrangement to another. For Marx, "history is nothing but the succession of . . . separate generations," each of which continues "the traditional activity in completely changed circumstances" and modifies "the old circumstances with a completely changed activity."[49] Because the specific ways time is tracked are social traditions and not objective measures, classical Marxism follows the changing social systems that produce each particular schema. Social systems are arrangements of subjects, objects, and relationships, and as such are not monolithic. This is a necessary consequence of Marx's rejection of abstraction, for consistency demands that Marx define history in terms of "material, empirically verifiable [acts] . . . which every individual furnishes" rather than "a mere abstract act on the part of . . . the world spirit."[50] History, the only constant measure of time Marx provides, is neither abstract nor definable in terms of one single measure; it is plural, renewing, and revealed through the ongoing shifts in material relations.[51] As Kołakowski writes, "Strictly speaking . . . there is no such thing as time in itself but only relations of succession (before and after), 'time' being a secondary abstraction from these."[52]

Marx's framing of his system in terms of conflicting groups and successive systems is accompanied by motive forces that determine how and why things change. One essential aspect of Marx's thought is the notion that subjects and objects follow a trajectory that terminates at a predetermined endpoint.[53] Society must be studied scientifically before any trajectories can be determined,[54] but it is a fact that all objects in a particular context aim at a definable goal.[55] The end at which things aim does not come from essences or utopian ideals. It originates from the interactions between objects and subjects situated in the same world.[56] Nothing outside or behind one's everyday actions and material situation determines this sequence of events, yet given the state of society there is no other possible telos but the one Marx describes.[57] Marx's telos is produced from below rather than instituted from above, yet it is a defining principle of the world he creates. The capitalist world is ripe for revolution because "by driving hitherto isolated workers into mills and factories, modern industry had created the very conditions in which the proletariat could associate and combine into a dominant force."[58] Individuals may play different roles in realizing society's goal, but everyone is pulled along by the collective weight of history as if caught in a tidal wave, with no hope of changing a direction determined by forces far outside their control.[59] Revolution is no exception; it results from many interactions that each express a purpose and becomes part of the social context that gives others purpose. The purpose revolution expresses is always a reconciling of contradictions,[60] for it is a massive restructuring that only appears at moments of transition. It is produced not by a system, but by the contradictions a system creates.

Classical Marxism outlines a world more accommodating to change than regulationism's. It is adaptive, interconnected, and self-motivated. Revolution is no longer used as a stopgap, for the supersession of boundaries that regulationism is designed to prevent is an essential characteristic of Marx's world and something to be embraced. Marx's revolutions do not confine change within specific parameters, but direct it onto a productive path. They stem the tide of destructive forces, motivating new social arrangements when the current one becomes untenable. Though capable of massive shifts, revolutions have historically only led to incremental changes. In the introduction to Marx's *The Class Struggles in France*, Engels says previous revolutions have only "resulted in the displacement of one definite class rule by another"; any marginal advances were overshadowed by the fact that, because "the proletarian masses . . . were still absolutely in the dark as to the path to be taken," their initial zeal quickly degraded into "a revolution of feeling as soon as illusion evaporated and disappointment set in."[61] Only now, after the modifications of previous eras, can a true communist revolution (which will finally "bring [human beings'] 'existence' into harmony with their 'essence' "[62]) occur. Revolutions have a clear social function—they provide a new organization to society that resolves previous inconsistencies and errors. Even when unsuccessful they can have a profound effect by opening "fractures and fissures" in society while denouncing the "abyss" that awaits if no action is taken.[63] Revolutions "are the driving force of history"[64] that act like elemental powers conditioning Marx's world. The boundaries of regulationism are replaced in classical Marxism with a trajectory, the endpoint of which revolution must ensure.

Classical Marxism avoids many of the problems of regulationism by embracing a historically evolving model of human nature. But does it capture the full possibilities of revolution by grounding it in a material world and endowing it with a telos? Revolution may not be put to work enforcing the ideal state of regulationists, but nevertheless its role as a motive force makes it speak for the forthcoming communist state. Because Marx's revolutions treat as unimportant anything not connected with the larger goals of Marx's project, they limit other forms of emancipation by privileging their own. The state Marx describes—ineluctably aimed at creating a communist society—dominates the discourse of emancipation.

Guiding Revolution from behind the Scenes

Marx reshapes the terms of political debate from a focus on justice to a focus on human existence. In so doing he casts liberal political theory—and its inauguration in the atomic individual possessed of rational thought and selfish desires—as ideological.[65] Political theory must capture the becoming of human existence, not rest on a set of regulative ideas.[66] Such ideas form enclosed systems of power around static concepts of humanity, yet in reality they are a piece of the larger movements of society. They must be understood within the context of the material environment that produced them. Revolution is centralized in classical Marxism as it enables Marx to connect different social hierarchies into one schema that presents them as part of an ongoing progression. Because enclosed systems of power are really part of a larger unfolding order, their inadequacy and downfall must be part of this larger order too. Revolutions are not the system in moments of crisis, but the system working as it should. Rather than being driven by the social contract, revolutions are the counterpoint to noncommunist societies and the classes that compose them, able to solve the inevitable problems that such societies intrinsically carry. The larger order that is ineluctably revealed in exigent moments narrows and focuses revolutionary possibilities. Overthrowing particular governments draws society closer to the point where it recognizes itself as it is, dissolves all classes, and creates a sustainable system for all. Revolution is still stewarded by the state, but rather than authorizing the same government that preceded it, revolution now operates as part of the same program as the state. The processes by which the world develops lead to communism, and both revolution and the state are committed to that goal, even if they are unaware of this fact.

Marx believed that during his lifetime he saw instances of the coming worldwide revolution that would overthrow the capitalist order, and his understanding of revolution is in part informed by these events. Both the Paris Commune and the revolutions of 1848 happened during his lifetime, and both reflect concerns similar to those he writes about. The revolutions of 1848, while having little direct impact on governance, developed a consciousness among the lower classes that persisted long after the revolutions were put down. Similarly, the Paris Commune was one of the first attempts to create a truly socialist society, complete with elections, feminist initiatives, workers' rights, and the separation of religion from governance. These revolutions were notable for the way they saw class and living conditions as important issues that revolutionaries should address. Demands should deal with concrete material conditions, not just formal aspects of governance. One also sees the concept of socialism developing, for despite the similarity in demands made by both revolutions the people running the Paris Commune had a better formulated idea of how society should function to be inclusive, democratic, and egalitarian. Finally, the harsh way in which each revolution was put down indicates how hostile established states were to transformative change, and how dangerous they felt these new ideas to be. These concerns are all reflected in Marx's writings, for like these revolutions Marx deals with material conditions, believes communism will develop over time, and is skeptical that states will reform themselves or accept revolutionary demands. The practice of revolution undergoes a shift in Marx's lifetime that parallels how Marx's concept of revolution differs from earlier ones.

Marx sees revolutions as a cure for ideologies. Throughout his work he describes revolution as "the alteration of men on a mass scale,"[67] the abolition of "the political character of civil society" that "set[s] free the political spirit,"[68] and the result of "material elements" and "productive forces" rather than ideas.[69] Revolutions are both part of society's progression and moments of becoming that destabilize repressive ideologies. They occur when conditions are such that the ideology of the present is at odds with the extant material forces.[70] Though previous revolutions wound up producing new ideologies and class divisions, the coming communist revolution will abolish both.[71] Revolution is a moment of anti-ideology. It may lead to a new ideology, but its principal function is to undermine established ideologies. Yet Marx imbues revolution with an ideology itself by fixing its trajectory. His descriptions of revolutions contain both form and direction, as by Marx's account they must occur in a certain way and aim at the same telos. Marx insists that peasants must be turned into proletariats before any revolution will succeed in overturning capitalism,[72] that the next major revolution will be economic in nature,[73] and that the state by necessity will be supplanted by worker councils.[74] Marx overloads his revolution with excessive preconditions in order to ensure a seemingly natural transition to communism. As Bernard Yack writes, Marxist revolution "does not arise necessarily out of the social experience of workers; workers must view their experience from a particular philosophical perspective, they must have a particular understanding of man's humanity and the obstacles to its realization, before they will even long for a total revolution . . . let alone actually revolt."[75] Marx speaks prophetically of revolution. Communism is for him inevitable and imminent because "society can no longer live under [the] bourgeoisie [as] its existence is no longer compatible with society."[76] The same unalterable laws that determined why and when the bourgeoisie revolted against feudalism also determine the nature of the proletarian revolution. It is necessary that revolution follow these rules for Marx to make the case that it fits into his larger project. As Kołakowski writes, "The future liberation on which [Marx's and Engels's] historical optimism was based was not merely a matter of abolishing poverty and satisfying elementary human needs, but of fulfilling man's destiny and ensuring his dignity and greatness by giving him the maximum control over nature and his own life."[77] The anti-ideological voice of revolution hides the ideological program that projects the creation of a classless, communal society onto every occurrence of revolution and portrays communists as the essential saviors of workers. The confines of the social contract are gone, but revolution is still dictated by the materialist framework that Marx places beneath the state.

Marx envisions revolution as predictable. For that to happen, revolution must follow certain knowable rules, necessitating that facets of the world remain outside revolution's reach. Such parts play a role in shaping how revolution occurs, keeping it on track within the program Marx describes. Revolution results from unsustainable material contradictions, such as when propertyless slaves are pitted against the property owners in communal societies, or when feudal towns must overcome resistance from the countryside to expand.[78] It is able to radically change material conditions in response to contradictions, as happened when the increasing amount of trade between countries transformed society from a feudal hierarchy to the capitalist opposition between bourgeoisie and proletariats.[79] The material conditions that produce the productive forces that form particular social arrangements are, in times of revolution, radically altered to create a new normality. What does not change is the character of the material world, which from beginning to end is the realm where social arrangements, ideas, and states originate. This character functions as an axis around which the world moves, but is itself stable and independent from the shifts and reversals Marx describes. For example, the *Economic and Philosophic Manuscripts of 1844* define nature as man's "inorganic body" inasmuch as it is "his direct means of life" and "the instrument of his life activity."[80] Humans have real desires, emotions, and needs, though the illusory notions of wealth or status found in capitalist societies turn these authentic expressions of our humanity into "abstract conceits" and "imperfections."[81] The *Manifesto of the Communist Party* says ideas stem from man's material existence,[82] while *The German Ideology* provides four premises—that existence is dependent upon satisfying needs, that satisfying needs leads to new needs, that the perpetuation of one's existence leads to the development of families and social relationships, and that social relationships occur in certain modes or forms that determine the direction of history—that specify how to approach writing a materialist history free of "political or religious nonsense."[83]

Throughout Marx's works a fixed character is given to the material world. Certain aspects of individuals' relationships to themselves, or between humans and nature, always behave according to permanent rules. Revolution is enormously effective at reorganizing the material world to produce new technologies,[84] governments,[85] and products,[86] but it is incapable of altering the basic facts of this world. As long as humans exist they will have wants that must be fulfilled. Ideas are always a product of materiality. Social orders will develop via the same processes that produced those preceding them. The material world is torn in two. One part is unchangeable and furnishes the material laws Marx describes; the other part contains the entities, forces, and relationships present in any particular social arrangement, and is where revolution operates. In a similar vein, Bernard Yack claims Marx's project relies on a dichotomy between "human powers and material forces" that sees the latter as indifferent to human purposes and the former as capable of being consciously directed.[87] This division of the material realm has a critical impact on revolution. Marx describes revolution as though it is produced by and produces all the entities and relationships found in the material realm. Yet a whole host of indispensable, permanent entities mark off parts of the material world as inaccessible to revolution. Marx's revolution operates only on parts of the material world (such as social arrangements and political systems), which allows the other parts (such as human nature and the relationship between the material and ideal) to maintain the consistency of the material realm. By wielding revolution as a scalpel, classical Marxism radically alters some things and perpetually keeps others the same. The positioning of revolution in this way makes revolution operative for Marx's larger program by only subjecting some parts of the world to revolutionary ire.

So sure are Marx, Engels, and the early Marxists that they know the path revolution will take,[88] they are dismissive of revolutionary projects incompatible with their communist vision. These ideological undertones have unfortunately so pervaded the communist movement that for many it is an expression of their devotion to undertake dangerous actions, including some that Marx would no doubt reject, to bring about Marx's communist state. These claims have been put forth on many occasions. For instance, some feminists criticize Marxism as patriarchal, while others have tried to revive Marxism as a tool for feminism.[89] Similar critiques have been leveled at Marxism by race and queer activists.[90] Meanwhile, Humans Rights Watch and Amnesty International have both criticized Cuba's ostensibly communist government for repressing the population, imprisoning dissidents, and executing political prisoners.[91] Solzhenitsyn's *Gulag Archipelago*[92] documents numerous abuses of Stalin's nominally communist state.

Putting revolution in service of the communist project, while excluding from discussion political or ethical concerns attached to illusory ideologies, creates the perilous potential for sanctioning brutal actions. No moral codes can justly restrain revolution if it can fundamentally alter the material conditions out of which ethics arises, and concerns over proper treatment of those here and now seem quaint when measured against the ultimate end of all history. The attempt to think revolution through becoming—rather than capture its being—deftly avoids the problems of the social contract, but the mechanisms Marx uses to do so result in new dangers.

Marx might object that humans do have consistent, natural traits, and that the relationship between the material and ideal is both describable and tested. Certainly experimentation has shown similarities between most, if not all, humans that contribute to economic and political processes. Similarly, we would be naive not to see correlations between the material world and the ideas held by society. Dynamic Anarchism and the liberated revolution don't deny that such is the case, but do qualify these statements such that they are contingent and not absolute. The similarities between humans in the economic and political sphere are conditioned by other factors. The relationship between the material and ideal is similarly conditioned. Changing these conditions to alter these similarities is not necessarily easy, but it is possible. It is inaccurate to treat either the conditions or similarities as essential. In addition, dialectic thinkers emphasize how the dialectic creates breaks between what was, what is, and what will be. It allows for development and growth. Can we say that the "natures" and "relationships" used in Marx's analysis will forever be unchangeable, even if we don't know how to do so now? We are learning more about how to modify the conditions that produce these natures and relationships from disciplines like psychology and biology. Over time, the technologies or ideas we develop could help us alter what is currently unchangeable. The dialectic's characterization as a break that signifies development must allow for this option.

Marx may also object that the liberated revolution sacrifices a scientific account of change for an open one that is vague and undefined. According to this criticism, the scientific account is preferable for its precision and applicability. It is true that the account of change I give is open, and as such is harder to apply to particular circumstances. Though there are guidelines to revolution that are discussed in chapter 6, there are few, if any, hard and fast rules in revolutions. Nevertheless, we shouldn't sacrifice accuracy for predictability. If revolution demands a stronger account of change, as I argue, we should give it one. The practice of revolution should be addressed after developing the best possible definition of revolution. If it becomes harder to apply to particular revolutions, but the predictions we make are more accurate, the tradeoff is worthwhile.

Rearranging the Marxist Trajectory, Part 1: Science versus Organizing Principle

The Marxist tradition is plural. Followers built on Marx's initial work, including by revising its understanding of revolution. The significant differences between Marxist theories indicate a possibility for a theory of revolution that escapes capture by the state. I will review the more popular theories to explore whether they succeed.

The revolution Marx envisioned did not happen as quickly as he predicted, and while his faith never wavered, as Marx grew older he accepted the likely necessity of a long struggle.[93] His philosophical progeny spread throughout the world, bringing the message of working-class liberation and communal ownership. Along the way, paradoxes, inconsistencies, and biases compelled a retooling of some basic principles, while new philosophical and scientific discoveries called for attempts at synthesis. Since Marx's death, his disciples have reformulated his project many times, adapting it strategically while trying to preserve its basic message. To see the effects of these alterations on the *visionary* revolution advocated by Marx, and to check whether they escape its contradictions, I will trace the development of Marxism through the party-centered conceptions of it by V. I. Lenin and Mao Zedong; the phenomenological variations of Alexandre Kojève, Jean-Paul Sartre, and Maurice Merleau-Ponty; Louis Althusser's structuralist interpretation; and the critical articulations given it by the Frankfurt School. Rather than recounting their philosophies wholesale, I will focus on the modifications each thinker makes to Marxism's foundations.

There are two principal ways in which the Marxist project is modified. First, the laws guiding its operation are adjusted. This includes the functioning of the dialectic, the manner in which ideology and materialism operate, and the method for producing a communist society. Second, the structure of Marxism is revised. This includes the overall shape of the world, relationships between established parts of the Marxist world (such as between the dialectic and individuals), and the specific places where forces like production and exchange are located. In the former, it is the process of Marxism that is engaged, while in the latter, it is its form. In regards to process, Lenin, Mao, and Althusser treat Marxism as a science, while Kojève, Sartre, Mealeau-Ponty, and the critical theorists treat it as a universal organizing principle. In regard to form, each thinker locates Marxism within a world substantially different than the world Marx himself describes. However, the degree to which the world is definite and determinate, and what about the world can be known, differs from theorist to theorist. The version of Marxism each thinker returns is ultimately located in a different world than Marx and Engels described. Though this results in new characterizations and roles for revolution by each thinker, in no theory does revolution fully escape the trajectory Marx prescribes. The nature of the state to which revolution is attached varies; but that it is attached to a Marxist state endures.

Those that emphasize Marxism's scientific character focus on how it works as a system to provide substantive knowledge about the social realm. Vladimir Lenin's interpretation of Marxism formalizes many of the disparate elements of Marx's writings, codifying them into a doctrine and expanding on a number of topics Marx left undeveloped. What is of importance to Lenin is distinguishing the exact path needed to get to communism and rejecting any formulation of Marxism that turns it into a policy or general approach to politics.[94] Marxism, as treated by Lenin, is a prescription, arrived at scientifically, that accurately recalls the movements of history in order to foretell the future. The "withering away of the state" that Marx and Engels refer to is necessarily "impossible without a violent revolution."[95] Any sort of strategic alliance or commonality with the bourgeoisie is a fundamental illusion, as the overthrow of the bourgeoisie "can be accomplished only by the proletariat."[96] Similarly, Mao Zedong claims that the revolution will only succeed upon firmly uniting "all the nationalities, democratic classes, democratic parties, people's organizations, and patriotic democrats" around the Communist Party's "fundamental law—the Common Programme."[97] This view of Marxism has been verified, Mao says, "not only because it was so considered when it was scientifically formulated by Marx, Engels, Lenin, and Stalin but because it has been verified in the subsequent practice of revolutionary class struggle."[98]

Marxism, for both Lenin and Mao, is demonstrably true as an objective and impartial description of the state of society. It exists independently of any form of constructivism, and its prescriptions have a scientific validity that has been achieved through the application of the basic principles that motivate humanity. Žižek discusses how Lenin thought that "while ordinary individuals are caught in historical events which surpass them, blinded to their true meaning, so that their consciousness is 'false,' a revolutionary cadre has access to the true ('objective') meaning of events, that is, his consciousness is the direct self-consciousness of historical necessity itself."[99] This manifests itself most clearly in the doctrinaire way in which they understand the dialectic, for both Lenin and Mao believe the dialectic is an observable phenomenon that operates in a determinate manner. When incorporated into the study of history, Lenin says, the dialectic produces a field as accurate as any of the natural sciences.[100] Mao goes one step further, emphasizing that every instance of motion results from a dialectical progression between the internal contradictions that make up every object.[101] Contradictions are universal—their particularity comes from the fact that they exist differently in particular objects[102] and that within each situation there is always one primary contradiction surrounded by numerous secondary ones.[103] Because the dialectic operates according to formal rules, Lenin and Mao emphasize teleology and the ability of the Marxist project to provide a definite understanding of the past, the present, and the future. Lenin predicts the necessity of two stages of communism (one where differences of wealth exist without exploitation[104] and a later one where the state is gone and freedom reigns[105]), while Mao is certain that communism is the only way that human civilization will survive.[106] Lenin and Mao interpret Marxism as a discipline that describes in absolute terms how society operates, and that conclusively determines society's trajectory. There is one revolutionary project that leads to communism, and any other paths will result in failure.

Though Marx sounds many of the same notes as Lenin and Mao, it is important to recognize that Marx himself was far less programmatic than either Lenin or Mao, and on numerous occasions puts in qualifications to his predictions and methods. For example, he admits that sometimes revolutions may be accomplished peacefully,[107] that future events will occur differently in different countries, that communists should partner with groups that do not have the same aims,[108] and that different countries require different tactics.[109] It is also worth mentioning that Marx's ideal vision of communism was much less violent towards the bourgeoisie than Lenin's or Mao's projects.[110] For Marx, reflection, not dogma, "is essential to draw inspiration from past revolutionary attempts, to learn from their mistakes, to revive in the imagination of contemporaries the moral effects of particular historical transformations and to orient them in shaping dispositions and powers currently unavailable."[111]

Similarly, Louis Althusser claims that Marxism functions as a "science of history"[112] that subjects social formations to a systematic and rigorous analysis. But while Lenin, Mao, and Althusser each say that Marxism is a science,[113] they differ in their understanding of how that order is arrived at and its relationship to the external world. Whereas Lenin and Mao argue that the external world obeys laws and that Marxism avoids ideology by studying the material world, Althusser argues that because it is impossible to ever truly grasp the external world or to practice science without a motivating ideology, Marxism must be constantly critical of any received doctrine.[114] Science means something very specific for Althusser, as he does not conceive of it as an empirical exercise but as a multileveled process of abstraction whereby different types of generality get transformed from "facts" into "theory."[115] Everything that a scientist works with is generalized to some degree, including immediate sensations, for even they are only comprehensible once they have been articulated through words.[116] The work of a scientist is to transform the "facts" that comprise the most basic level of generality into concepts and theories that have explanatory power. Marx's scientific project is not to describe the real qua one's sensations, but to operate on several levels and through several stages of generality to construct a knowledge about the social world.[117] Importantly, Althusser avoids rooting Marxism in any concept of what it means to be human, claiming that Marx gave up any such notion after 1845.[118] The scientific approach that Althusser sees in Marx's work necessitates a critique of any received doctrine, including those that come with a static or essential concept of human nature. For him, all such ideas are ideological in nature.[119] The true starting point in Marx's science is materialist praxis, and its purpose an ongoing critique of ideological assumptions of all kinds.[120]

Other Marxists claim that viewing Marxism as a science is too superficial, and that Marx's doctrine acts as an organizing principle. For those who hold this view, Marxism is not just an approach or a method that uncovers or systematizes how the world functions—it *is* the process by which the world becomes consistent. When conceived as an organizing principle, Marxism is not something that distills and formalizes reality, but the mechanism by which the reality we experience forms. French existentialists Alexandre Kojève, followed shortly afterwards by Maurice Merleau-Ponty and Jean-Paul Sartre, reject the Leninist, Maoist, and Althusserian approaches by questioning the possibility that the world can be given an objective form in the manner that Lenin and Mao believe, or that Marxism can constitute the subject in the way Althusser claims. Kojève gained recognition for his attempts to synthesize Hegel, Heidegger, and Marx. Kojève argues that the dialectic is a part of Being, and in particular how Being is known. While "pure and simple Being" is not dialectical, being as revealed through thought and speech is.[121] In every act of knowledge, there is a two-part structure: a subject knowing the object, and an object being known by the subject. Thus while reality is a unified thing, it is constantly produced by two opposing beings—in other words, it is both double and single.[122] Hegel's inability to admit this—and instead to see his method as a scientific one that passively watches and describes as Being unfolds—means his thought is not truly dialectical. It doesn't realize how, upon humans bringing thought to bear on the world, a different ontology is revealed than nature has on its own.[123] In other words, the true dialectic is one where humans engage the world and reveal it through discourses. In doing so, they try to capture its concrete becoming. Marx's influence here is clear, for Marx gives a more substantive account of the development of humans through interaction with the world, just as Hegel gives a more substantive account of how knowledge and its development is possible. Rather than make the world or knowledge dialectical, Kojève insists that it is through the human interaction with the world that Being itself—including both the subject and object—becomes dialectical. To treat Marxism as science rather than organizing principle is to ignore the constitutive role of the subject in every act of knowing.

Sartre argues that things in the world are in themselves meaningless as they are capable of an infinite number of different appearances, and so the transcendental ego is necessary to provide them with any value.[124] Similarly, Merleau-Ponty states that any quality can only be apprehended within "a whole perceptual context"[125] that affects how it is perceived, and that meaning in sensation must be understood as "a process of integration in which the text of the external world is not so much copied, as composed."[126] For both, the subject is an integral part of any experience of the world, and no knowledge can be developed without it. Thus there is no possibility of neutrally observing the external world, or studying it scientifically without at the same time constituting it. Marx's system can only be saved by changing it from a means of studying the world to a means of producing the world. As the principle by which the world is created, Sartre claims Marxism incorporates everything, including human consciousness and the dialectic, into its theory.[127] As Merleau-Ponty shows, the failure to do this inevitably places knowing outside dialectics (and thus outside the Marxist system), giving it an absolute character and placing Marxism in tension with itself.[128] Dialectics must be able to explain its own development as well. For Sartre, this means that it needs to be able to justify itself without referring to anything outside it.[129] To refer to external forces implies a separate order beyond dialectics, one which works according to an old model of motion that sees movement as an accidental occurrence. Dialectics provides the only explanation for motion that conceives of it as an internal principle,[130] and only by justifying itself will dialectics not end up invoking an absolute foundation that precedes it. Sartre's dialectics is not a science, as unlike science it cannot refer to principles or beings outside itself; instead, dialectics is the only principle that must be determined a priori and without relation to anything else.[131]

Merleau-Ponty agrees with Sartre in his criticism of materialist dialectics qua science, but diverges in part on the role dialectics plays within the world. For Merleau-Ponty, dialectics is an organizing principle of the world, but not *the* organizing principle of the world. According to Martin Jay, Merleau-Ponty denies that there is any "normative totality which could be used as the critical vantage point from which the present might be judged."[132] For Merleau-Ponty, Marxism is "essentially descriptive" and "used to make sense of what was," but its task is infinite in nature.[133] Materialist dialectics appears at the intersection of subjects in the world, as a principle by which a field of experience is formed and by which objects and subjects are always opening themselves to others.[134] Unlike Sartre, Merleau-Ponty does not think dialectics is totalizing, and in fact argues that the dialectic itself is dialectical inasmuch as it goes through stages[135] without ever reaching a final totality.[136] Though the dialectic is constituted, Merleau-Ponty emphasizes that the relationship between the external world and the subject does not leave the outcome of history radically open. History is ambiguous and yields no definite meaning, yet it has a vague trajectory that is revealed in moments of crisis. This trajectory does not determine, but rather guides, society, while at the same time human actions affect the course of history. The movements of history and the significance of human action are so interwoven that at a certain point they become indistinguishable. It is for this reason that we can lose neither the dialectic—and the idea that it has a telos—nor the idea that humans are free to their own destiny.[137] Even though no totalizing ever occurs, the dialectic encourages or motivates history in a vague direction while being open to a modification of the ultimate goal.

The critical theory of Theodor Adorno and Max Horkheimer is comparable to the works of Sartre and Merleau-Ponty inasmuch as they all resist seeing Marxism as a science *of* the world by emphasizing the dialectic's ability to call into question the coherence of the world. But unlike Sartre and Merleau-Ponty, Adorno and Horkheimer do not ground the dialectic in the constituting capacity of subjects. Instead, they see dialectics as an inherent, real, and necessary process grounded in the nature of the world. As Adorno writes in the introduction to *Negative Dialectics*, dialectics is not programmatic or rule based, but real and existent,[138] so it should not be reduced to a set number of steps or to an operation. Dialectics is becoming—not just in the sense that things are constantly moving from place to place or gaining and losing qualities, but that things are constantly not what they are.[139] Dialectics is a process by which newness enters the world, and through it any identity is open to radical change. As Adorno puts it, dialectics is the manner in which "all concepts, even the philosophical ones, refer to nonconceptualities."[140] Yet this is only half the process, for dialectics continually traps the nonconceptual in the conceptual since any attempt to point to something outside the conceptual inevitably requires a concept to complete itself.[141] Dialectics cannot follow a program, a rule, or any conceptual model without limiting itself, thus negating its very purpose. Because of dialectic's openness, Adorno questions the need for a predetermined end in communism[142] and, like Althusser, posits instead a need for constant critique in order to keep all concepts dynamic.[143] As Martin Jay writes, "Adorno . . . seems not to have hoped for the complete overcoming of reification, that special bugbear of Hegelian Marxism. Yet in much of his writing, he used reification as a term of opprobrium, contending, for example, that 'dialectics means intransigence towards all reification.' "[144] There is no positive content to dialectics that can be permanently delineated, as the nature of dialectics is to sublimate anything of that type. Adorno radicalizes Marx's dialectic by removing it from the traditional Marxist program. Dialectic becomes a principle in itself.

This perspective on dialectics, while reminiscent of other Marxist philosophers, ultimately separates Adorno from all of them. In his description of scientific Marxism, Althusser only talks about the different levels of generality that come out of an encounter with the world. Dialectic is one such abstraction, and it constitutes a theoretical practice. By contrast, Adorno talks about dialectic not just as a theory, but as a force that mediates between the conceptual and nonconceptual. Similarly, at first glance there seem to be a number of similarities between Merleau-Ponty and Adorno with regard to their descriptions of the dialectic's openness, inclusion of the nonconceptual, and application of critique to the dialectic itself. Martin Jay writes that both Merleau-Ponty and Adorno "proposed an essentially negative dialectic without the likelihood of any positive resolution"[145] and felt that the idea of a harmonious end to history was an idealization of death.[146] A. T. Nuyen argues that both Adorno and

Merleau-Ponty claim the nonconceptual (or nonreflective) make reflection and thought possible.[147] The primary differences between the two thinkers are twofold. First, Merleau-Ponty grounds his dialectic in a constituting intersubjectivity and life-world (which, according to Herbert Reid, is why Merleau-Ponty can give a more convincing account of social change),[148] while Adorno denies the dialectic is constituted by subjects at all (he says the dialectic precedes subjectivity and is part of the how the world operates).[149] Second, Merleau-Ponty believes that the dialectic furnishes us with a vague, incomplete, yet somewhat positive trajectory, while for Adorno that trajectory is always only towards negativity and nonidentity.[150]

Rearranging the Marxist Trajectory, Part 2: What Is the World?

The debate over how Marxism operates is connected with the question of the world's being. Each Marxist thinker I've mentioned modifies the form the world takes as a part of their attempt to update Marx's theory, and while they each retain a large majority of Marx's insights in regards to how the world is experienced, their descriptions of the world in itself differ radically. The fundamental character of the world goes from being law-driven and determinate to unknowable and contingent as one moves through the different Marxists.

First, Lenin's analyses are grounded in a belief that the world obeys specific laws, that it can be described accurately without bias, and that a study of these descriptions and laws will reveal the right (and the only realistic) revolutionary project. Lenin underscores this in stating, "There is no trace of Utopianism in Marx," since Marx "takes the actual experience of a mass proletarian movement [the Paris Commune] and tries to draw practical lessons from it"[151]—in particular, the requirement of armed revolt against the state. The laws that the world necessarily follows are described by Marx. No room for variation exists in this program, for to open the program to different ideas is to bring about "eclecticism and absence of principle," resulting in a lack of revolutionary theory without which "there can be no revolutionary movement."[152] Althusser describes Lenin's faithfulness to Marxist thought in a couple essays, claiming that Lenin saw the materialist dialectic as the "one thing in the world which is absolute"[153] and was "profoundly convinced" that every philosophical worldview "represents the class struggle" Marx laid out.[154] The foundations of Marxism were for Lenin an unquestionable truth. Mao's Marxism is also grounded in a determinate world. For him, dialectical materialism is an objective rule operating in the world in predictable and determinate ways. As he says, "The fact is that the unity of identity of opposites in objective things is not dead or rigid, but is living, conditional, mobile, temporary and relative. . . . Reflected in man's thinking, this becomes the Marxist world outlook of materialist dialectics."[155] For both Lenin and Mao, neither the objectivity of the world nor the idea that the laws it follows can be clearly delineated are open for question. The world, as we observe it, is what is.

The determinacy of Lenin's and Mao's world is questioned by Kojève, Sartre, and Merleau-Ponty, as it fails to account for the role of the subject in producing its experience. Perception, consciousness, thought, intentions, and other factors play a role in creating the world as it is encountered, including creating the Marxist schematic that explains phenomena like alienation, property, and capital. Marxism does not exist independently of this constituting project but is an intrinsic part of it, as the dialectic is necessarily a part of what is generated. So while the world itself is not determinate like Marx imagined, the world as it is experienced is Marxist in nature. Kojève, Sartre, and Merleau-Ponty reconcile Marxism with phenomenology by stating that, while there is no world without a constituting subjectivity,[156] and while meaning comes out of an interactive process between the subject and the phenomenon within a particular situation, it is still the case that the manner in which the world is created follows particular processes. It is not possible for the world to appear in whatever way a subject chooses it to, as while the subject plays a constitutive role in composing the world, one is also thrown into it and composed by it in turn.[157] An interaction of opposing material forces—the Marxist dialectic—is a prerequisite for the appearance of the world. For Kojève and Sartre, this is true because the knowledge of the world is only possible through a dialectical relationship[158] between the unknowable external world[159] and the subject (similar to Merleau-Ponty's view that the development of history comes from an encounter between the ambiguous trajectory of history and the constituting power of individuals).[160] Kojève insists that "vulgar science" only deals with an abstraction inasmuch as it studies the entirety of the object as known by the subject, not the object itself. Such science cannot be the basis for truth itself, since that must be unchanging and eternally valid. It is impossible to uncover the object-in-itself, since all knowledge involves an act that reveals only the object that results from interaction.[161] For Sartre, such subject/object produced knowledge is not ordered and structured, but totalizing and synthetic. In other words, there is no possibility for objective knowledge—that is, knowledge not constituted by a subject and that definitively captures the external world—since every subject is of the world she or he wants to understand, but can only develop objective knowledge by holding the world and herself or himself apart. The subject and the external world are in constant dialogue, which is why Sartre claims that the encounter with the world, from a phenomenological perspective, inevitably implies the Marxist dialectic.[162] The dialectic does not work in a realm that can be scientifically observed from afar, for it sweeps up everything in its path. Though coming from a similar perspective, Merleau-Ponty rejects this view as it negates alternative possibilities in its constant push to capture everything. For Sartre, the dialectic, and as a result all beings and all knowledge, aim at drawing together and incorporating everything into one cohesive whole;[163] it is a constant process of unification. Merleau-Ponty's dialectic is as much an opening onto new differences as it is a bringing together of differences into a coherent unity. What Sartre claims is an inexorable push for unity is for Merleau-Ponty a vehicle for bringing separate entities into dialogue with one another, the result of which is the possibility of new meanings, significations, and contexts.[164] The dialectic is necessary for a unified field of experience inasmuch as such a field can only be formed by differentiating one element from another, yet any meaning resulting from the field is only temporary. The same is true for knowledge of the dialectic, which is constantly being superseded.[165] Merleau-Ponty opposes any systematization or institutionalization of the dialectic, as doing so would reduce the dialectic to what it establishes—a field of knowledge.[166] Dialectic cannot be enshrined within the proletariat nor terminate at the end of history without becoming flat and lifeless—in a word, nondialectical. Whereas for Kojève and Sartre the dialectic is the only process by which the world develops, for Merleau-Ponty it is a necessary, but not the sole, means by which the world becomes cohesive.

Relative to Kojève, Sartre, and Merleau-Ponty, the constituting subject plays no role in the world Althusser creates. Rather than look into subjectivity for a new grounding of Marxism, Althusser tries to establish the conditions that must be necessary for the world to operate as described by Marx. This means foregoing experience and beginning with the world as a complex whole, made up of many smaller relationships and contradictions.[167] It is, as Martin Jay says, a whole that has "neither a genetic point of origin nor a teleological point of arrival."[168] Althusser claims it is impossible to delve beyond this complex whole, or even to elaborate it further, for the world is given as a complex, structured unity and not as an original, simple unity.[169] The lack of simple unities means there are no essences and no concepts from which particular instances of things are drawn; rather, instances are at the base of any abstraction or generality developed. As the complex whole of the world is impossible to experience without concepts, Althusser posits ideology as an irreducible part of the world.[170] Althusser claims ideology is an artifact of culture, meaning that it acts as a lived relation between man and the world, and not a function of consciousness.[171] Humans require ideology to engage the world, and so their experience of reality is nothing other than social relations, which get their meaning from real and concrete interactions within the complex whole of the world.[172] It is impossible to approach the real with no concepts, for while the real is what exists apart from human knowledge, it can only be defined with human knowledge.[173]

In addition, Althusser says ideology turns individuals into subjects and allows them to recognize themselves as such. It is through ideology that we learn how to function in society, as it constantly "hails" us to engage with others by taking on certain roles.[174] In our engagements with friends, teachers, police officers, and other members of society, our behavior begins to conform to the expectations of society as we are rewarded or chastised for our actions. Ideology is thus the mechanism by which we recognize that we are subjects, and that certain things are demanded of us. Althusser reverses the Sartrean and Merleau-Pontean subject-ideology relationship, as ideology constitutes the subject rather than vice versa. Yet he agrees with them that there is no possibility of objective knowledge, insisting that there is no getting outside ideology. Ideology constantly surrounds us and conditions our knowledge and actions, so much so that even saying one has escaped ideology is a function of it.[175] Because ideology lets us recognize the existing state of affairs, it is a vital part of our social existence,[176] not something that can be got rid of. The point of Marxism is not to begin with abstract ideas and search for their confirmation, but to forge new concepts in your encounters with real objects.[177] And because human knowledge is pulled so much from culture and society, rather than being determined by intentions, perception, and consciousness, the influence an individual has over how the world is presented is, according to Althusser, much less than Sartre and Merleau-Ponty claim. To be truly faithful to the relationship to knowledge and the approach to praxis of Marx's project, we must return to the conceptual architecture of Marxism itself.

The critical theorists continue the trend of questioning the possibility of objective knowledge, though their critique does not rest on an examination of the subject or the ideological lens through which the world is seen. Of all the post-Marxist thinkers, they say the least about the world, refusing to posit it even as a dialectically constituted phenomenal realm or a complex whole composed of contradictions. Any description of the world—even the minimal ones given by Sartre, Merleau-Ponty, and Althusser—would, if taken as foundational and necessary, become incapable of being superseded by the dialectic. A contradiction would appear, for this necessary foundation would be held apart from the world inasmuch as it is not subject to dialectical sublimation, yet be held a part of the world inasmuch as it is the only essential piece of it. Horkheimer corrects for this by claiming the world has no necessary meaning that can be objectively found. All ideas are socially determined,[178] and no model is excluded from these influences. The world can only be grasped from a socially conditioned perspective, as no theory can exist apart from the mediating influences of culture and history.[179] Though an external world can be posited, the role it plays in composing the world we experience is unknowable, since any theory dealing with that topic would be prejudiced by history and culture. As Jay writes, Horkheimer "always acknowledged the existence of a natural object irreducible to the objectification of a creator subject and resistant to all attempts to master it conceptually."[180] This view separates Horkheimer from the view held by Merleau-Ponty. Horkheimer believes our knowledge of external objects is only negative, whereas Merleau-Ponty claims an ambiguous positive knowledge. And while Merleau-Ponty claims that the horizons that disclose the world to us have an irreducible social element,[181] Horkheimer says that it is theory (as a product of society and culture), rather than our experiential dialogue with the world at the bodily level,[182] that primarily forms the world. For Merleau-Ponty, the world we experience is constituted when we are called by the external world to complete it, and in doing so to form a complete Gestalt. This is possible because in its most basic form the subject and object—the perceiver and the external world—are not independent but completely inseparable.[183] Horkheimer rejects this approach, as for him it is impossible to know absolutely the relationship between the subject and object, including whether the two are intricately linked. Because our knowledge of subjects and objects is always affected by society and culture,[184] and because there is no way to excise the influence of society and culture from knowledge, Horkheimer does not believe it is possible to say what the primary relationship between subjects and objects is.[185] The phenomenological foundation that Merleau-Ponty wants to give for our experience does not for him arise from society and culture, and the knowledge that the body is "a general medium for having a world"[186] is not a socially conditioned concept (even though for Merleau-Ponty the body is, ontologically, irreducibly connected with the other bodies in society). By contrast, Horkheimer does not believe any theory of the subject, object, and their relationship can ever found knowledge or experience, as each one is conditioned by society and culture. Because all claims to a fundamental ontology, even a thoroughly social one such as Merleau-Ponty's, are so conditioned, there is an "irreducible tension between concept and object"[187] that makes any theory of beginnings suspect.

Yet Horkheimer is not advocating a pure and absolute relativism such that any idea about the world can be applicable at any time. Such a claim reduces the view of the world to a function of subjective reason (the type of reason that makes rational actions possible through deduction, inference, and classification),[188] and leads to fascism inasmuch as all views—even those that are hegemonic or intolerant—are allowed in.[189] This is because subjective reason is individualized, able to operate within any particular world without being beholden to it. To prevent the fascism that could come from an approach that privileges personal or group interests over the principle of social cohesion, Horkheimer argues that the world should be kept a function of objective reason, which aims at denoting the structures inherent in reality.[190] Both subjective and objective reason are socially constituted and contingent, but only objective reason works to understand the composition of the world. Horkheimer believes that by keeping the world within the sphere of objective reason it is possible to preserve a notion of a world that is common to all. In other words, the idea that the world has absolute meaning should be retained, just not any particular idea of what that meaning is.[191] To some degree, an "anything goes" approach remains inasmuch as what can be true is unconstrained by external influences, yet it does not come at the expense of, but rather enhances, community. This, again, contrasts with views held by individuals like Merleau-Ponty, or, in the world of science, David Bloor, who both posit different mechanisms to prevent absolute relativism. As I mentioned, Merleau-Ponty says our beliefs and experiences are conditioned in part by the world just as we condition the world, while for Horkheimer such a claim cannot be known. Similarly, Bloor would oppose the relativism of Horkheimer with the claim that there is an unknown yet ordered external world—or a "common core of people, objects, and natural processes"—that calls into question any claims that we can ever know something absolutely or completely.[192] Horkheimer does not think we should abandon a "common core," but unlike Bloor he does not think there is only one "common core" against which our knowledge is continually measured.

The world is not something that can ever be satisfactorily defined, but the attempt to define of the world cannot be given up without a completely relative world resulting. This is different from Althusser, who, while admitting that knowledge about the world is ideological and never truly captures the real, nevertheless believes that certain concepts are more accurate than others. His advocacy for a scientific approach leads him to advocate for concepts that are "practical" and forged when "you are face to face with your real object."[193] Such concepts developed are not eternally valid, but as products of a "science in development"[194] are subject to change. Yet for a period of time they are more accurate than abstract or utopian concepts developed apart from the real. Critical theory, unlike Althusser, does not claim that a methodological devotion to the real determines which ideas are dominant, as such a claim assumes an outside world against which your ideas can be measured, and that is not the product of cultural prejudice. Ideas may be more or less accurate at a point in time, but it is due to historical circumstances, rather than epistemological superiority, that they become so.[195] Apart from any contingent meanings we invent, the only things that can be said about the world are that it is not separate from thought and theory[196] and that it is not static but is changing.[197] Unlike the subjects or contradictions that compose the other post-Marxists' austere worlds, these two characteristics do not form a theory of the world, but act as critical operations that call into question any such theory. Apart from the movement of the dialectic the world is unknown, and our necessary attempts to try to know it will inevitably fail.

Rearranging the Marxist Trajectory, Part 3: New Revolutions

Each thinker responds to the possibilities and challenges their theory raises with new revolutionary strategies. As both Lenin and Mao believed themselves to be updating Marx's program for their particular situation (respectively, imperialist Russia and colonialist China), they each adjusted Marx's vision for revolution and the particular role the Communist Party plays in it. Lenin's belief that the revolution requires a vanguard party to succeed is drawn from Marx's writings, but plays a more centralized and programmatic role in Lenin's vision than Marx ever intended. As Lenin says, "A small, compact, core, consisting of reliable, experienced and hardened workers, with responsible agents in the principal districts and connected by all the rules of strict secrecy with the organisations of revolutionists, can . . . perform all the functions of a trade-union organization."[198] Professional revolutionaries are necessary[199] to bring together the variety of people, jobs, locations, and interests in society and unite them behind a common purpose. Power should be centralized, but with connections throughout society. Unlike Lenin, Mao does not view the party as sacrosanct. Dedicated revolutionaries are needed to bring about the transition to communism, but Mao's ultimate goal is to institute a "New Democracy" where all people are encouraged to participate in politics regardless of party affiliation.[200] Mao's well-known saying that one should look to the Communist Party to find bourgeoisie[201] implies that Communists should continually go to the peasants and workers in society to reinvigorate their revolutionary fervor and commitment to democracy. A successful revolution must undergo a transition toward socialism, which necessitates a renewal from outside to prevent the bourgeoisie from undermining it.[202] Were the revolution to become controlled by the Communist Party, it would lead to another bourgeoisie, and not to a recognition of the dynamic contradictions inherent in the materialist world. Another difference between Lenin and Mao is that while Lenin believes communism requires an immediate and unwavering opposition to the bourgeoisie, Mao believes that for the revolutionary program to succeed in China the bourgeoisie and peasants must first unite to throw off their colonizers. Left mostly untouched by Lenin and Mao are the materialist, dialectical, and ideological components of Marxism, as they focus primarily on developing and formalizing the revolutionary program.

The possibility of developing such a revolutionary program is endangered by the philosophies of Sartre and Merleau-Ponty. Writing in response to the events of the USSR and the doctrinaire way the Soviets applied Marxism, their claim that knowledge and the knowing subject undergo dialectical progression[203] means that a revolutionary program is not easily predicted, systematized, and localized. Merleau-Ponty believes

Marxism is torn between two views of revolution, one that sees it as an incidental expense of historical development (i.e., as progress) and one that sees it as a permanent overturning (i.e., as rupture).[204] Inasmuch as Marxism wants revolution to escape the situation it comes from yet tries to make it obey another situation, revolution is put in tension as both pro and anti situation. Its very nature means that it is necessarily correct about what needs to be done yet possibly wrong at the same time.[205] This leads to a revolutionary antinomy whereby the Marxist revolution, which is created to resist power,[206] produces revolutionaries—completely convinced of the justness of their cause[207]—who work to create a recognized and ordered power structure. Thus the revolutionaries in the USSR ended up using revolution to justify a governing body that was completely unrevolutionary.[208] What is needed, according to Merleau-Ponty, and what will be truly revolutionary, is a noncommunist left that resists the problems of both capitalism and communism. This left should not follow a plan dictated in advance, for to be true to the nature of the world the ambiguity and plurality inherent in our experience must be incorporated into the revolutionary program. If Marxism is to be revolutionary, it must be open to reinterpretation. Just as Merleau-Ponty claims the meaning of paintings must remain open, Marxism must be recognized as an "advent" that leaves itself open to "a future man not even outlined in our present life"[209] (i.e., to the possibility of new things to come not predictable by the present). Like Merleau-Ponty's hyperdialectic—the dialectic that does not resolve everything or follow a set path, but embraces ambiguity and partial synthesis while admitting the possibility that "progresses" can be made[210]—Marxism should not contain absolutes or be formulaic, but be willing to surpass itself. Similarly, Sartre demands that resistance occur not via a vanguard party or doctrinaire program, but a revolutionary praxis that transforms collectives into revolutionaries.[211] Sartre's philosophy is a philosophy of action that demands the development of a praxis to bring about a different situation, in part through the development of new group identities.[212] Sartre and Merleau-Ponty both separate Marxism from its programmatic elements, and as a result try to reconceive of revolution as something without a particular doctrine, but that follows from such a doctrine's absence or undoing. Revolution is not a formula, it is an event in the world that exceeds any formal system.

Situated between Lenin and Mao, on the one side, and Sartre and Merleau-Ponty, on the other, is Kojève. Kojève doesn't write much about revolution, but emphasizes that to practice the dialectic as he recommends (i.e., to embrace the role we have, as thinking subjects, in producing the world) leads us to similar conclusions as Marx. This is made clear in his interpretation of the master-slave relationship from Hegel's *Phenomenology*. Kojève argues that the best way to understand that passage is by seeing the Master as one who is meant to work for himself or herself, not others. Yet because work necessarily puts one in relation to others, no one can fulfill this role. One overcomes this challenge by creating the Master as a legal entity, such that one's biological self works for one's legal self. This is notably similar to how Marx says people work for property and capital rather than satisfying their species-being.[213] Like Hegel, Kojève advocates overcoming the master-slave relationship, and his descriptions of doing so reference revolution numerous times. Kojève emphasizes that the slave can transform the world and herself or himself through work, as shown by the French Revolution. Such active labor recreates the slave in line with an idea of herself or himself as free, just as it remakes the world.[214] Revolution, then, is the work of the slave transforming the world to achieve freedom. Kojève draws an analogy to the Christian worldview, which he argues is one of slavery. It can only be overcome after it is instituted, for that worldview provides the ideal of freedom as something to be achieved. Only once the experience of Christian slavery is had, and the institution of freedom found inadequate, is it possible for the slave to know for what she or he risks her or his life.[215] These statements demonstrate that Kojève is more doctrinaire than Sartre and Merleay-Ponty while less so than Lenin and Mao. Kojève agrees with the idea that development goes through clear stages but also emphasizes that it is through participation in the creation of the world that these stages appear. It is not historical forces, but the dialectical creation of reality that animates these stages. In short, Kojève suggests the existence of stages while not necessitating any,[216] and gives more of a role to the participants in the creation of the stages than Lenin and Mao did.

The high degree of skepticism critical theory proposes in order to be faithful to the constantly changing world means no revolutionary program is wholly endorsed. Many of the critical theorists were themselves witnesses of revolutionary activities,[217] and held a sympathy for revolutions, but were skeptical of dogmatic programs of revolution.[218] Their experience with the Nazis had shown them the danger of fascism that arises from dogmatic adherence to a political program. Critical theory was presented by Horkheimer as a revolutionary tool in the sense that critique, when properly formulated and inserted into society, can be the catalyst for change.[219] Small, incremental progress being unsatisfactory for the achievement of a better world, a revolution must move beyond the schema at work in the present, a task that critique can help to begin. Yet the danger of fascism that follows from a complete openness means that to some extent there must always be some schema at work in revolution, even if the schema itself is problematic. The insight of critical theory is the identification of the antinomies—between chaos and dogmatism, between critique and fidelity, and between totality and otherness—at the heart of the Marxist project of revolution. The practice that critical theory recommends is to stay in between the bounds of the antinomies to avoid the dangers that come from embracing one side or the other. Revolution is a constant, ongoing exercise, in need of regular criticism and renewal.

Althusser's comments on revolution were made as a response to the French Communist Party's dilution of Marxism into a liberal humanism. Althusser believes Marxism is a scientific theory capable of transforming the structure of society, not an ideology aimed at determining what policies best fit the constitution of the subject. Part of Althusser's concept of revolution is his emphasis on how it is vital to ensure the theory of Marxism is correct, for theory is a potent weapon in the promulgation of communism.[220] The other place Althusser discusses revolution is in "Contradiction and Overdetermination," where Althusser uses the example of the Russian Revolution to discuss how revolutionary conditions originate. The key point he makes is that revolution is not the result of a general and hegemonic contradiction imposing itself on society, but rather the "fusing" of many disparate "circumstances" and "currents" into one "ruptural unity."[221] The general contradiction (such as that between the proletariats and bourgeoisie) can perhaps define the revolutionary situation, but it cannot bring it about. A revolution is enacted from below, as the surging, shifting masses of people begin to reflect similar contradictions throughout. As more and more of the relationships within society become defined by the same contradictory characteristics, the opposing groups become unified, merging together until a revolution becomes inevitable. Althusser is careful to claim that these relationships are not pure phenomena, but, as Marx would say, derived from the relations of production and conditions of existence in society.[222] Althusser uses the term "overdetermination" to emphasize how the contradiction that brings about a revolution, even as it determines society, is itself determined by the various instances within the social body. It is "overdetermined in principle."[223] The Russian Revolution, Althusser claims, was the first instance of an industrial nation directly experiencing a communist revolution because of how prevalent, overwhelming, and thus exacerbated the contradictions between the elites and the workers were.[224]

Althusser's other relevant discussion in regard to the question of revolution is his recommendation about how radicals can use ideology productively. Because ideology and practice are intimately intertwined, even a slight misunderstanding of a concept can significantly affect the outcome of an event. A successful revolution is one that has a well-developed theory that underlies it, while a revolution lacking a strong articulation is easily subverted or undermined. Words and concepts are for Althusser sites of struggle—the ways they are used represent continual battles between the bourgeoisie and proletarian masses. Althusser's revolution is one that operates not only in the streets, but in the textbooks and classrooms of the university. It carefully constructs ideas and concepts as weapons that can be used to undermine oppressive systems. The Marxist revolution will only succeed "on condition that it fights both about very "scholarly" words (concept, theory, dialectic, alienation, etc.) and about very simple words (man, masses, people, class struggle).[225]

Beyond the Dialectical Revolution

We now turn to our final assessment of dialectical theories of revolution. Though the criticisms given here apply to all visionary theories, they focus on Marxist ones for obvious reasons.

We saw Marxists astutely diagnosing paradoxes and contradictions in Marx's program, which in turn yielded important revelations about the nature of revolution. But can dialectics be saved simply by varying the character of the dialectical world? Challenging overly doctrinaire revolutionary programs or mechanistic views of history gives revolution some independence to explore different possibilities, but as long as a dialectical trajectory remains, is revolution truly free? Or rather, is it possible that the variations on the dialectic free up new possibilities only by placing other possibilities beyond the bounds of revolution?

An interesting feature of the variations on dialectics is their increasing engagement with contingency and nothingness. We see this most clearly in Marxism. Whereas Marx's accounts in *The Manifesto of the Communist Party*, *The German Ideology*, and *Grundrisse* are histories of necessity, their retelling by Lenin, Mao, Kojève, Sartre, Merleau-Ponty, Althusser, Adorno, and Horkheimer increasingly presents Marx's discoveries as outgrowths of his time that now must be rethought. In addition, Sartre's claim that negation conditions the possibility of individuals becoming socially engaged[226] and Adorno's claim that philosophy draws its legitimacy from the negative[227] illustrate that the role of nothingness is of increasing concern to Marxists as a condition for the possibility of their projects. Nothingness, as portrayed by these thinkers, is what keeps Marxism—and philosophy as a whole—going, as it represents the irreducibility of the material world to any program or doctrine. To varying degrees, every Marxist thinker mentioned attempts to prevent the solidification of Marxism into an orthodoxy by preserving the dynamism of its structural elements like ideology, revolution, and dialectic. Lenin and Mao update the description of how the communist revolution will occur, taking into account contexts (such as the continued existence of peasants in some industrial societies and the worldwide scope of the European imperial system) that Marx himself was unaware of. Kojève, Sartre, and Merleau-Ponty apply the dialectic to the very constitution of objectivity and the knowledge of it that humans have. Althusser presents a world that is unknowable aside from its being a whole composed of contradictions. And Adorno removes any sense of identity between the material and the conceptual, presenting the dialectic as an ongoing encounter between the two. Each theorist seeks to maintain Marxism's ability to speak substantively of social and political systems while beginning from foundations often vastly different from the one Marx did. In order to take into account all the potential contingencies of history and philosophy, the certainties of Marxism have become increasingly minimalist while its method extends beyond the limits of knowledge to the point where nothingness is encountered.

Even the fascist dialectics mentioned at the beginning of the chapter follow this pattern of engaging with nothingness and resisting doctrine. First, they begin by reframing thought as an act or process, emphasizing that what matters is not the content but the operation. The specifics of what the dialectic says are less important than the fact that thought is saying them dialectically. In addition, both Croce and Gentile emphasize the emptiness of the world absent thought, and note the importance of realizing that thought is actively creating the world. Finally, the doctrine of fascism as given by Gentile resists patterns and established meanings. Humans and the state are adaptive, while the fascist lifestyle disciplines us to embrace this fact. Life is about mastery, not about following established codes of conduct. Whether it is the content of thought, the nature of the world, or the essence of being human, fascists similarly incorporate the ideas of contingency and nothingness into their thought.

Yet as a foundation for revolution, even these revised theories fall short. Revolution still follows a dialectical pattern, and is conditioned by a stable, if mostly unknown, world. As dialectical, revolution is always a harmonizing force, bringing together the polar opposites of a dichotomy even as it creates new ones. Marx says the reconciling of the feudal classes leads to capitalism and the opposition between the worker and the bourgeoisie;[228] Lenin believes that overthrowing capitalism will at first lead to a contradictory form of communism where everyone is treated equally rather than according to one's ability and need;[229] and Sartre believes reconciling an individual with his or her history ultimately requires the development of new structures that oppose the individual to his or her group membership.[230] Fascism doesn't condone revolution, saying the synchronizing elements of the dialectic—between one's willpower and one's environment—are contained within the state. Revolution's transformational and creative power is limited by the nature of the dichotomy itself, and the potential changes that can occur upon the dichotomy's supersession. The revolutions conceived of by Marxists and fascists, because they are motivated by class conflict or nationalism, are circumscribed by the nature of class and the nation such that other concerns become secondary or ignored. Few Marxists have theorized issues of race, gender, or nationality except inasmuch as they can be attached to the Marxist critique of capital, nor articulated a vision of revolution that does not position the working class as the primary architect and beneficiary. Systematic disparities or programs of injustice unrelated to class are unimportant, as they will ostensibly be solved upon the reconciliation of class disparities, once humans are returned to their actual lives and the conditions of their existence. While Fascists discuss race as an outcome of their nationalism, they ignore the inequalities of class, gender, and similar issues as an impediment to true harmony.

Even among contemporary Marxists who substantively diverge from Marx on the question of telos and the program of revolution, this difference between the ideological and actual remains, and revolution is always portrayed as an attempt at harmonizing these two realms. Social or political concerns that do not primarily deal with the relationship between these two realms are irrelevant to Marxism, while revolutions that occur in relation to such concerns do not even qualify within Marxism as revolutions. Instead, the natures of the ideological and actual operate as a given to condition what counts as a revolution. And a truly transformative revolution, which could radically change the rules governing the ideological and actual, is impossible.

Revolution is always put in service of the dialectic's larger program, whether that is the overcoming of class inequality, the ending of national disunity, or the continued attempt to find an objective meaning in the world. *Visionary theories*, unlike *regulationism*, do not attempt to capture revolution in a predetermined world, but do attempt to describe a normative operation—the dialectic—by which revolution always functions. This operation can greatly affect the overall shape of the world, but is itself never affected by any changes in the world despite its location there (Croce and Gentile excepted, who claim it is located in the mind; that said, they similarly do not allow the mind to shape the dialectical operation). Though Sartre's and Merleau-Ponty's philosophies claim the dialectic affects itself, and that the form of the dialectic is not formulaic, this only varies the specific shape of the operation, but does not overturn it. The dialectic itself, in its most generic form as the contestation between and reconcilement of two opposing forces, persists. Revolution is embraced by Marxism and presented as a function of the world. It is synchronized with the world's basic structure such that revolution reaffirms a dialectical and materialist outlook even when it opposes itself to specific shapes that society takes. But in making revolution conform to the Marxist project, it becomes bound to the goal of Marxism to return the ideological to the actual. New things can be created in the process of achieving this goal, but radical change is still only a means to an end. It is not the boundaries of the world, but its trajectory, to which revolution is put in service. In fascism, the reconcilement is between opposing thoughts as the mind creates reality. The dialectic produces thought, which in turn produces reality. Thought returns to itself, just as the exploration of thought produces oppositions. Fascist politics is about disciplining the state and one's body to society's will; to the extent that radical change exists, it begins in the mind before attempting actualization in the state, and ultimately a synthesis of the two. It is still just a means to an end. In either case, revolution remains chained to the state.

There is another problem with the theories of revolution enabled by the dialectic. Dialecticism presupposes a common plane through which oppositions encounter one another and become unified, or a common vernacular that allows for the transmission of information from one to the other. Only in this way does reconciliation become possible. This plane or vernacular is different for different thinkers. For Hegel, the harmonizing takes place in Spirit, and is done through the medium of the human person, who can encounter both objects and ideas. For Marxists, the harmonizing takes place in the material world or in a particular account of Being, since that is where they see the actual and material coming into contact (depending on whether they believe ideas come from the material world, or whether they believe subjects and objects are both constitutive of reality). For Fascists, the harmonizing occurs in thought, which in turn constitutes reality. This shared plane presents revolution as an event that occurs on it, one that facilitates interaction by enabling dialogue between—and ultimately the harmony of—opposites. Revolution is incapable of overturning this plane, or rewriting the vernacular that allows for the opposites to communicate. While the planes and vernaculars that dialecticians describe allow for a lot, they don't—and can't—allow for anything. They thus tend those who operate with them towards certain states over others. In this way, revolution becomes captured again by a state; though in this case, it is not a particular state so much as a telos or a tending-toward that the state is supposed to follow. To give a few examples, consider the dialectical programs of Hegel, Marx, Gentile, and Merleau-Ponty. Hegel's dialectic tends toward a consideration of others, for any reaching outwards will encounter other humans as relative equals to oneself. Hegel's political program must of necessity involve one that conceptualizes humans as relative equals, which makes it no surprise that Hegel indicates a slight preference for a constitutional monarchy. Though this is not the only government that a consideration of humans as equals would lead to, it is one of several, while other forms of government (dictatorship) clearly don't meet this criteria. Marx focuses on the material needs of humans, and his dialectical program shows society wrestling with how best to satisfy them. Any state that doesn't think about these could not be one that Marx's dialectic tends toward. Thus it is obvious from the outset that Marx will not end in a society advocating basic liberalism, for those societies are the outcome of focusing on peoples' ideal needs (i.e., freedom). Gentile's plane is one of thought, considered robustly as foundational of all reality. His telos or tending-toward is going to be one that trains thought to control rather than be controlled. A state that allows for maximum freedom doesn't do this, but one that focuses on developing willpower does. Clearly, his dialectic necessitates a state different than the one produced by Hegel's or Marx's. Finally, Merleau-Ponty's dialectic focuses on Being as product of subject and object, where its horizons are constantly being shaped and reshaped over time. The state that is produced by this plane is one that resists totalization, but that constantly tries to capture everything nonetheless. Hegemonic states and loosely regulated states could not be the outcome of this dialectic. As all this shows, dialectical theories of revolution tend toward states, or types of states, even if they refuse to prescribe correct ones. The visionary model of revolution becomes restricted by the way in which dialectical thinkers understand and pursue their ideals. The revolution is not freed, though it is given more autonomy in deciding which state to advocate.

By making these criticisms, am I fetishizing revolution, as some might suggest? Radical change has obsessed many revolutionaries, sometimes to a revolution's detriment. Yet my critiques don't demand we abandon all programs, but rather rethink the relationship revolution has to them. The problem is not the goals of revolutionary programs or emancipatory politics, but the manner in which revolution is put in service of them. At its best, revolution is a tool of the oppressed. When the oppressed and dialectical thinkers desire the same ends, they can use revolution and work for emancipation together. But visionary thinkers demand revolution always service the emancipatory program. This can lead to revolutions working against the oppressed when emancipatory politics go awry. As part of a visionary program, revolution cannot adapt as needed. It becomes tethered to the program, inhibited from addressing the needs of the place where it is being implemented. By liberating revolutions, a stronger visionary program is created. Revolution can change the program to suit the needs of the oppressed, just as revolution itself can tailor its actions to the situation to which it is applied. In short, the liberated revolution creates a more resilient and less mechanistic visionary program. This will not only do more to help those who are oppressed, but also increase the chances of success for visionary programs as well.

The failure of dialectics implies that to incorporate revolutions into definite systems, even if there is no definite world to which it is yoked, is still problematic. The rules of the systems become constraining, leading to the privilege of certain concerns and the ossification of processes governing change. Recovering revolution requires excepting it from the world and finding a description that does not subsume it under a larger project. Spaces wholly removed from the world, from its processes, and from its movements must be uncovered. The profound impact dialectics has had on history and theory has maintained many of the chains of the state even as it worked to remove them. Only beyond dialectics, once the notion of trajectory has been left behind, will we be able to begin thinking about how to remove these bonds.

This analysis of *visionary* theories makes clear that we need to understand how ruptures like revolutions can incorporate the processes of the world as well as specific figures in it. This type of radical change has been explored by numerous thinkers the tradition called "evental theory." It is to their work that I will look in the next chapter.

4

From out of Oblivion

Evental Thought and the Liberated Revolution

Breaking with the State

The desire for radical change has found expression many times, and in many ways, throughout the generations. Revolutionaries have advocated for complete liberty and equality, an egalitarian distribution of resources and power, and an end to corporate greed and political malfeasance. Yet the actual results brought about by radical groups often differ, sometimes substantially, from their rhetorical visions. The frustrating, fascinating curiosity of revolution lies in its inability to be predicted, irreducibility to normative rules, and impossibility to manufacture. Iconic tomes of revolutionary thought have been unable to yield much in the way of a consistent and foreseeable program of revolution, while the tactics that once worked well yield vastly different results when applied in another time and place. Revolutionaries are constantly returning to the beginning and heading out in a new direction. A dogmatic and unthinking revolution peters out into disconnected, inconsistent actions that lack a firm message, and is easily appropriated by the state it opposes. Finding a transformative revolution will require a new approach to the subject.

Thus far this investigation has yielded several points: (1) the liberation of revolution requires separating it from all states, (2) separating revolution from the state entails conceiving of change as an agent or motive, and (3) this agent or motive of change cannot use revolution as a means to any particular end by putting it in service of any one thing. The strain of thought most helpful for this project consists of theories that attempt to disconnect events from a necessary ontology or epistemology, and that see events as producing massive changes within the state. I call this "evental theory." The defining feature of evental theory is a focus on discontinuity, as meaning comes from processes that can change radically. For evental theorists, revolutions are ruptures with what came before and the creation of a new set of meanings. What sets evental theory apart from other theories of revolution is that it portrays radical transformations as restructurings of the rules determining what exists, not as reorganizations of what is into new groups. According to evental thought, dangerous and unjustifiable states arise from essentializing the relationship between the state and its conceptual ground rather than from having an inauthentic relationship to that ground. If politics has an intrinsic ground, the states built on top of it will always be remarkably similar. To be capable of producing massive transformations, revolutions must be beyond the order that defines the state. Consequently, and in order for radical change to be possible, the state—understood as an order that defines both what takes on political significance and the manner in which it does—is wholly contingent. No entities, relationships, or ideas inevitably remain in it forever. Though the state persists, no part of it will out of necessity do so. Looking at the ways evental thought makes this case will provide clues about how to liberate revolution.

There is a difficulty that all evental theories must deal with. As citizens, we live within the boundaries of the state; we are only citizens inasmuch as we do so. Our understanding of politics is constituted by the character of the state in which we live (even a communist living in a capitalist state organizes her or his actions, policies, and political knowledge as a response to the state in which she or he lives). If revolution is defined by its novelty, and founded on a ground that is not the state, how is it possible for us to encounter it such that it can play a meaningful role in our society? As the Althusser-inspired political tradition would put it, how is it possible to "think the new"?[1] This problem is composed of several, interrelated issues that must be addressed before a complete answer is possible:

1. What grounds the possibility of evental thought? Why is it possible to claim that events have this massive transformative power?

2. What is the nature of an event? What characteristics does it have, and what language is appropriate for describing it?
3. What is the state? What logic defines it?
4. What relationship does the event have to the state? How is it possible to trigger such a massive and transformative action, and what are the effects of that action?

Despite the similar approaches evental thinkers take to understanding revolutions, there are multiple disagreements within the corpus of evental thought that ultimately yield different political visions. Before describing Dynamic Anarchism's theory of revolution in the next chapter, I will recount the framework of evental thought, drawing out the disparities between each thinker, by posing to it these four questions. This will provide a basis for comprehending Dynamic Anarchism and how it diverges from extant evental theories. To make my explanations of evental theory clear, I will be framing my answers to these questions around Alain Badiou's philosophy, bringing in other theorists to draw out the conflicts within evental thought. The thinkers I reference are not unified by adherence to any particular political tradition, and at times strongly disagree with one another. I draw on them because they each have a theory of radical change that can be categorized as evental (though they do not comprise the entirety of that list), and because a discussion of their theories will best situate the eventual introduction of my own. The purpose of this chapter is to provide an explanation and critique of evental theory, demonstrating that while it provides useful tools for studying revolution it does not go far enough. Additional descriptions of evental theory—primarily those of Deleuze and Badiou—will be given in the next chapter as a way of framing my own novel theory.

Finally, a couple of terminological notes. First, in previous chapters, I have used the words "state" and "world" fairly interchangeably. This is in part the result of my attempt to tailor my language to those from whom I am quoting, and in part to emphasize the pervasiveness of the state as a totalizing entity that determines both the space in which and the nature of how politics occurs. However, for the sake of consistency and clarity, in this chapter and the next I will revert to using "state" rather than "world," and will endeavor to make my summaries of other authors reflect this change. It must be kept in mind that the term "state" refers to the order that politics takes as such, and not just a juridical framework or set of people inhabiting a commonwealth. This should be differentiated from the sphere of politics and the apparatus of politics. Next, while I emphasize contingency (both here and in the next chapter), this does not mean that any combination of things is possible at any point. What is contingent is the defining order and operation of the state, but this does not mean that any composition of the state is possible at any time. The theorists I cite in this chapter hold similar views of contingency (that is, what is contingent is the characterizing form the state takes, not the entirety of its composition). When I explain my theory in the next chapter, I will further elaborate upon both of these concepts.

Question 1: Grounding Radical Change

Transformative events have reorganized society from top to bottom. Changes like these are generally not predicted by extant models, leading researchers to search for what produces them. Evental theorists uncover their ideas when studying the dynamics preceding and following these radical shifts.

Answering the first question about the grounding of events requires looking beyond appearances, as the theories of evental thought present a radically changeable state. Very little is absolute or universal. New objects and ideas produced by radical shifts remake the state and its contents in fundamentally new ways. Foucault studies how madmen that were seen as vehicles for lyrical truth before the seventeenth century became patients to be locked up and studied in order to uncover psychiatric truths.[2] Said delineates how the Orient transformed from an object of study to a danger to be controlled because of changes in commerce and politics throughout the nineteenth century.[3] Beings, subjects, institutions, practices, ideas, and meanings all undergo radical alterations due to events. Badiou begins his argument for radical shifts with the claim that the attributes, characteristics, and parts of a thing are encountered prior to the idea that there is a being in which they inhere. He describes his insight by saying "what *presents* itself is essentially multiple; *what* presents itself is essentially one," concluding that if being is naturally one and multiplicity a fiction we end up with the contradiction that we are able to engage with a being beyond what appears. Yet because it is not contradictory to hold that being is essentially multiple and the unification of being only what we declare it to be, we must hold that "the one *is not*."[4] Everything we encounter as a single being has only been declared such, and is not actually so. To put it another way, unity is a function of appearing and not a natural part of being. This is why, in his later work *The Logic of Worlds*, Badiou claims that what counts as a unity is the result of a transcendental that is neither subjective nor constitutive, but rather a special logical machinery that can account for "the intra-worldly cohesion of appearing" (i.e., the appearance of ones).[5] Because our knowledge of a being's attributes is conditioned by the decision to count it as a being, it is possible that any particular understanding of the state (defined by Badiou as a set in which all the parts are counted as one and the structure of the set is counted as one) is radically alterable were we to follow a different set of rules in determining what counts as a being. Badiou grounds radical transformations on the premise that any organization of the state depends upon a changeable set of rules that determine how to cut up, divide, and categorize multiplicity. Multiplicity should not be understood as a meaningful realm, as the nature of multiplicity prohibits comprehending it as a single thing. Badiou says, "The multiplicity from which ontology makes up its situation is composed solely of multiplicities. . . . In other words, every multiple is a multiple of multiples."[6] As Oliver Marchart explains, for Badiou definitions "do not refer to any empirically given 'object' outside the processes of thinking."[7] The ontological primacy of multiplicity removes the need to think about what meanings being possesses as such, and opens being to many possibilities.

Other evental thinkers replace the transcendental rules that determine what counts as a being with the notion of difference. Derrida claims that meanings originate from interactions between and differences with others, so it is impossible to develop a discourse about a being (or to have any knowledge about it whatsoever) without looking at how it relates to what surrounds it. In addition, the potential meanings of a word, gesture, or sign of any kind are open and always "to-come." Permanent rules, such as found in other theories of revolution, must be subject to change. Ethics and politics carry impossible demands, because we cannot institute any principles without also admitting they can be radically different.[8] We can only ever make a meaning present by referring to its fundamental absence.[9] Because there is no central locus of meaning, everything becomes "a system in which the central signified, the original or transcendental signified, is never absolutely present outside a system of differences. The absence of the transcendental signified extends the domain and the play of signification infinitely."[10] The implications of this are that there are no essences to be discovered. This concept is applied politically by Antonio Negri and Michael Hardt, who discuss the importance of the encounter for political struggle. They resist seeing the multitude as atomic individuals, and instead use Spinoza's ideas of mixing and composing. These ideas occur through encounters, which result "either in decomposition into smaller bodies or composition into a new, larger body."[11] Encounters in turn form singularities, as the latter only exist and gain meaning through their relationships with other singularities.[12] Evental theorists emphasize that one cannot approach the world with the assumption that there are constants to what constitutes a subject, society, or state. Historical events and objects have no meaning, no essence, and no form apart from the context from which they arose; our ability to see meaning, essence, and form in them is conditioned upon the possibility of them to be different. As Foucault explains, "So many things can be changed, being as fragile as they are, tied more to contingencies than to necessities, more to what is arbitrary than to what is rationally established, more to complex but transitory historical contingencies than to inevitable anthropological constants."[13] Though similar in their understanding of meaning, Foucault and Derrida use different strategies to investigate the production of meaning and apply their investigations to different fields. Foucault looks at how changes in discursive formations and power-regimes transform concepts like subjectivity, punishment, and sexuality. Derrida studies how discussions of philosophical theories invoke a whole "metaphysics of presence" and impose privileged binaries. Applying his deconstructive method to questions of democracy, linguistics, and death, he overturns the privileged binaries within them by demonstrating how what is present or privileged is conditional on the absent and subordinated, and that fundamentally different orders are necessarily possible. Radical transformations are possible because that which conditions meaning leaves open the possibility for the new.

All evental thinkers conceive of their systems as transhistorical, inasmuch as each system operates within yet persists apart from any particular sociohistorical context. This means that, while Badiou's rules governing what counts as one, Foucault's power relations, and Derrida's play of signs change moderately in response to their context, they do not change as radically as the beings they produce. Despite the ways they appear, their basic function and mode of operation persist. Power is a constant in Foucault's analyses from his genealogical period onward, but his analyses show it functioning in diverse ways throughout history, from the physical tortures effected on the body[14] to the bureaucratic procedures that regulate society and impose state racism.[15] Similarly, for Deleuze and Guattari the plane of consistency and strata appear differently in biology than in linguistics, but they always perform the same task.[16] That the forces creating the state are open and plural in their appearance explains why they are never fully theorized. For instance, Foucault says that he is giving an analytics of power rather than a theory of it,[17] and Derrida claims deconstruction is not a theory in itself, but the recognition of the fiction of origin (or the "trace") that appears whenever a theory is put forth.[18] Like with Hardt and Negri, applying these processes to politics yields the same result. Rancière's concept of dissensus, which draws from Foucault and Derrida, among others, operates similarly in all situations. Dissensus is a gap in the sensible that places something from one world in another (e.g., using protest to turn a factory into a public sphere). In all situations, dissensus brings something new into the sensible by creating an image or phrase that doesn't fit with what's around it.[19] Evental theorists must examine productive forces anew at the beginning of each new state.

Evental theorists ground the possibility for the event by developing methods that can only be described in terms of how they affect the state. They use forces that can appear within the state in numerous ways to emphasize that there are no subjects, objects, concepts, or institutions that condition the state. Showing the contingency of all potential grounds is the first step in finding a way to decouple revolution from the state, for it clears the foundation of the state of specific forms that could be used to resist transformative change.

Question 2: The Potential of the Event

Exempting the event from the state starts to explain the transformative power of events, but begs the question of how to understand the event. There are many examples of radical transformation, so capturing them all under one theory requires a detailed discussion of how events work.

With regard to question 2, all evental theorists agree that true events are separate from everyday occurrences. Many happenings transpire constantly that do not rise to the level of event. This is because events shake up the foundations of the everyday and prescribe new foundations in their wake. They are a rupture with the previous circumstances, and yield new ideas, practices, and institutions that become the state's foundation going forward. Alain Badiou's *Being and Event* describes the event as "a *singular* multiple,"[20] irreducible to any situation and about which "ontology has nothing to say."[21] It is a "radical transformational action" that "originates in a point" known as an "evental site."[22] Evental sites are obscured and singular places within the state, and what counts as an evental site is contingent upon the state itself such that there are no permanent evental sites. It is also worth noting that events will at times take on the state of the situation rather than the situation as such. The difference between the situation and the state has to do with what is presented (the situation) versus what is represented (the state). For Badiou, events are incomprehensible until an "interpretive intervention"[23] arrives. This theory stays largely consistent throughout Badiou's corpus. There are some differences in terminology (e.g., Badiou does not use the term "interpretive intervention" in *Logic of Worlds*, but says the event "sets off the stepwise recasting of the transcendental of the world"[24]), and new ideas that complement those in *Being and Event* (e.g., Badiou's typology of subjects), but in general this explanation of event does not change.

Interpretative interventions declare the event to be part of a new state by redescribing the rules determining what exists. The insight that leads Badiou to describe events in this manner is the fact of multiplicity, or the idea that there exist no ones or unities within the world.[25] There are only the unities that we declare. Yet as any declared unity is incapable of capturing the totality of things (since no totality exists to be captured), there is always a remainder—what Badiou calls the void—that escapes our declaration of something as a unified being.[26] Events occur when a multiple within the state is not fully presented, or when there are parts of it outside the state. The inability of the state to explain this partially presented multiple means that the state must be changed to fully present this multiple within the state. At that point, something may happen that reveals a need to develop new rules about what exists (i.e., what can be declared as a "one"). Events come from people within the state considering and reacting to the void revealed by this partially presented multiple. Standing in between the state and the void, events demonstrate the need for an original or radically transformed state to be developed that follows a new logic incompatible with the old one. Those who recognize the need for a new logic, by remaining faithful to this need and disseminating the new logic, actively work against the extant state. As Badiou says, "One can again think fidelity as a counter-state: what it does is organize, *within* the situation, another legitimacy of inclusions. It builds . . . a kind of *other* situation, obtained by the division in two of the primitive situation."[27] The event is a caesura that originates from a particular place without conforming to it, and prescribes a new logic that through the actions of militants leads to a new state with new beings and practices. As Oliver Marchart writes, "A political organization of militants (i.e., the subject in the field of politics) is nothing but the collective product of a process of fidelity towards an event. . . . A truth is produced by the decision of a subject to remain faithful to an event."[28] Within the field of evental thought it is the ideas of caesura and incompatibility, more than any other, that are used to describe revolutions.

Like Badiou, other evental theorists emphasize the disconnect events produce and the incommensurability of the preceding and subsequent states. Michel Foucault says of revolutions that they both "belong to history" and also "escape from it."[29] Hardt and Negri build on this point, saying that revolution is both continuity and rupture, and belongs to the present (rather than the future) yet exceeds it.[30] There is no necessary outcome to revolution that will be achieved in the future, but neither does revolution make complete sense within the horizons of the present. But whereas Badiou is concerned with the declaration of the event, Foucault tries to understand events through a study of their effects. Foucault sees a difficulty in trying to unravel events, as they do not come in the form of a single break but as a contemporaneous collection of several transformations that may take centuries to unfold.[31] For example, Foucault says that the French Revolution acts as a "complex, articulated, describable group of transformations that left a number of positivities intact, fixed for a number of others rules that are still with us, and also established positivities that have recently disappeared or are still disappearing before our eyes."[32] While it is a difficult task to pinpoint an event in space and time, it can be tracked through its effects on society in the form of the discursive formations and regimes of power that grow out of it. No matter what happened at the time of the event, it is possible, by studying texts written before and after it, to see how the event changed the state. Notable events develop new and incommensurable *dispositifs*, or frameworks for knowledge,[33] that present us with entirely different orders.[34] Thomas Nail says that this happens by harnessing already occurring breakdowns and exclusions in order to transform the dominant political order rather than by creating ex nihilo or through a transcendental process.[35] Because the statements, ideas, and objects found within these orders obtain meaning from their differences with others, in a new framework the same statement will not necessarily mean the same thing it meant in the old. There is no common measure that allows us to judge one framework right or wrong, but progress is possible when a new framework can explain what were before considered anomalies without erasing the explanatory power of earlier viewpoints.[36] Revolutions must be tailored to their specific circumstances. Using Foucault's notions of biopower and revolution, Hardt and Negri argue that the age of biopower will only be overcome if the struggle focuses on the unique problems created by biopower.[37] This point is made all the more clear in Hardt's and Negri's criticism of Marxism's tendency to develop uncritiqued superstructures. Hardt and Negri laud the work of Althusser and the Frankfurt School to subsume the superstructures within the material bodies of the world, dissolving the boundaries between them and returning the transcendental to the immanent.[38] Thomas Kuhn takes a similar position about radical shifts in science. He describes shifts as "reconstructions of the field from new fundamentals"[39] that occur in periods when there are significant anomalies unexplainable by science's theoretical assumptions. Like Foucault and Badiou, Kuhn claims every new paradigm is incommensurable with earlier ones, for models and statements do not mean the same thing in one paradigm as they do in another.[40] Fred Evans explains the notion of incommensurable paradigm by saying, "We could possibly translate the Newtonian's idea of the conservation of mass into Einstein's language about the conversion of mass into energy ($e=mc^2$). But we could not do so without considerable distortion of the translated position."[41] Like Foucault, Kuhn does believe paradigms can be preferred over others by their ability to solve more problems than earlier ones.[42]

These thinkers differ in the degree to which they conceive of the event as unified. Badiou provides it with the greatest sense of unity, saying it is a recognized multiple that prescribes a new set of operations for a new state. For him, the event is very clearly delineated from the situation that came before. Kuhn sees events as more ambiguous, as the anomalies produced by the failure of a paradigm are not readily separated from that old paradigm. It takes time to develop a conceptual and perceptual system that allows events to be seen. There needs to be a process that brings about the event.[43] Foucault says the unity of the event is a function of the contemporaneity of numerous transformations, which over a period of time aggregate to produce a massive effect. Any unity the event has is contingent. Badiou recognizes the event more easily, as for him it occurs all at once in the form of a new multiple (i.e., a being whose parts have never been recognized previously as all belonging to the same entity). It is wrestling with the effects of that multiple, and how to be faithful to it, that takes time. By contrast, the events Foucault describes take years, if not centuries, to be realized. Rancière leans more toward this side as well, for while sensation can tell you when something does not belong, the consequence of such an appearance is a struggle over enunciation and appearance that can take place in any location at any time.[44] The redrawing of the "natural" lines of enunciation can take a long time, and is often a messy process. Kuhn thinks they can be relatively quick or excessively long to develop, depending on how quickly a new paradigm can be developed and spread throughout society.[45] As Ian Hacking writes, Kuhn became "lukewarm about [the notion of] discontinuity, holding, plausibly enough, that even if some revolutions occur in a trice, many others do not. . . . The new-world problem is not about working in a new world after a moment or a week of illumination and transformation."[46]

The event is an important tool for thinking revolution as it erases the idea that there are necessary meanings or figures that constitute the state. Instead, the state comes from processes that draw connections, create relationships, and narrate themes in many different ways. When these connections, relationships, and themes are shown to be significantly inadequate, events create new ones. Events present the foundations of social contract theory and Marxism as functions of these processes, and thus alterable given the right circumstances.

Question 3: The Origin of Order

Once evental theorists have a concept of the event, they can start to describe its relationship to the state. And just as evental authors use different methods to describe events, they approach the question of the state's constitution in several ways. The state is understood by Badiou as the operations that determine how entities are categorized and counted, or the establishment of transcendental rules by which things can happen and beings can function.[47] As Badiou writes, "The State is in fact the measureless enslavement of the parts of the situation, an enslavement whose secret is precisely the errancy of superpower, its absence of measure."[48] This is the political version of what Badiou refers to in *Logic of Worlds* as a "transcendental of a world,"[49] or what in *Being and Event* he calls the "state of the situation."[50] It consists of the formal rules by which things are included or excluded from presentation, or appearance.

Using his set theory inspired ontology, Badiou shows that the state is not concerned with individual people, but with the organization that those individuals take. The state does not look at people as unique members of society, but rather the class they belong to, their designated gender, their occupation, and so on. As Badiou says, "The State is simply the necessary metastructure of every historico-social situation, which is to say the law that guarantees that there is Oneness, not in the immediacy of society . . . but among the set of its subsets."[51] The state arises from the sociohistorico situation that determines what is and is not visible, but yet is separate from it.[52] And inasmuch as it determines how things are categorized within society in a top-down fashion, its function is wholly repressive. Politics and revolution cannot be incorporated into the state, as that would turn them into forms of domination. To be liberatory and free they must be opposed to the state, not functions of it.[53] For Badiou, politics and revolution are instrumental in revealing the workings of the state. As Adrian Johnston puts it, "A genuine political event causes the previously mysterious, spectral, and (most importantly) immeasurable excess of state power suddenly to become something with a precise and known measure."[54] Or, to put it another way, "Politics, thus, is the art of making the impossible possible."[55]

While Badiou talks about the state as a categorizing operation, other evental thinkers talk about it as a logic that intervenes to allow or disallow certain incidents, behaviors, or beings (and thus, unlike Badiou's state, it does deal with individual beings by controlling their formation). Thinkers such as Rancière, Foucault, Deleuze, and Kuhn depict the state as a vehicle for organizing society in a specific way. In doing so it has repression as one of its primary functions (though, contra Badiou, not its only function). Rancière describes this in his "Ten Theses on Politics," when he gives a definition of "police" that approximates how political philosophers like Foucault and Deleuze discuss the state. He says, "The police is not a social function but a symbolic constitution of the social. The essence of the police lies neither in repression nor even in control over the living. Its essence lies in a certain way of dividing up the sensible."[56] Only via an outside force can the contingency of the state be shown and the authority of the state resisted. Again, Rancière's philosophy illustrates this, as his notion of "politics" is directly opposed to that of the police. For him, politics disrupts the state and the whole notion that there is a first principle or beginning to government. Democracy—the institution of politics—is not a form of government either, but the liberation of the people from any ordering of society. It challenges the idea that any individual or groups of people are more entitled to rule than any others, and posits a form of radical equality in opposition to it. To search for who should exercise democracy is likewise a fruitless task, for the subjects of politics are as uncountable as the subject who should rule. Politics and democracy seek those not included in the state (or by the police), and thus have no designation.[57] Those who seek to separate the state (i.e., order) from politics (i.e., the disruption of order) are bound to fail, just as those who seek a new state in political action will perpetually be disappointed. The two concepts are inextricably connected yet opposed. Politics, as a disruption of the state and institution of something new, only exists where there is a state, but yet it can never be captured by the state. Were it to be so, it would be a process of consensus, and the application of state apparatuses to society.[58] In order to enable change, there can be no state to politics, only a perpetual opposition.

Finally, Foucault's state is the formation of discursive practices and power relations immanent to the world. As he says, "Power produces; it produces reality; it produces domains of objects and rituals of truth."[59] The state is best understood within Foucauldian terminology as a particular codification of power, or a specific episteme, that produces subjects, institutions, and a society that cohere with its rules. For example, the monarchical power that defined punishment in the seventeenth century produced a state with an absolute and infallible ruler,[60] while the biopower that appeared starting in the nineteenth century operates through a multiplicity of institutions that invisibly disperse their power throughout society.[61] The state, as a particular ordering of power and knowledge within society,[62] is set up to allow certain practices and statements within society while disallowing others. In this manner it is inherently repressive. At the same time, because power always operates with resistance, it is always possible to oppose a particular ordering of the state by contesting the processes that produced it (opposing power with power, or knowledge with knowledge). It is structurally possible, by referencing the outside, to oppose the repressive power of the state.

An important corollary of each thinkers' definition of the state is that its presence is irreducible. To abolish the state is to abolish all political structure. The state is necessary, but not any form of it, and evental thinkers are generally hesitant about prescribing an ideal form the state should take. Badiou proposes an abstract vision of communism that leaves much open to be decided. Foucault is the most reticent about prescriptions, and refuses to endorse any form. Instead, Foucault will often suggest possibilities, with the caveat that they must be critiqued. None of these thinkers say the state is simply a political remnant of earlier philosophies that can be cast away. Despite the state's repression, it is only via participation in it that actions, ideas, or institutions are possible. Butler describes this problem by saying that democratic politics are constituted through exclusions that prescribe who can appear in the polity.[63] Žižek agrees, saying that it must be clear that universals are unavoidable.[64] One cannot forego the state without becoming completely incapable of relating to others or to oneself. Yet these thinkers disagree when it comes to the amount of human agency involved in the formation of the state. While individual actions are intimately involved in the production of the state, such actions are not entirely controlled by the subject. Foucault relates actions back to discursive formations and power structures, claiming that subjects are constrained by historical and social forces that restrict every action they perform. Creating a new state is not an easy task, for a revolution will only come from a movement that effectively utilizes the political tools described by evental thought.

The evental concept of the state is important for a study of revolution by virtue of its lack of permanent foundations. Evental thought shows how all of the state's institutions, ideas, and practices are open to structural change. The theoretical models that evental theorists use to build the state reject the idea that any meanings or policies are intrinsic. There is a radical openness to this approach that encourages the development of new models rather than constantly demanding revolution return to the old. By thinking the state through these concepts, we are one step closer toward escaping the rigid boundaries of the state.

Question 4: Connecting Order and Change

The ideas covered so far illuminate how to understand events as radically transformative, but beg the question of how that transformation occurs. Radical change that restructures the world requires a nonworldly account of revolution, and brings evental theorists to the ideas from which their tradition gets its name.

The fourth question about how the event and state interact boils down to a question of the nature of change. What process or situation generates radical change, and how does such change appear to those who live through it? Badiou draws out the nature of evental change by contrasting it with three other types of change: modifications, facts, and weak singularities.[65] Modifications are "the rule-governed appearing of intensive variations which a transcendental authorizes in the world"[66] and are akin, in the realm of politics, to the passing of a law. Such changes are fully expected to happen, and occur as part of the normal routine. Yet other changes fall outside the normal routine, and cannot be understood by referencing only the facts, ideas, and beings that are already recognized. These extraordinary changes alter the normal routine. Depending on how drastic the alterations are, they can be called facts, weak singularities, or events (with facts having the smallest impact and events the greatest). Events have an enormous impact because they "make exist within [the state] the proper inexistent of the object-site"[67] by changing the rules governing what appears as a being. The Paris Commune of 1871 was an event, because it made the French government recognize the working class as a significant group. Previously unrecognized by the state, the working class (as organized through the Commune's Central Committee) became a massive political force capable of transforming the Parisian political landscape. For all intents and purposes, the episode of the Paris Commune made this formerly inexistent group exist.[68] From the perspective of the state, events provide a glimpse of what Badiou calls the void. When an event occurs we see how our worldview is inadequate for the task of capturing being, as something presents itself that cannot be explained. As Bosteels puts it, "The inexistent serves as an index of the strict contingency of everything that appears,"[69] meaning that our seeing into the void logically demonstrates the contingency of all that appears to us. New explanations must be developed to give the inexplicable phenomenon a place. Because explanations circumscribe multiplicity to create a coherent narrative, and thus all explanations contain a similar "remainder," there is no complete explanation to be sought. Reactions to seeing the void differ: some follow the event to its conclusion, some reject it, and others deny its existence.[70] Yet no matter the choice one takes, society is left to wrestle with the "phantom of inconsistency"[71] the event reveals for a long time to come.

Kuhn's notions of "normal science" and "paradigm shift" closely resemble Badiou's differentiation between "modifications" and "events." Kuhn describes normal science (what I would term the state) as a set of models that provide the foundation for a scientific tradition, like Newtonian dynamics or wave optics.[72] When a paradigm shift occurs new models are substituted for old ones and a new state is revealed. Kuhn emphasizes that paradigm shifts do more than just rename objects, as new beings are revealed that were previously unseeable. Speaking of astronomy, Kuhn writes, "Can it conceivably be an accident, for example, that Western astronomers first saw change in the previously immutable heavens during the half century after Copernicus' new paradigm was first proposed? The Chinese, whose cosmological beliefs did not preclude celestial change, had recorded the appearance of many new stars in the heavens at a much earlier date."[73] Kuhn's focus in *The Structure of Scientific Revolutions* on how paradigms allow one to see new things is supplemented in his later work by a study of how linguistic change occurs. According to Paul Hoyningen-Huene, "In the first case, it is perception that grounds the connection with the world; to encounter the world is to see it. . . . In the second case, by contrast, the connection with the world is a product of language; to encounter the world is to capture it linguistically."[74] Kuhn and Badiou emphasize that we should not think about rule changes and paradigm shifts as simply psychological operations, as they have an effect on perception, experience, and being as well. They are more than conceptual heuristics, as they affect any and all engagements we have with what is outside us. Badiou and Kuhn differ on several points. Unlike Badiou, Kuhn believes a well-defined material realm exists outside paradigms,[75] though he implies that the nature of that material world is impossible to get at.[76] Outside rules, Badiou is only willing to posit "multiples of multiples."[77] Additionally, Kuhn does not distinguish degrees of change as Badiou does. There are no equivalents in Kuhn to Badiou's notions of "fact" and "weak singularity," though inasmuch as they all affect the foundations of a normal situation, it is likely Kuhn would categorize them as paradigm shifts of a different quality.

The inconsistencies of being that for Badiou give way to change are described by Kuhn as anomalies that violate "the paradigm-induced expectations."[78] Kuhn's anomalies reveal the limits of a theoretical model, just as Badiou's events expose the threshold of knowledge. The primary difference is that Badiou's events are instantaneous and lack ontological standing, while Kuhn's anomalies are "extended episodes" that appear as "novelties of fact" that can be reproduced and examined.[79] In *Logic of Worlds* Badiou says the event is that which "makes what did not exist in a world appear within it"[80] and later on, when describing the event of the French Revolution, says "the unknowns of the Central Committee, politically inexistent in the world of the eve of the insurrection, exist absolutely on the very day of their appearance."[81] For Badiou, events are instantaneous, even though our wrestling with them and their implications may take a long time. No such distinction is present in Kuhn. Yet for both the abnormality disappears upon its incorporation into a new theoretical model. Neither Kuhn nor Badiou believe that one model will account for everything, and they consider it important to continue to develop new models to account for any inconsistencies the old revealed. For Kuhn, people react to anomalies by forming different schools of thought that inform different research programs.[82] The research program that takes hold is the one that incorporates the anomalies most effectively. And while Badiou identifies three types of reactions to the event, Kuhn (perhaps because he refers to the field of science rather than politics or history) claims that all reactions attempt to incorporate the event in some form. This state of confusion, trial, and error is excellently translated into the field of politics by Deleuze and Guattari, who in *A Thousand Plateaus* describe how groups within states often have "fringes or minorities" that produce a furor against the state's sovereignty and lead to an epoch of revolution. As they say, "There are always periods when the state as organism has problems with its collective bodies, when these bodies, claiming certain privileges, are forced in spite of themselves to open onto something that exceeds them, a short revolutionary instant, an experimental surge."[83] The revolution is "confused" and causes the state to analyze the surge and shift itself to reinscribe its order back over the revolution.[84] Yet just as Badiou and Kuhn emphasize the productivity of events, so do Deleuze and Guattari conclude that revolutions are not defined simply by hostility to the state's authority, saying revolutions "can make war only on the condition that they simultaneously create something else."[85] As Thomas Nail puts it when developing a "constructivist theory of revolution" from Deleuze's and Guattari's work, revolutions break free from existing states by "creating a prefigurative alternative composition within and alongside older ones."[86] Similarly, Negri and Hardt say political change only happens by organizing the singularities found in a political situation.[87] They argue for the creation of altermodernity, or the production of a new concept of humanity drawn from three lines of philosophical thought: the enlightenment tradition that critiques dogma in the name of freedom, worker movements that challenge capitalist hegemony, and anti-colonial movements that work to create a more inclusive understanding of humankind.[88] The goal is not to improve concepts and categories drawn from the latest iteration of capitalism and biopower (what they call Empire), but to pass beyond them. Reforming the categories such that there is equality between them does not erase the operations of dominant forms of power; instead, what is needed is "an abolition of identity itself."[89]

The transformative understanding of change detailed by evental thought is useful for a study of revolution because it shows how change can be triggered without referring to doctrines. It inscribes radical change into the structure of the state, but resists attempts to plan out that change in advance. Change will happen when there is a need for something new, and such needs are indispensible. The confusion, debate, and uncertainty that surround events are a positive attribute to be embraced by revolutionaries. It is in the opening this disorder creates that the building of a new state unshackled by the old is possible.

Breaking up the State, but Holding on to the Pieces

With the account of evental theory complete, it is time to examine how these ideas affect the project of liberating revolution from the state. Can we now see beyond the limits of the state to a liberated revolution capable of changing anything?

Evental thought is a way to think beyond the limits of the present. The seemingly intractable confines of being are broken apart so that its infinite possibilities can be approached. Evental thought has much to offer revolutionaries, for it is able to reveal the limits of any state without at the same time prescribing a definite form for the state. As understood by evental thought, revolutions are not stained with meaning, forced to perpetuate a particular state, or made to advocate for a future society. The radical politics of evental thought advocates freedom and openness, not just with regard to specific policies but also to what populates the state. Programs, doctrines, and well-defined goals are excised from revolution as such. The state is not gone, but while events remain its ability to oppress is always threatened. When interpreted by evental thought, Marxism becomes a tool for building the state after an event rather than descriptions of the only justifiable state. Badiou embraces communist thought, though he reinterprets the materialist dialectic as a carrying forth of a truth that can create a new world. Deleuze and Guattari makes a similar point in *What Is Philosophy*, saying that Marxism is a way of reterritorializing things.[90] Though the danger of turning the nonfoundationalist, flexible, and constantly changing ideas of evental thought into dogma must be guarded against, they are nevertheless valuable tools that allow for the rethinking of dangerous ideas.

But if events are to be wholly separate from states, evental thought, as it has been construed so far, is still problematic. Even though evental theorists do not posit rules or ends that circumscribe revolution, they still use the state for their descriptions of the forces that produce events. In order for multiplicity, difference, and openness to theorize revolution's ability to transform the state, it is necessary that they each be separate from the state. Yet as part of the state, evental theorists can only encounter and describe those ideas inasmuch as those ideas are also a part of the state. Because there is no possibility of thinking beyond the state, or of perceiving the world in a manner unaffected by the state, it must be the case that these forces and operations can be perceived within the confines of the state. The answer that evental theory provides for how it can view what is beyond the state from the state is that the operations it describes are held within the interstices of states. They are not present as things, but as relations or as processes that states must follow in order for our experience of states to be consistent. Yet these operations that construct states and hold them together are not just found behind states, they are found behind revolution too. Revolutions are produced through the same operations, processes, and forces that produce the state. This creates a dilemma for evental theory, for its theories are only tenable if the operations, processes, and forces are perceivable from within the state, yet revolutions are not free as long as they are conceived of as the product of operations, process, and forces. Thus, despite evental thinkers' best efforts to escape the state, evental thought ultimately reproduces the equivalent of protostates. A protostate is a formal, transcendental architecture responsible for forming beings, subjects, and all other appearances found within the state. It consists of consistent forces or process that condition both the state and revolution. These protostates are less determinate than the states of social contract theory and Marxism, but nevertheless bind revolution to an abstract order.

Because the projects of Badiou, Kuhn, Foucault, Deleuze, and Derrida are so varied, engaging their projects will be an effective means of illustrating the different possible manifestations of a protostate. By examining how their protostates still control revolution we will see what still needs to be done for revolution to escape the state. As I will show, evental thought determines the process of revolution by promoting protostates that create change in a specific way. A longer argument is forthcoming in the next chapter, but for the moment let's consider how change is conditioned within the work of Badiou and Foucault. First, Badiou's theory of revolution relies heavily on the declaration. As Badiou says, "By the declaration of the belonging of the event to the situation it bars the void's interruption. But this is only in order to force the situation itself to confess its own void, and to thereby let forth, from inconsistent being and the interrupted count, the incandescent non-being of an existence."[91] Badiou's revolutions must be attached to a truth procedure, for there is no radical change unless a new set is declared and the truth of that set propagated.[92] But is it not possible for there to be revolutionary change that goes unrecognized in language or thought, or for such change to occur in the relationships between extant beings rather than through the creation of a new set? The American and French Revolutions have had unexpected effects on society throughout history up to and including today, even though by Badiou's logic the multiples they constitute were declared long ago. Politicians, military leaders, and social movements have been inspired by them in ways those involved with the revolutions never imagined, and the messages inherited from the revolutions have been revised numerous times. Badiou's reliance on the logic of multiplicities, and in particular on the fact that transcendental rules determine which multiplicities are recognized as ones,[93] sets up a state that determines how events occur. Even accepting Badiou's system doesn't necessarily lead to his conclusions about change. Yiju Huang argues that Badiou's advocacy of fidelity—and in particular his practice of adhering to the Chinese Cultural Revolution's legacy—is a common response to the trauma of loss. Rather than holding to a truth, Badiou reacts to the pain of the Cultural Revolution's outcome by developing a "transferential relation with Maoism [that] becomes itself an object of desire for many leftist intellectuals today."[94] By this account, holding to a truth is just as much an act of mourning as abandoning it is.

Foucault's notions of power and discourse return a substantially different concept of events. Unlike Badiou's truth-procedures, Foucauldian power and discourse are located within the social realm.[95] Creating an event is not about the reworking of a set's logic but rather the organizing of points of resistance in order to deploy new power relations throughout society. The rule of immanence that Foucault follows in his study of events means that contestation and strategy are irreducible parts of power, and that as a result power can be both seen and manipulated. As Foucault writes, "Rather than analyzing power from the point of view of its internal rationality, [my project] consists of analyzing power relations through the antagonism of strategies."[96] Events for Foucault involve radical reversals in power dynamics, the production of new behaviors, and the reworking of old habits to make them more amenable. They are like "games" that involve a "complicated interplay" between power and freedom.[97] Yet Foucault's attempt to see the system of differences at the heart of power relations[98] means that it is difficult for him to appreciate revolutionary militancy. There may be a shared vision of a future to come that inspires a revolution, as Foucault believed was present during the Iranian Revolution,[99] but danger of misusing power means that such a vision cannot be safely codified. Any program or strategy needs to be subjected to critique, and so Foucault's ideal revolutionaries are those who experiment instead of rigidly following a program. Foucault points to the dichotomy between the creative, intrepid revolutionary life and the militant programs of revolutionary parties in his lecture series *The Courage of Truth*, saying that it would be interesting to study "how the idea of a cynicism of the revolutionary life as scandal of an unacceptable truth clashed with the definition of a conformity of existence as the condition of militantism in the so-called revolutionary parties."[100] As these examples show, the protostates of evental theorists determine the state and how revolution should function in relation to it. Movement is subordinated to the protostate's prescription of how it occurs.

These protostates of evental theorists thus pose several problems that indicate the need for a new theory of revolution. As the examples of Badiou and Foucault show, there is no qualitative change in how the processes and operations of evental theorists work at different levels. The logic of multiplicities and the nature of power follow the same principles at the pre-individual, individual, and societal level. This conflicts with the phenomenon of emergentism as described by systems theory, or the idea that new beings, rules, and functions arise as systems become more complex and interconnected. I'll discuss this more in the next chapter; for now, it suffices to say that this conflict raises questions. Next, for some evental theorists the logic of change within a state and between states is roughly the same. Revolution is one type of change produced by multiplicities, power, encounters, and so on, but it is not a unique type of change. While revolution displays unique properties, the same forces and operations that produce revolution also produce change within the state. This links revolution and the state in a way that limits revolution's capabilities.

In sum, while the change proposed by evental theorists is more open and less controlled than any other changes studied so far, it still limits revolution. Instead of ordering revolution (as regulationism did) or making revolution tend towards something (as visionary theories did), it takes one aspect of being (power, multiplicity, etc.) and stabilizes that as an unchangeable foundation such that they can launch their analyses of society, ontology, truth, and so on. While this is not bad—in fact, it is indispensable for an analysis of any sort—it does predispose the revolution they describe to certain forms of change over others. Specific behaviors and actions become more important and necessary for change; others less so. To give an example, the power relationships described by Foucault and encounters described by Hardt and Negri are open-ended and require two different entities such that an exchange can occur. Paradigms and sets (Kuhn and Badiou) are closed and the discovery of them requires only one entity. Additionally, the former types of change focus on a more networked order, and the latter on a more categorical order; the difference being that one is more decentralized and autonomous, and the other more unified and dependent. Because of these differences, the appearance of novelty and the resolution of it operate differently for each thinker, rendering certain types of state formations more or less optimal. Specifically, states that privilege the same sorts of procedures or tactics that the thinker describes (e.g., declarations or encounters) will be more likely to take hold after the revolution is over. While this doesn't necessitate any type of government per se, it does encourage governments to operate in certain ways over others. Governments that privilege declarations are going to be substantively different than those that focus on relationships and encounters. Thus we see that the protostates used to understand revolution end up becoming part of the state. Evental thinkers also differ as to the relative importance of the material or ideal, and the immanent or transcendent. The ways they arrange these realms in relation to each other and to revolution will dictate both practice and theory during and after a revolution. Should one seek to free extant changes by embedding them in a new order, or should one seek a new order by which to understand such changes? Should one focus on prefiguration of the to-come or combatting the forces preventing it? To prevent the protostates from seeping into the functioning of the state, the type of change we describe with revolution must be qualitatively different than the type of change described in the state.

Evental theorists may worry that I reject any normative framework for revolution. Such frameworks supposedly increase a revolution's chances of success and avoid the pitfalls of the past. Describing radical change as open or closed, ongoing or instantaneous, helps us develop effective strategies for change. I affirm evental thinkers in their desire, and my project is undertaken in part with the same goal. My rejection of the normative guidelines does not imply there should be none, but rather that we must seek them after liberating revolution. In the next chapter I discuss complexity and dynamism, which are intrinsic parts of an ontology that liberates revolution. The failure of evental theorists to address these characteristics generates the protostates I critique. I give normative guidelines in chapter 6, after first reframing evental theory.

A state of any kind acts to restrict change, and is as a result hostile to revolution. A revolutionary state is a contradiction in terms, for all states project a stagnancy before them that oppresses. A theory of revolution that escapes the state will need to find a way outside this dilemma. Perhaps an answer will be forthcoming if we begin by inverting the strategy that has been used so far. Political philosophy—including evental thought—explains the state by referring to its parts or the processes that compose it. This is what it means to search for foundations. But what if by delving deeper and deeper into the molecular constitution of the state we are prevented from finding the answers we need? What if, instead of explaining the state by referencing its parts, we begin with the notion that the parts must be explained by reference to the state? This question, and its implications for a theory of revolution, will be taken up in the next chapter.

5

Dynamic Anarchism's Revolt

Turning the System against Itself

Introduction

It is now time to lay out a new theory of revolution. But because this theory must avoid perpetuating any part of the state, my claim is that nothing grounds the possibility of revolution other than the state itself. There are no beings, no pieces, no processes or forces that, in composing the state, also condition radical change. The description given to revolution must preserve the three traits, mentioned in chapter 1, of incommensurability, unpredictability, and indiscernability. The state itself leads to radical change, just as radical change leads to the state. As I will show, by conceiving of the state as dynamic and generative it is possible to resist the pressure to hold a piece of the state apart from change or to theorize a protostate. I will lay out my theory in several steps. First, I will contrast it to the event ontologies of Deleuze and Guattari as well as Badiou, focusing on how an ontology based on systems theory can better explain certain phenomena we can observe. Other event ontologies will be referenced as needed. Second, I will describe the essential features of a systems-theory based approach to the study of revolution. These include a distinction between ones and wholes, the concept of a metastate, and the proper role of dynamism. Finally, I will show how this approach can solve the problem of revolution raised by this book.

Completing these tasks requires taking up several issues. First, a new concept of the state must be found. If even the protostates of evental theory are problematic, our new theory must present states as wholly dynamic and changeable, yet also primary rather than derivative. *In short, this theory must be able to explain change by referencing states themselves rather than their pieces.* As I will show, I consider events to be endemic to the nature of states, or a widespread yet contingent part of how they function. It is how states operate as a whole, and not a part of or process producing them, that should be studied to see how events appear. The next problem that needs to be addressed is why evental thought is wrong to assume processes external to states (i.e., the protostates referenced in the last chapter). Though such processes condition both the state and revolution, they are only a serious problem for revolution if they privilege the state by circumscribing the possibilities for change. A new theory must show why the creation of protostates is unnecessary or dangerous for revolution.

Third, this approach requires a new path to radical change. In order to adhere to the stipulations of the first and second problems, we must find a way to theorize revolutionary change without making its existence conditional. Radical change cannot simply be the expected product of forces and beings coming together; it must have a character unique to itself that is not apparent by looking at the state's composition. As I will show, the key to solving these problems is to rehabilitate the notion of "system." By defining states in relation to systems it is possible to see how states, by themselves, can be wholly changeable without positing a protostate. This can work because systems, properly understood, do not come from a stable ground but are related only to themselves. Because this is the case, any part of them is open to change. A new understanding of system developed along these lines not only will provide the concept of the state needed, but also the necessary context for a new theory of revolution.

In using systems theory, I am not saying that it, itself, is a new theory of revolution. Rather, there are several ideas revealed by the study of complex adaptive systems that suggest the philosophy of Dynamic Anarchism. But whereas systems theory is treated primarily as a tool used to understand observable and testable phenomena, Dynamic Anarchism is an innovative philosophy that attempts to describe a new approach to change and dynamism. To clarify this point, I will describe the differences between systems theory and Dynamic Anarchism in more detail throughout the chapter, starting with the origin and current uses of systems theory.

Systems theory is used primarily in mathematics and science. It began with mathematical tools (such as those found in calculus, trigonometry, and set theory) that help to track chaotic and unpredictable movements.

While it began at first with minor deviations and examinations of how small interactions could alter fixed trajectories, over time it has grown to encapsulate studies of massive systems composed of numerous entities, each operating according to a certain set of rules. Currently, systems theory is employed by physics, biology, sociology, political science, and numerous other fields. In addition, the field has developed to the point where the predictions it makes are more comprehensive, and concern the system as a whole rather than individual elements within it. Finally, some traits observed in systems (such as emergence) do not have mathematical correspondents, but, as they can still be observed, they are allowed in scientific studies of how systems work. What systems theory indicates is how important traits like complexity, interconnectivity, and adaptation are to the functioning of the whole. In addition, it provides insight into how we can begin to make sense of movement through the judicious understanding of functions and sets. Yet systems theory as it is studied within the hard sciences focuses on determinate objects that tend to follow fixed rules. The point of most systems modeling is to make something comprehensible and predictable. To the extent that it does this, systems theory embraces scientific realism and sets aside questions of being, structure, and change. It generally accepts the conventional understanding of these terms while focusing on how, within the world these terms describe, we should understand the systems the terms' referents are part of. What I will show is how the understandings of change and being that these systems reveal requires challenging the conventional ways we use basic terms.

Systems Theory, Deleuze, Guattari, and Badiou

Systems theory—especially discussions of how nonlinearity, complexity, and interconnectedness produce phenomena like emergence, resilience, and heightened diversity—describes change that is not reducible to a state. Broadly understood, systems are radically interconnected networks composed of creators of change, objects that are changed, and mechanisms for change in such a way that each and every member is composed of and reflected within the others.[1] Melanie Mitchell defines systems as "a collection of interacting elements that together produce, by virtue of their interactions, some form of system-wide behavior."[2] It is notable that Mitchell says immediately following that this definition "can describe just about anything," for that is exactly the point. The only thing the concept of system cannot describe is a unified and static object (which, as I will show later, does not exist except as a concept), for if there is trackable change there is an interaction occurring. Contemporary systems theory positions change and movement in a markedly different place from any of the event ontologies discussed in the previous chapter. Before describing why this is, it is important to show how systems theory challenges other ontological accounts of change.

Badiou, on the one hand, and Deleuze and Guattari, on the other, represent different paths within event ontology: the former favors universals and the latter untotalizability. As the important details of each were discussed in the previous chapter, I will only rehearse their outlines here. Badiou describes the One as "not a being, but a predicate of the multiple"[3] that exists as an operation[4] that brings one-ness into being. In *Logic of Worlds*, he says a transcendental gives a being variable degrees of identity and difference with other beings in the world, and "that every being is in a world only to the extent that it is indexed to this transcendental."[5] Since what is given in experience is multiple, we need an operation to unify it, and this operation is the One. It makes an inconsistent multiple consistent. This unification gives us the structured situation, or the idea that the multiple we've been presented with is sound.[6] Within a structured situation, both individual elements and several elements together can count as a group (the latter are called submultiples); this means there are more groups in the situation than there are elements. Badiou calls this theorem the point of excess.[7] To grasp how a situation has more groups that can be included in it than actually belong to it, we structure the structured situation, leading to the state of the situation.[8] The state thus decides which submultiples are included in our representation of the structured situation, and does so by counting them as unified beings. These included (as opposed to belonging) multiples aren't presented, only represented; in other words, they are ideological.[9]

By contrast, Deleuze and Guattari describe multiplicities as lacking unity or subjects and objects, having only "determinations, magnitudes, and dimensions," saying that unities appear "only when there is a power takeover in the multiplicity by the signifier."[10] In reality things are rhizomes, meaning they are "composed not of units but of dimensions, or rather directions in motion" and "can be laid out on a plane of consistency, and from which the One is always subtracted."[11] We get beings through cutting up the plane of consistency, forming the plane of organization, or strata. Strata articulate the intensities on the plane of consistency, and from those articulations we get abstract symbolic components we use to understand existence. It is important to realize that strata do not articulate what already is; they form both a content and an expression at the same time (i.e., something to symbolize and the symbols used to represent it).[12] Within any given strata, there are always assemblages that, while part of the strata, also form a unique semiotic system that can be used against the strata by creating lines of deterritorialization that show how the strata itself is connected to other assemblages. Any given assemblage contains not only the lines that form it, but lines that connect it to other things that reveal the inconsistency of the assemblage. Deleuze and Guattari call such lines rhizomes, saying they "pass between things, between points."[13] Finally, there are lines of flight that don't form beings or connect beings to one another, but destroy beings by showing how the strata are inadequate. Deterritorialization can be absolute, bringing one back to the plane of consistency, or relative, when new strata appear to reterritorialize what was deterritorialized.[14]

Badiou, Deleuze, and Guattari insist that talking about their ontologies is problematic, since one must use language, which removes one from what is actually there.[15] And while they both oppose the logic of one-ness that has historically defined ontology, they give different accounts of how the One operates. For Badiou, the One grounds unity and any understanding of multiplicity. Without the One, you are left without an operation that can make sense of the multiplicities that present themselves. For Deleuze and Guattari, there is a tentative unity to the plane of consistency.[16] This unity is incomprehensible until a symbolic One is imposed upon it, which divides the plane into an understandable order. Badiou's Ones bring together; Deleuze's and Guattari's divide. Badiou's One precedes relationships (which are prescribed by the state of the situation); Deleuze's and Guattari's One follows relationships (which challenge the One and point to the plane of consistency or other strata).

A whole systems ontology is impossible here, and distracts from my goal of liberating revolution. So I will focus on how systems theory contests important parts of these ontologies while giving a better account of revolution. What systems theory shows is that Ones neither bring together nor divide; neither precede nor follow relationships. Ones create the possibility for both Badiou's logic of multiplicity and Deleuze and Guattari's logic of difference, and are also separate from Wholes. Ones create an index and relationships by holding something constant, but when set in motion form organic wholes composed of agents, relationships, dynamics, and outcomes. The Whole, rather than the One and its relation to an outside, should logically be the focus of event ontology. Making this point requires translating concepts from systems theory into ontological terms. Since systems theory and ontology have historically studied different things, this will require an argument by inductive analogy to show how the concepts employed by systems theory have currency here.

Systems theory uses two tools that bear strong similarities to Badiou's state of the situation, or Deleuze and Guattari's plane of consistency. They are, respectively, phase space and vectorfields. Phase space is a term used to indicate all the possible states of a system.[17] By contrast, the state of the situation brings unity to any composition of elements (one-multiplicities) that form a consistent part. In other words, both catalog the different forms the thing they are studying (a system or a structured situation) can have. Second, by unifying presented multiplicities the state of the situation gives us terms we can use for comparison (e.g., the structured multiplicity of a person produces the concept of height and allows us to measure ourselves). Similarly, phase space prescribes axes of measurement that can be used to compare different systems or pieces of a system (e.g., when you track a system's change over time, you prescribe time as an axis for measurement). Finally, just as elements in a structured situation can be presented and represented, presented but not represented, or not presented but represented, phase space can show a system in states that actually exist, can omit things about a system that do exist, or can predict the system moving into states that don't exist (e.g., the climate's future).

Vectorfields are similar to Deleuze's and Guattari's plane of consistency. Vectorfields are prescriptions of velocity vectors at each point within a state space,[18] vectors being expressions of movement. Deleuze and Guattari refer to the plane of consistency as "smooth space" that consists of "relations of speed and slowness between unformed elements" and wherein "continuums of intensity or continuous variation" exist. While vectorfields contain measured movement rather than unformed movement, they are indicators of movement and direction, the entities that comprise Deleuze and Guattari's plane of consistency. Vectorfields consist of an infinite number of measures of the intensity of movement, where each vector within the vectorfield exists within the same space and is connected to others through this space. A vector itself has no being, as it is only an instantaneous calculation of the rate of change occurring at a particular point at a particular time.[19] One finds vectorfields by taking what exists—movements that one can observe and track—plotting it within a space, and then using equations (such as the tangent calculation) to determine velocity at any particular point.[20] Again, this is similar to Deleuze's and Guattari's notion of territoriality, where beings are the formation of intensities below the plane of organization. But whereas vectorfields are plotted along a plane organized along numerous axes measuring the movement, Deleuze's and Guattari's notion of "smooth space" precedes any such axes or measurements, as they argue becoming necessarily exists prior to any measurement of it. Finally, while vectorfields are static pictures of what's occurring at a particular moment in time whereas the plane of consistency is a place where becomings are forever drawing "themselves into zones of proximity or undecidability," if a vectorfield could present forces over time, it would have many of the same traits the plane of consistency does. The vectors would be affected by each other and change their motion with no particular telos.

Where these analogies diverge, and where systems theory has something to add, is in how these concepts operate. Badiou's One operation fixes beings and gives them a definition.[21] The state of the situation orders them in a closed typology (as evidenced by Badiou's description of truth as the gathering together of all investigated terms by a generic procedure of fidelity supposed to be complete).[22] Phase space does not operate in this way. There is no closed typology, for the beings a system describes are constantly taking up new roles and discarding old ones.[23] Presented traits regularly disappear and reappear. In addition, within the phase space of a complex system elements often display behavior that is aperiodic and unpredictable—a fact that is predictable.[24] Finally, phase space itself can be represented in several different ways, such that it has different characteristics.[25] Patterns within phase space are not predictable simply by looking at the underlying math. The nature of complexity means that even when one knows the attributes of something very well, its behavior is not necessarily foreseeable. Badiou gives no indication in his descriptions of the state of the situation that the hierarchies it prescribes are predicted to change, that the agents can be expected to alter the roles the state prescribes, or that the state of the situation can itself be revised dramatically not by instituting a new truth but by following the trajectories of the beings within the state of the situation to their conclusion.

Systems theory's critique of Deleuze and Guattari comes from the fact that vectorfields can be represented in many different spaces. Deleuze and Guattari are correct that you can't see intensities without being organized into strata, assemblages, or rhizomes, but they don't fully account for how the strata, assemblages, and rhizomes can themselves change the operation of intensities. They say the plane of organization only "translates" or "transverses" the plane of consistency; not that the former "produces" the latter. But within systems theory, strata, assemblages, and rhizomes (to borrow Deleuze's and Guattari's terms for different modes of being) determine the plane or space upon which to show vectorfields. The vectorfield for a metronome is often presented in cylindrical space, while that of an object being pulled to the ground by gravity can be presented in Euclidean (noncurved) space. Formed objects influence the shape of the space upon which their motion is presented, and many spaces are manifolds (i.e., curved, non-Euclidean spaces). In other words, the same vectorfield will appear differently on flat space than curved space, and it is primarily the motion of objects on the plane of organization that determine the shape of the space, not the vectors or intensities.[26] Because the space where becomings exist is partially produced by the space where objects exist (i.e., the plane of consistency vs. plane of organization), and because space can exist in many forms with many dimensions,[27] their relationship cannot be the one Deleuze and Guattari suggest. Accepting the premise of Deleuze and Guattari's philosophy while bringing in the insights of systems theory would suggest a reciprocal relationship of production between the planes they describe.

What systems theory adds to this debate is the idea that there is a better way of explaining the relationship between being and change than given by the two schools of event ontology represented by Badiou and Deleuze and Guattari. Whereas Badiou conditions beings on the operation of one-ness applied to the incomprehensible field of multiplicity, and Deleuze and Guattari on the becomings of the plane of consistency, systems theory conditions it on becomings within the context of the whole that is a complex, interconnected system. And while Badiou can account for the changes I mentioned by referring to his typology of singularities, and Deleuze and Guattari can accommodate the phenomenon I've described by saying the plane of consistency contains space and what occupies it in a coextensive state, I believe systems theory shows that these arguments are inadequate. Without delving into the whole ontology of systems theory, I can only indicate why that is. First, both Badiou and Deleuze and Guattari ignore the role of a *function* in systems theory. Badiou ignores how functions relate sets to one another such that we can see a trajectory forming between them. Badiou's state of a situation misses how beings are both presented and represented as things that have potential paths as the result of their interactions. Deleuze and Guattari ignore how functions prescribe space, and that no understanding of space can exist lacking a function. You need a function to know how a particular space works, including how many dimensions it has, how things can develop or move, and what exists at all. (Though they lack the mathematical formulation of the functions systems theory uses, Deleuze and Guattari's descriptions of their two planes play the same role a as function, confirming my point.)

Similarly, both Badiou and Deleuze and Guattari omit the concept of emergence, or the idea that more can come out of a system than went into it. Emergence challenges Badiou's idea of the state of a situation and, indeed, of One-ness as a whole, for it shows how the interactions between already structured elements/parts can itself yield unpredictability, not just singularities or events. Emergence also questions the idea that systems can be resolved into becomings on the plane of consistency. While the plane is described in abstract enough terms that it doesn't preclude the possibility of emergence, neither is there any indication of how the plane could produce emergence. In short, Badiou has trouble explaining the role of aggregated movements and trajectories of becoming, while Deleuze and Guattari have trouble explaining radical shifts. Systems theory can explain both.

The Nature of Systems

Systems theory gives us perspective on the role difference, becoming, and multiplicity can play in ontology. This is the first step in moving away from protostates, as we can now start to see how systems theory is not dependent upon these elements to describe radical change. Before we can see the alternative ontology I propose, we must explore other relevant parts of systems theory, especially the ideas of nonlinearity, chaos, and emergence.

I will start by describing the development of systems theory. Systems are highly diverse. They go from simple and mechanical (e.g., a pendulum) to complex and unpredictable (e.g., the ecosystem). It was the exploration of the latter that led to the discovery that complex systems exhibit qualitatively different behavior from the former. Early modern physics primarily presented systems in terms of laws and linear processes.[28] Complex ones featuring nonlinear dynamics were indecipherable using the tools of the time.[29] Only with new technologies and mathematical concepts were more complex systems studied. It is now widely accepted that adding many agents and relationships to systems yields phenomena quite different from the models of classical physics. Ladyman, Lambert, and Wiesner argue that complex systems regularly display "nonlinearity, feedback, emergence, local organization, robustness, hierarchical organization, and numerosity," and exhibit "a diverse range of behavior over time i.e., [they have] many causal states."[30] Complexity itself is defined by Yaneer Bar-Yam as consisting of interconnected or interwoven parts such that we must understand not just the behavior or the parts but how they act together to form the behavior of the whole.[31] If complex systems were composed simply of the sum of their parts, having an accurate understanding of each part and how it behaved would yield an understanding of the system as a whole. Yet that is not the case. Complex systems behave in unexpected ways even when they are composed of parts we have comprehensive knowledge of. New agents come into being, groups operate according to different rules, and forces that played a major role in a smaller scale are replaced by fundamentally different ones when moving to another scale.

The reigning theory for why this happens is chaos, or the idea that small differences add up such that minor changes aggregate into massive differences at the systemic level. Among the first to articulate this is Edward Lorenz. In one of his works on the subject, "Deterministic Nonperiodic Flow," he looks at the possibility of predicting overall weather patterns when the basic forces composing them are deterministic and predictable. He says that global weather systems "exhibit either periodic or irregular behavior when there is no obviously related periodicity or irregularity in the forcing process," concluding "prediction of the sufficiently distant future is impossible by any method, unless the present conditions are known exactly."[32] The principle that complex systems are "inherently unpredictable" was uncovered when the same idea was observed in fluid dynamics, population biology, chemical reactions, electrical circuits, and more.[33] More recently, this principle has been expanded to say that complex systems are not just unpredictable, but produce novelty. Phenomena that don't exist at the agential level appear at the systemic level, while phenomena important in studying agents play no part in the whole. Bar-Yam sums this up, saying, "The collective system has a behavior at a different scale than its parts."[34] Emergence is only one of many ways complex systems exhibit novel behavior when taken as a whole and put in motion from when the static system or any of its moving pieces are viewed separately.

The dynamism I describe here needs to be related to the ongoing discussion within systems theory about open versus closed systems, for it may seem like I am claiming a system is either closed or dynamic, when what I am actually claiming is that all systems—whether closed or open—are dynamic. Let us define open systems as those "characterized by outputs that respond to inputs but where the outputs are isolated from and have no influence on the inputs," and closed systems as those characterized by a "loop structure that brings results from past action of the system back to control future action."[35] Open systems are those that receive inputs from outside the system, and closed systems are those that receive their own outputs as inputs (it is possible for a system to be mixed, and receive inputs both from beyond itself and from itself). In both closed and open systems, as they were classically conceived, the inputs go through the same set of steps, or the same processes, as all previous inputs. While over time the output can yield drastically different results, the steps or processes that inputs undergo never change. What Dynamic Anarchism claims is that this classical conception of systems is inaccurate, and that all systems are actually dynamic, such that the processes that define them are subject to fundamental change as well. Although it seems that some systems are determinate rather than dynamic, this is a function of the fact that some systems are not very complex or interconnected, or that the outcome of the complexity is easy to predict despite the complex forces creating it (a phenomenon known as emergent simplicity). Simple systems generally operate formulaically, though over a long enough period of time they express dynamic attributes, while emergent simplicity can come and go as systems evolve. Complex and highly interconnected systems are better examples of the issues under discussion here. Whether closed or open, it is not unusual when a system is highly complex, or if it is given enough time, for the processes defining it to shift, to reverse themselves, or, in rare occasions, to dissolve entirely.

John Holland writes of complex systems that "the interactions between the parts are nonlinear, so that the overall behavior *cannot* be obtained by summing the behaviors of the isolated components. . . . In this sense, more comes out than was put in."[36] The difference between rigid systems and the transformative systems Holland describes has to do with whether the order governing systems is formulated from beyond the systems themselves, or whether the order is part of the system. When the order comes from without it is impossible to change, yet when the order is generated by the system itself it can be completely rewritten. Although each individual system follows rules, when the right context comes along every one of those rules can be overthrown. Nothing—no beings, rules, forces, or guidelines—defines systems as such except the fact that they are dynamic. This approach reveals how even the most determinate system will over time produce diversity and generate new structures, operations, and functions. Scott Page writes that if one begins with systems that are composed of "*diverse, interdependent, networked* entities"[37] capable of change, then one sees that complexity and a rich array of new phenomena can emerge even from a relatively minimal number of parts. Page concludes that "*fundamental diversity* is not required for complexity. *Emergent diversity* is."[38] Importantly, because these systems are dynamic rather than static, they react not just to the rules governing them but to their products, the behaviors of the subjects and objects composing them, and the network of forces that allow them to function. Determinate systems thus often yield unpredictable effects because of what scientists have termed the "multiplier effect" and the "recycling effect," whereby small accretions or deficits can over time accumulate to the point where they invalidate a theretofore intrinsic part of the system. Holland writes that the multiplier effect "jeopardizes long-range trends based on simple trends"[39] and says that the "overall effect [of the recycling effect] on a network with many cycles can be striking."[40] Though these claims are made with reference to biology, studies have shown that these principles hold true for all complex systems.[41] Phenomena such as emergence, unpredictability, and dynamism are the result of complex interdependent networks, so this description is just as easily applicable to the field of politics as it is to biology.

This account of systems theory indicates a new approach to the study of systems. Perhaps most importantly, systems theory argues for holism, or an irreducible becoming only visible when the whole system is in motion and not connected to intensities, multiplicities, or other ontological components. It is for this reason, I argue, we should differentiate between the idea of the *One* (as put forth by Badiou as well as Deleuze and Guattari) and the *Whole*. If the One is an indexing of what is, the Whole is the organic outcome of that indexing when set into motion. As systems theory illustrates, the two are rarely the same. Demonstrating why that is requires giving a more comprehensive account of systems, which I will do now. First, why is it incorrect to see the world as composed of atomized, individual beings, or to use a nonsystem based ontology? The reason why the idea of systematicity must be brought in is because it is the only way to explain dynamism without resorting to a protostate. The rationale for a system's motion—and for the motion of every piece of a system—must be explained, but without creating a transcendental architecture that generates it. The only answer is to see the motion as an intrinsic part of the system, and not as the product of eternally present processes. There must be a system, as without it the goal of liberating revolution is impossible. Second, what keeps the pieces of the system from going their separate ways? While this is a potential outcome of a revolution, it is true that most systems do not break apart easily. They have a tendency to stay connected. The reason for this is that the system is responsible for constituting its parts, just as the parts constitute the system. Connections exist not just between the different agents and objects of the system, but between these elements and the project of the system at any particular point in time. Though in the right circumstances a being will leave a system, it is this relationship that tends to keep the system bound together.

Also integral to this theory is that while every particular system has agents of change, objects of change, and means of change, none of them necessarily persist. These features can always be overthrown. In describing what a system itself is it is impossible to say any more than that it is interconnected and dynamic. Even to say that systems contain agents, objects, and means of change is partly inaccurate, for by treating these elements as separate the indivisibility of the system is hidden. Though the system is not a simple unity, neither does it easily differentiate into rigid and atomic parts. Either choice presents the system, or a piece of it, as firm and unchangeable. Rather, the system is a complex whole of continually differentiating and merging parts, the movement of which can be helpfully understood through the four elements I describe in this chapter. It is both dynamic (understood as constantly changing in all aspects) and emergent (understood as the ability to develop novelty as a result of such change). Fred Evans makes a similar point in reference to society, which he says is a "multivoiced body" that operates as a "unity composed of difference."[42] The voices of society are always "'in motion'" and "exist as responses to one another," and while it is possible to identify the individual voices, every "voice is shot through and partially constituted by the other voices of the community."[43] The same principle Evans points to with regard to societal voices applies to systems, for just as societal voices are always drawing from and reflecting each other, so too is each part of a system a reaction to and product of the rest. A system is not a rigid and hegemonic unity, but one comprised of many ingredients that both constitute and are constituted by change and whose character and function is not set in advance. As I will show, it is the radical interconnectedness and interdependency of these ingredients that allow me to make this claim. There is both sameness and difference—both unity and plurality—in the system, but what constitutes each is in flux.

This account of systems is different from the way systems have traditionally been discussed. Though the diversity of philosophical systems makes generalizations difficult, it is possible to find ways in which great systems thinkers of the past have impeded or formalized the dynamism of systems. Kant, for instance, describes how external input is ordered through time, space, and the categories of pure reason. Because these categories are conceived to be unchangeable, there is no possibility of his system developing. Hegel, according to one reading of his system, formalizes the manner in which knowledge can be reached. When he says "knowledge is only actual, and can only be expounded, as Science or as *system*,"[44] one interpretation of this claim is that he believes a systematic examination of knowledge predicts the dialectical movement of "externalizing . . . the Notion"[45] and subsequently reincorporating the externalized concepts into a philosophically "comprehended organization."[46] Because Hegel knows the rules of the dialectic, he can foresee the trajectory of knowledge—not just in the sense of reaching its telos in absolute knowing, but in the sense of predicting its constant externalizing motion. Reflecting on this project, or on systems thinking in general, some have said that it reduces becoming to a mere formula. Michel Foucault describes his project as trying to flee Hegel,[47] and criticizes the dialectic for guaranteeing that difference will always be recaptured.[48] In broader terms, Nietzsche criticizes systematicity as such as showing "a lack of integrity."[49] Even those who reject this, arguing that Hegel is much less deterministic than such a reading would imply,[50] maintain that change, movement, and truth always come from a conflict of opposites[51]—claiming in essence that dynamism is produced in a necessary way even if becoming itself cannot be reduced to a formulaic piece of knowledge.

Though past systems thinkers have a restrictive understanding of systems, anti-systems thinkers do not escape systems thinking. Many contemporary philosophers identify systems with form, order, and the normal way of doing things. According to this approach, systems must be fought to get change. Instead of capturing the definitive nature of the state, systems take what is irreducible to thought and turn it into something determinate. In portraying certain elements as stable, and all change as the result of fixed causes, systems miss how nonidentity, dialectical sublation, and difference undermine all determinations. Adorno writes that "the pedantries of all systems, down to the architectonic complexities . . . are the marks of an a priori inescapable failure," concluding that the necessary outgrowths of all systems reveal "the untruth, the mania, of the systems themselves."[52] Similarly, Foucault asserts that systems of knowledge have led to enslavement and domination,[53] while Derrida claims that the goal of his project is "to seek new concepts and models, an *economy* escaping this system of metaphysical oppositions."[54] Anti-system philosophers claim all systems are incapable of doing what they set out to do.

Yet we should question whether these thinkers really escape systems. The tools they develop to disrupt systems (such as the nonconceptual, power/resistance dynamics, and the idea that meaning is always "to-come") only function because the tools have a presence within, or are a part of, the systems they are disrupting. Without this being the case it would be impossible for these tools to undermine any system. These tools are not beyond systems per se, but rather are presented as parts or attributes of all systems that previously went unseen. More importantly, these tools cause change—by subverting and creating new identity—in a specific way. In Foucault's philosophy, for instance, power is always immanent but masks "a substantial part of itself,"[55] creating change through the tactical utilization of relationships for the purpose of instituting a new regime of order. The tools described by anti-systems thinkers operate as part of a determinate system that may be unfamiliar within the history of philosophy, but it is still a system. And as a system, every element of it is interconnected and interdependent. Changing one thing in the system can create a ripple effect that changes other pieces of it as well. If these tools are part of the system, they are just as subject to being changed by an alteration in the system as any subject or object within it. The tools of anti-systems thinkers cannot affect things within the system while remaining apart from the movement of the system. Anti-system thinkers may undermine rigid and determinate systems of earlier philosophers, but in doing so they create systems of their own. To an extent anti-systems thinkers admit this, as Foucault describes power as being able to change in how it functions, while Deleuze presents his ontology differently within different fields. Thus the tools of anti-systems thinkers are not monolithic. For now, my point is just to show how systems are still vital elements of anti-system thinkers' philosophies, and that the working of systems affects their tools even as the tools change systems.

Metastates and States

This concludes my account of what constitutes a system. It is now time to consider what constitutes a state. Though as I will show a state is composed of all the elements of dynamic systems, it needs to be distinguished from dynamic systems as such. This difference is necessary because a dynamic system cannot be overturned without a constant that transforms it into a state. If every element is interconnected with and produced by every other element, then there is nothing fixed or determinate, as all things are perpetually evolving. For a state to be toppled and another to come into being, we have to identify something determinate that has been changed. Unless this happens, we cannot conclude that a state has ever ceased to exist. At some point, the definitions of dynamic system and state need to diverge. The primary difference between a system and a state comes from the fact that a state is characterized by a metastable state, or metastate. This *metastate* is what is held constant in a particular system, and thus operates like a function. Though systems are properly dynamic and contain no necessary constants, they are stabilized by creating one. Only with a metastate can we see how other things are moving in relation to the constant, and thus start to form an idea of coherent system. This term comes from physics, and in particular the study of dynamics in reference to natural systems. An early paper to use the term describes it as "a natural ensemble, analogous to the state-space measure describing a chaotic dynamical system" before going on to say that it is not equivalent to many states, because there is something fixed that connects "the structure of the metastate and that of the replicas."[56] The metastate approach is valuable because it "explains, connects, and unifies such concepts as replica symmetry breaking, chaotic size dependence and replica non-independence" in physical systems.[57] Example metastates include ideas about how things work and what is to come. Metastates are a slowing down of the motion within a system, since something that is properly in motion is treated as immobile for the purpose of tracking the motion of other things. Certain motions of a system are eschewed in order to highlight others. In doing so, we capture a web of relations that can be used to represent and prescribe the order politics takes.

Where my definition of metastate differs from a function is in its capacity for elaboration. Conceptually, elaboration occurs as the ideology for a system develops. As systems theorists have discovered, plotting a function on a graph can yield new insights that help to develop the math further. Similarly, experiments show how the same equation has different attributes on different charts, while different equations can produce the same graph.[58] Materially, one sees elaboration occur as a system operates, for as the various parts interact they develop and grow in complexity. A nascent political state inevitably encounters problems and challenges that require new solutions, and that lead it to create new laws, organizations, or structures. The United States' Constitution only alludes to the president's ability to appoint a cabinet, and the first time one was formed there were only four positions (secretary of state, war, treasure, and attorney general). As the government developed, the cabinet grew in complexity to the point where it now has fifteen positions (and another twenty cabinet positions have been proposed to address lacuna in federal government oversight). These new positions do not contradict, oppose, or otherwise immediately undermine the political organization of the United States; rather, they are conceived of as helping to grow and preserve the country's ability to meet its constitutional requirements. A metastate should not be equated with any particular formulation or rendering of a system, but with the set of tools, depictions, operations, and movements that are used with regard to the same set of affairs. Similarly, a state consists only of those movements that develop, enhance, perpetuate, or preserve its metastate. In other words, a state is a dynamic system inasmuch as it consists of all the same elements as one, and inasmuch as it grows in complexity like one, *yet* anytime the system moves in a way that undermines the states' metastate, that movement cannot properly be included within the constitution of the state. In short, a *state* is the movements, concepts, beings, and interactions related to the metastate of a dynamic system.

The idea of a metastate as a constant has a basis in systems theory. Poincare describes the principle of relative motion in *Science and Hypothesis*, saying that the acceleration of a thing in a system depends on its movement and position relative to other objects in the system, and that absolute velocity or position is a myth.[59] Similarly, in *The Value of Science* he says that what is considered objective must be transmissible, and that anything nontransmissible is nonobjective.[60] Taken together, this means the value of a thing only arises through comparison, and that objective value comes from its being shared in a context that allows for comparison. In other words, a system's values are necessarily relative, and only exist because we can compare them to something for the purpose of measuring those values. What we compare the values to must be objective insofar as we must be able to share it with others. Thus, something needs to be expectable in order to predict other things. This thing must be sharable, otherwise there is no basis for things in a system to interact. Systems theory itself yields such predictable movements when it creates models, as they reveal points or lines toward which things tend to move (called attractors). One also uncovers cycles that can occur periodically and ways in which things can spiral out of control. Social or political metastates include such phenomena too. For example, in a democracy, politicians are supposed to move toward—that is, they are attracted to—public opinion.[61] Similarly, corrupt systems often increase in corruption over time, since being successful requires that one be as corrupt, if not more so, than those preceding one; this can continue until the state becomes unsustainable.

There are two reasons why this definition of state differs from other theories. The first has to do with the placement of the metastate, which does not precede the state; the metastate and many of the agents and relationships that perpetuate it come into being at the same time (other agents and relationships will appear as the metastate goes through elaboration). The metastate is not imposed on, nor does it bring together, what we encounter. Instead, it slows everything in the system down by holding something constant. While there is always a choice in deciding what part of the system to hold constant, the system also influences that decision, since some movements are more prominent than others (though that isn't known until after the metastate is established, nor is such knowledge absolute). Periodic movements, movements that are predictable or easily trackable, and movements directly experienced more easily serve as archetypical ones. Yet metastates are not only representational, as once they emerge they can play an agential role in preserving the state. They become the measure against which actions are judged, or institutions are formed, and they prohibit those things that do not meet their guidelines (just as how in Hobbes's theory it is inappropriate to question the unitary authority of the sovereign).[62] Thus unlike the states of social contract theory, for which the order of states is determined in advance, the states of Dynamic Anarchism have no predetermined metastates. Nevertheless every metastate is still able to play a role in disciplining the system to act in a particular way, and in resisting radical change.

The second reason the state of Dynamic Anarchism is different is because it is not static. While it does follow a certain order, the movements that form and the complexity of that order are always evolving. The particular processes that form the order at one point may be swapped out for others later on without any discernible change in the metastate itself, assuming the product of each set of processes is the same. This means that Dynamic Anarchism would reject the Marxist claim that economic relationships always determine the form the state takes. It also entails the rejection of the Marxist base-superstructure theory, for the order of the state is not inherently hierarchical, nor does the metastate define a separate realm from the processes and movements of the state (as the base and superstructure do in Marxist theory). States are mobile, and as such cannot be modeled simply as a "universal" or "one."[63] Any account of them must be able to illustrate both what is allowed to change and what is required to stay the same. As long as states contribute to the perpetuation of a certain political arrangement, there is no necessary way or domain through which they form that order.[64]

We can now show why the protostates discussed in the last chapter are unnecessary. As I mentioned in my first critique of evental thought, protostates act as a transcendental architecture within states. They do not determine what specific beings appear in the state any more than the gothic style of a cathedral determines which biblical scenes will appear on the walls. However, protostates provide a space for and a form by which beings and meanings appear. This is now unnecessary, because by viewing states as dynamic and complex systems we avoid the need to posit transcendental processes that act within yet exist separately from the state. Though a more comprehensive account of change will be given in the next section, we've already seen how emergence, nonlinearity, adaptivity, and chaos, as well as my concepts of metastate and elaboration, are inherent conditions of systematicity. As long as the system does not come from a stable ground, but is related only to itself, then any part of it is open to change. And if we remember that parts of states are interdependent and that states themselves are dynamic, then that change does not need to be produced externally but is an intrinsic characteristic of a state's existence. When we properly conceptualize states as systems, then we can see that what motivates radical change is not a transcendental process like Deleuze's deterritorialization or a perpetual condition like Badiou's concept of multiplicity. That which is wholly immanent, as long as it stays in motion, can produce radical change. As John Holland writes, "perpetual novelty is still typical"[65] even in systems that are essentially comprehended.

This new model of the state contradicts Badiou's and Žižek's ideas of universality and one-ness. Similarly, this model challenges Deleuze and Guattari's idea that "representation is a transcendental illusion"[66] and that liberating difference means we must no longer subordinate it to the identity of the concept and the thinking subject, to the similar within perception, to the negative, and to the analogy of judgment.[67] Because the state is an adaptable system, all notions of stability and normativity, as well as notions of difference and openness, come from operations immanent to the system. The notions of universality proposed by thinkers like Žižek and Badiou are problematic, for when they oppose unity, or "the one," to the radical openness of the "real" or "multiples of multiples," they assume a universal that is uniform and hegemonic, and whose notions of stability and normativity are transcendental conditions that come from beyond the universal itself. Badiou makes this point in discussing the need for a metastructure that structures all ones, saying, "In order for the void to be prohibited from presentation, it is necessary that structure be structured, that the 'there is Oneness' be valid for the count-as-one."[68] The state, for Badiou, regardless of its historicosocial situation, is always involved in the operation of guaranteeing "that there is Oneness . . . among the set of its subsets."[69] And Žižek claims that signifiers devoid of content still can have an effect as empty signifiers.[70] What constitutes the state is for them nonadaptive and formulaic. What Žižek and Badiou miss is the fact that the function of signifiers and forms depends on their context, and that in a complex system it is predictable that the function of a signifier will change as a system evolves. Peter Hallward traces this deficiency in Badiou to his reliance on set theory, saying, "Set theory obliges us to think that 'there are only multiplicities, nothing else. . . .' Not only is relation thus conceived as little more than a variation on the elementary relation of order (greater-than or lesser-than), there is no clear sense that it can qualify, shape, or otherwise affect the objects related."[71]

By contrast, Deleuze and Guattari miss how the difference they want to liberate only exists on a plane brought together by a function or functions, and how the plane itself is changed by the beings (or content and expression) produced by their abstract machines. Deleuze and Guattari posit an openness that precedes a unifying function in order to avoid the formulas and hegemonies ontology has been reduced to in the past.[72] The assumption they make is that Ones must be formulaic and hegemonic, and that the only way free of them is to position difference outside of a One. In one example, Deleuze and Guattari use the Koch curve to demonstrate the existence of fractional dimensions, arguing that this shows how in smooth space the line and the space it occupies are coextensive.[73] Deleuze and Guattari are right to argue that space and what occupies it are interrelated in the Koch curve, but omit how the curve only comes into existence after the Koch curve rule.[74] This rule operates as a function that creates both the matter and space that Deleuze argues precede it. To use the language of systems, the function is the metastate that generates the planes and spaces Deleuze and Guattari describe. Systems theory, and in particular ideas like chaos, emergence, and dynamism, show that ones give way to wholes, which aren't hegemonic. A whole can contain the irreducible difference Deleuze and Guattari want if we can show that the whole is unpredictable, wholly adaptive, and capable of bringing forth natality without reference to a plane where difference resides. In short, what needs to be opposed to radical change is not something uniform and hegemonic in its emptiness, nor plural and different without any unity, but something that is plural and variable at the same time that it is unified.

The real need for a theory of revolution—one that escapes the notion of state entirely—is not just to question the determinacy of appearances and beings in the state, but to question determinacy itself. It is not enough to displace order from the things in the state to the processes that compose them; it must instead be shown that determinacy itself is not determinate. Systems, and all the pieces found within them, must be seen as evolving, emergent, and capable of developing novelty without reference to a protostate. Building off of the idea of Merleau-Ponty's hyperdialectic, we need to find a way to understand systems that is not simplistic and reductive, and that does not prescribe a form for systems but allows for their change and creativity. This openness to change must include the forces, operations, and processes that produce the state as well as the things within it. We need, in a word, hypersystematicity.

The Proper Role of Dyanamism

At this point, we're almost ready to unveil Dynamic Anarchism's concept of the liberated revolution. We have covered what system and metastates are, but we still need an account what dynamism is and how it works. This is a crucial piece of the puzzle inasmuch as it is the way we will avoid grounding revolution in a protostate.

As a study, dynamics can be hard to define. In broad terms it deals with change or movement,[75] but in practice there is nothing one can say about it without first connecting it to a being. This is why the study of dynamics in physics is divided into different fields like fluid dynamics, aerodynamics, molecular dynamics, and so on. Scientists also explore different equations used to model motions uncovered when studying these beings (linear, nonlinear, periodic, emergent, etc.).[76] But short of having a being to study, the only thing to be said about movement is the self-evident "it moves," or some equivalent concept. The question of what dynamism is can best be answered through a comparison of two different philosophies that attempt to synthesize the insights of continental philosophy with empirical science: speculative realism and relationism. For the former, I will use Quentin Meillassoux's philosophy of speculative realism as my interlocutor, and for the latter I will use Karen Barad's agential realism.

Speculative realism opposes "correlationism," or the idea that philosophy must begin with the relationship between being and thought. Correlationism's argument is that relationships produce determinate being and knowledge, both of which change as relationships change. The problem with this, according to Meillassoux, is that it cannot relate to "ancestral" statements, or those relating to existence before human life. If determinate being and knowledge come from correlations, and correlations exist only after human life arises, then everything beyond humans is unknowable, and studies like geology become untenable.[77] This problem extends all the way back to Kant or Berkeley, whose philosophies challenged the idea that being exists in and of itself independently from humans.[78] Meillassoux wants to return to the concept of primary and secondary attributes developed by Descartes and Locke, where primary attributes are those that exist independently of the subject's relation to an object, and secondary attributes are those dependent on it. Where Meillassoux adds something is in his concept of what counts as each. Rather than primary attributes being those related to extension and geometric proof, Meillassoux says they are "all those aspects of the object that can be formulated in mathematical terms," or those that give rise to formula or digitization, while secondary traits are those that arise from relationships (especially relationships to humans).[79] The outcome of this philosophy is that all notions of being come after we formulate laws, and it is improper to assume being in advance. This is a declaration of ex nihilo creation, for there is no universe, no "Empire of Matter beneath the gullible delusions of an autonomous biological or cognitive sphere,"[80] in which the potential for life and thought exist. Life and thought emerge from nothing and for no reason; only with their advent do laws about them form. For those who argue that mathematical formulas are thoughts and thus cannot discuss what preceded them—an apparent contradiction Meillassoux admits to[81]—Meillassoux deploys a two-step proof. The first is to argue that correlationism is conditioned upon an absolute, albeit an unknown and unknowable in-itself that might obey a rationality with the same traits. The determinacy of reason and being is undermined by displacing those to an a priori realm that conditions their existence. Meillassoux refers to this absolute as hyperchaos, a realm where nothing is impossible, even the unthinkable.[82] This absolute is pure contingency and, as such, is the only thing necessary.[83] Contradictory as this sounds, it is the logical outcome of ex nihilo creation. If no laws predetermine life and thought, then they are by definition undetermined. Importantly, this claim is not metaphysical, because it is not about first principles but an argument that all first principles are subject to the speculative or factial (or, as Meillassoux puts it, "a moment of sheer irrationality"[84]). That there are facts (i.e., a facticity or metaphysics) is not itself a fact. The second step is to demonstrate that this understanding is exactly the same as the one revealed by set theory. Specifically, set theory demonstrates it is not possible to provide a universal foundation for all mathematics, and that concepts of indeterminacy and infinity only arise in an already existing set that follows axiomatics (or laws). There is no axiomatic governing contingency as such, which is what correlationism argues in its advocacy for contingency being a function of relations. To claim contingency arises from relations is to turn it into a metaphysics rather than making it a condition for metaphysics.[85]

Karen Barad's agential realism derives from quantum physics and the research of Niels Bohr. Particle entanglement indicates an irreducible relationality between entities, so much so that it is inaccurate to posit entities prior to relations. Barad emphasizes that existence is indeterminate prior to its "enacting" of "boundaries, properties, and meanings" and the relationship those create with "specific material phenomena."[86] Barad uses the concept of discursive practices—drawn from Michel Foucault but explained in material terms to avoid anthropocentrism[87]—to argue that the core of matter is not substance but agency, by which she means that it is in a process of ongoing becoming by which relationships and understandings come into being and pass away. "Matter is not a thing but a doing, a congealing of agency"[88] inasmuch as dynamism is visible at the smallest possible level one can observe and it determines particles as much as particles determine it. Matter is, in Barad's term, "intra-active," because it contains activity within it that is irreducible to linear cause-and-effect understandings.[89] When we define or conceive of something, what we are grasping is an "apparatus," or specific material-discursive practices that produce boundaries but that are open to change. Our understanding of an apparatus itself evolves as we uncover new relationships and agencies involved in producing phenomena. Barad illustrates this with a description of the Stern-Gerlach experiment, where a silver atom beam was projected through a magnet in hopes of seeing the particles diverging depending on how the magnet affected them. Barad recounts a notable event during the experiment that occurred when Stern was smoking cheap cigars with lots of sulfur: the silver became more visible. The atoms combined with the fumes of the cigar to form silver sulfide, a jet-black substance. This is notable because it illustrates how apparatuses are not isolated machines, but combinations of many intra-actions occurring in many places. In addition to the cheap cigar, Barad says the Stern-Gerlach experiment depended upon "class, nationalism, economics, and gender, all of which are part of this Stern-Gerlach apparatus."[90] In short, boundaries are outcomes of intra-actions, matter is agential, and indeterminacy is an irreducible part of existence.

Barad's ontology has important consequences for understandings of possibility. While rejecting pure relativism whereby anything is possible anytime, she does argue that accounts of existence that take place within space-time are to be viewed with skepticism inasmuch as "topological manifolds of spacetime-matter relations" are part of what intra-activity produces.[91] Causal accounts must be viewed as outcomes of agency and not vice versa, because such accounts are temporal in nature. This also means that accounts of what is possible are subject to the development of agency. As agency is the defining feature of the world, and can never "run out," it is also the "space of possibilities opened up by the indeterminacies entailed in exclusions."[92] As boundaries in space, time, and matter are temporarily fixed, so too are possibilities. When boundaries change, possibilities change. At no point do the boundaries disappear altogether, as it is essential that agency both create and rework them. Novelty is an ongoing outcome of agential matter, not the product of eliminating boundaries.

The speculative realism of Meillassoux and relationism of Barad diverge in several ways. First, in the placement of relationships. Speculative realism sees them as the outcome of axioms. relationism sees them as foundational to both being and knowledge. Second, in the creation of novelty. Meillassoux argues for ex nihilo creation in the sense of saying being follows math, and nothing can be known in math without first having a set. Dynamism is trackable only within a set, and nonexistent outside. Barad argues for indeterminate creation where all specific existence arises from material agency. This movement is ongoing and produces knowledge as intra-actional matter becomes congealed. Finally, in the understanding of possibility. Meillassoux sees possibility as the outcome of a set, and while the possibilities there may be infinite, there is no set that includes the infinite possibilities of all sets. Barad sees possibilities as originating from material arrangements and apparatuses; change those and possibilities also change.

Both Meillassoux's and Barad's projects resemble the systems theory account discussed above. The math of systems theory relates to Meillassoux's argument that mathematics precedes any discussion of being. The highly interconnected and radically changeable nature of systems resembles Barad's discussion of indeterminacy and movement. Both thinkers have ideas I will incorporate into my account of dynamism. Nevertheless, before proceeding I will review criticisms of each project to illustrate why I think both are inadequate. Specifically, I argue that both Barad and Meillassoux leave a system intact at the foundation of their project. Rather than conditioning systems, the phenomena they describe depend upon systems.

Barad's argument is that indeterminacy is composed of agency, a material becoming. *Being* and *doing* become undistinguishable at the quantum level such that being is indeterminate and doing is always happening. The two concepts cease to make sense except as material agency. This is analogous to Bohr's resolution of quantum physics' wave-particle duality paradox. Bohr said that we only see a paradox because we are using classical concepts developed by mutually exclusive apparatuses. What exists at the quantum level is consistent, but only appears different due to our instruments, among other factors.[93] Barad argues similarly about being and doing; they are the same thing viewed from two different apparatuses. Yet this raises a question: Is it possible to use an apparatus that doesn't differentiate material agency into being and doing? Barad seems to indicate otherwise, since determinate being and doing are outcomes of the "boundaries, properties, and meanings" enacted upon indeterminacy and the congealing of agency. Being and doing are outcomes of all apparatuses. If this is true, what do we make of phenomena like waves and photons that don't seem to have any materiality at all? Regarding particles versus waves, Barad says, "Particles are localized objects that occupy a given location at each moment in time. Waves have an entirely different nature: they are not even properly entities but rather disturbances in some medium or field."[94] Similarly, quantum physics tracks massless particles like photons that seem to be comprised of pure energy.[95] To trace waves and photons, as nonentities, back to material agency, we would need to posit that the boundaries, properties, and meanings apparatuses give to nonmaterial phenomena do have a basis in materiality that is invisible. In other words, these phenomena are presented to us as separate from matter, yet in a way that allows for them to interact with being. This is hard to reconcile with the idea that intra-actions "leave marks on bodies" that have materialized through the enactment of cuts,[96] since waves and photons don't have material bodies and are primarily known through the marks they leave on others. It is necessary to say that apparatuses *also* "decongeal" or "dematerialize" agency, but these are not traits Barad gives to apparatuses.

More significant is the idea that phenomena are "material-discursive"[97] is hard to reconcile with the idea of agency as an enactment of iterative changes through the dynamics of intra-activity.[98] Barad posits an indeterminate entity—material agency—that is material, discursive, intra-active, and agential, yet only does so by referencing these four disparate notions. Discursivity is the "specific material (re)configurings of the world through which the determination of boundaries, properties, and meanings [are made]" as well as "ongoing agential intra-actions."[99] Matter is "agentive and intra-active," and "never sits still."[100] Intra-activity is "the mutual constitution of entangled agencies."[101] Agency is "a matter of intra-acting; it is an enactment, not something that someone or something has" and "is 'doing' or 'being' in its intra-activity."[102] In other words, Barad tells us to understand discursivity as agential and intra-active matter; matter as intra-active and agential discourse; intra-activity as discursively agential matter; and agency as intra-active and discursive matter. Barad tells us we should equate these terms with one another, but it seems more accurate—following her lead—to see them as intra-acting such that they coconstitute but are not the same as each other. These four phenomena are an interconnected system composed of different states that refer to and transition between the others to make sense of themselves. Why posit a material entity that reconciles these four forces when evidence only reveals their relationships and dependency upon each other? Why assume being and doing coexist when they are in tension at every level we observe? This alternative—that a system of relationships between states is a possible replacement for indeterminate being/doing—is supported by Einstein's alternative to Bohr's solution to the wave-particle duality paradox. Rather than assume a material basis for both waves and particles, Einstein suggested "decoherence" as a process by which waves become particles and vice versa.[103] In other words, agential and intra-active processes connect being and doing via systems. This is more plausible than positing a nebulous indeterminacy that is processual, material, and active. The foundation Barad describes should be understood in systemic terms.

Meillassoux refers to the mathematical to explain being and doing, since he argues thought is impossible without axiomatics. Indeterminacy, becoming, being, and doing all occur once a set has been defined. Sets produce both contingency (understood as the entities, including possible entities, it contains) and facticity (understood as the laws defining the set).[104] Meillassoux's understanding of axiomatics is drawn from Zermelo–Fraenkel set theory, or a set of approximately nine axioms that describe the proper ordering of sets. Meillassoux properly describes how set theory reveals a multitude of infinities, but fails to note how the indeterminate forms of mathematics are not part of any sets. Indeterminate forms are limits to a function, and as such not members of a set.[105] Examples of such forms are $0/0$ and ∞^{∞}. These forms are not theorized by the Zermelo-Fraenkel axioms, but are theorized by functions.[106] They cannot be revealed from within a set, but can be by comparing sets. In other words, by using set theory's axiomatics, Meillassoux is ignoring "primary qualities" (to use Meillassoux's term) of being we can think of. As Nirenberg and Nirenberg say, "ZF set theory admits objects and sets of a very restricted sort: numbers, structures, and in general those objects that are, or are taken to be, always the same and not affected by any conceivable event."[107]

Another issue Meillassoux's project raises is whether sets and axiomatics are all that is necessary to fix being in a way that allows it to be understood. According to Meillassoux, outside sets and axioms exists only chaos, or the institution of a "there are laws" metaphysics that is, itself, not demonstrable. Yet if we cannot encounter entities until there is a set, neither is it clear what types of entities we will encounter after we have a set. Sets can be depicted in multiple ways (as points, numbers, charts, diagrams, etc.), as I discussed earlier in the chapter regarding phase space and vectorfields. Additionally, there are some mathematical symbols that set theory cannot represent. An axiom doesn't necessitate beings, only possibilities (albeit a smaller number of possibilities than chaos). The set remains indeterminate until an intervention determines the set's presentation. The axiom fixes what will appear once the manner of presentation is decided, but does not indicate a manner of presentation. This, too, is an indeterminacy that is not symbolically represented in a set or mathematical formula. The introduction of mathematics as a primary quality thus does not eliminate indeterminacy internal or external to a set and axiom. Math itself shows that being cannot operate as Meillassoux describes.

Moreover, set theory is not the only theoretical foundation for mathematics. Type theory and category theory are rivals, and advocates argue for them due to their ability to perform operations and avoid paradoxes that set theory cannot.[108] It is possible to understand set theory through type theory inasmuch as sets are described as a type in type theory. Types within type theory are potentially a set within set theory too. Again, positing math as a primary quality does not guarantee being will act as Meillassoux describes. Meillassoux's ontology is already limited even if we accept Meillassoux's definitions of primary and secondary qualities. We are left, then, with various systems of axioms that by their very existence have an impact on what is and how being operates. To the extent that these systems can be interpreted through the lens of the other, there are also relationships between them,[109] though these relationships should not themselves be considered axiomatic systems (though they can be considered systems). What Meillassoux says guarantees math's ability to speak about the ancestral is chaos, or pure contingency and possibility. This is separate from empirical contingency, whereby things that exist will perish, as it includes things that may never come to be.[110] If chaos guarantees math, it does not guarantee the mathematics described by Meillassoux. All chaos guarantees is systematicity, since the concept is equivalent to the idea of pure change, inasmuch as change without any limitations admits of all possibilities. As I demonstrated above, change—even qua concept—is impossible without plurality and interaction. Contingency cannot be thought without difference. Systematicity underlies Meillassoux's concept of contingency.

In sum, both Meillassoux's and Barad's philosophies are dependent upon systematicity, but their insights regarding agency, chaos, and relationship are well-equipped to frame my concept of dynamism. I have shown that (1) materiality and agency (as defined by Barad) are conditioned upon processes and relationships such as decoherence; and (2) relationships, being, and indeterminacy are not properly understood by set-theory. We are left with systematicity, or networks of agents and relationships that have no materiality or agency prior to the existence of a system. Since all comprehensible systems require at least one function, absent that there is systematicity as such. Systematicity is in motion, plural, interconnected, untotalizable, and decentered. No objective description can be given of it without creating/describing a stable relationship, which in turn means that one cannot track changes to this relationship until one views the system using another relationship. Using set theory rather than type theory, or presenting a set as numbers rather than on a plane, is an act of holding stable the relationship between being and itself (or, to use system theory's terms, the creation of a function indicating agents and relationships). Systematicity keeps Barad's sense of indeterminacy, but separates it from the material agency she describes. It keeps Meillassoux's description of how math is necessary for knowledge and being, but not its dependency on set theory as the foundation that enables this. Material agency and set theory are replaced with systematicity. To the extent that materiality and being are intertwined, Meillassoux's ex nihilo dynamic is maintained. To the extent that they are separate, Barad's indeterminacy is preserved. Perhaps the best way of describing this quickly is to say that I argue for creation *ex systema*.

We have, then, an equivalence drawn between pure systematicity and pure dynamism. We have, also, a similarity between these concepts and indeterminacy and nothingness. The way to reconcile these seemingly irreconcilable notions is to find a way to explain indeterminacy sans materiality and nothingness sans emptiness in a way that connects them to dynamism and systematicity. This leads to my next argument regarding dynamism, which is that it is, itself, equivalent to a dynamic nothingness and immaterial indeterminacy. It gains substance and content only when attached to a being or, in the context of a system, when we hold something constant. About dynamism itself we can say nothing, not even that it exists.

This theory bears a similarity to the idea of the outside, or the idea that our inability to explain all we have evidence for, combined with the significant developments, shifts, and transformations observed in history, necessitates the existence of a fecund realm beyond human experience that is the source of these changes. Two oft-used models for this outside are the Kantian noumenal realm and the negative moment of the Hegelian dialectic. In the former, our experience and knowledge point to a realm where things exist in a manner that is incapable of being understood by humans. In the latter, our ability to describe something necessitates that something else remains to be described. Speaking schematically, the difference lies in whether the outside is underneath appearances or beyond them. In both cases the outside is the place where what exists resides in its most basic form. We do not encounter it directly, but its presence conditions all knowledge and experience.

For example, Schopenhauer equates will with the "*a priori* cognition of the body,"[111] and as an incomprehensible way in which the body is given to one,[112] while Nietzsche argues that will is a determination to command oneself to obey[113] that asserts itself via ideas about the world.[114] Similarly, Foucault says that knowledge, discourse, and power are dependent upon an absent being that constitutes their "outside." "Power is everywhere" such that we cannot escape it.[115] Because power and knowledge are inextricably intertwined and, together, "invest" things with meaning (e.g., they invest the human body with a political significance),[116] we are forever incapable of knowing anything about what exists outside our knowledge. Yet, as he says in "The Thought of the Outside," the very capability of knowing and saying anything point outside themselves to "a thought that, in relation to the interiority of our philosophical reflection and the positivity of our knowledge, constitutes what in a phrase we might call 'the thought of the outside.' "[117] The idea of determinacy "was fabricated in a piecemeal fashion from alien forms,"[118] and instead there is only a founding subject who deploys meanings as it is itself formed and an object "both incorporeal and indefinitely multiple."[119] Finally, just as Deleuze posits the plane of consistency[120] and Badiou the realm of pure multiplicity,[121] Kuhn claims there is a world beyond what our paradigm allows us to see.[122]

In the philosophies of evental thought, these outside realms are manipulated by a protostate to produce what appears. For Foucault power cuts up the outside world in different ways, while in Deleuze the territorialization of the plane of consistency produces new strata. The outside is not altered by engaging it, but encountering it produces new beings, ideas, meanings, and signs. There are no limits to how this outside realm can create meaning, as for all intents and purposes it is immeasurable and unbounded. This is why Derrida can speak of meaning as something "to come"[123] and Žižek can claim that there are multiple ways of instantiating the universal notion of a master-signifier.[124] As Žižek says of the Real, "It is simultaneously the Thing to which direct access is not possible and the obstacle which prevents this direct access, the Thing which eludes our grasp and the distorting screen which makes us miss the Thing." Phenomenologists, Lacanians, Hegelians, Marxists, theorists of identity, and more have all posited an outside and debated how it works to produce meaning.

My claim about dynamism draws on this tradition but takes it a step further. Instead of arguing that being or beings exist in some way irreconcilable with our perception,[125] I argue that there is an aspect to motion separate from being or beings, and that is similarly inconceivable until it has been connected to an ontology. Moreover, I argue that the right way to understand the "outside" is not as an outside at all (since the outside described by event ontologists has being, albeit one that is unknown and indeterminate), but as absolute dynamism and indeterminacy/nothingness. Finally, pure dynamism is not a condition for meaning and being, but a nonexistent ground out of which both become visible after implementing a metastate. In making this argument, I am again drawing on the study of dynamic systems. As we've already discussed, emergence is the "organized behavior [that] arises without an internal or external controller or leader" at a system's macroscopic level.[126] A common phenomenon cited as an example of emergence is human consciousness, where the building blocks of neurons form something unpredictable: awareness and reflection.[127] There is no central actor organizing the neurons into consciousness, but still their interactions produce it. Emergence, as a phenomenon, is a motion or change. It marks the creation of something that was not previously there but now is. It is not a change that is a function of parts of the system, nor of relationships and processes producing those parts. It is not even a function a complete yet static system. It is a change that arises when the system is in motion, and as such is not connected to a being.

One could object that the motion I am describing is not separate from Being or beings, as it is still connected to the whole of the system. There are several reasons to reject this claim. The first is by referencing the argument, made in previous chapters, that to do so is to reduce revolution to the state. But by itself this claim is tautological and insufficient, as it amounts to saying that revolution should be free from the state, and thus it is free. The second is to explore how we understand the being of systems. As event ontology argues, without a principle of unity there is no possibility of comprehension. But this principle of unity only gives us an index, not a system. A system only arises when there are interacting elements, as only then can we start to see how different parts of the system respond to one another (recall that interaction was an essential part of the earlier definition of systems). In other words, dynamism is not an outcome of the creation of being qua system; it is a fundamental condition for the existence of a system. Within the context of a system, Being (including the Being of the Whole) has no necessary preexistence in relation to movement. And if phenomena like chaos and emergence are any indication, our experience of the world depends as much on the unpredictable movements that form the beings we encounter as it does on a principle of unity. Dynamism produces being qua system; being doesn't preexist it.

(This is, again, an argument for holism in the sense that more arises from a system than its parts suggest. And this idea is supported by contemporary studies in quantum physics. While the relation between complex systems and quantum physics is still being debated [in part because systems display nonlinearity and quantum particles do not], people exploring how quantum physics changes ontology have said that concepts like superposition, particle spin, and the ability of particles to affect each other at a distance require us to accept a holistic view since quantum physics challenges the idea that all characteristics of beings are caused according to conventional laws. Peter Lewis, for example, says that "the various correlations between the results of possible spin measurements cannot be expressed in terms of properties of the individual particles, as we have seen. But nothing follows from this epistemic holism about the actual properties of the particles."[128] In other words, the movements of these particles [the spin being measured] are independent of the being they express [the results of the measurements] such that the truth of the whole is not reduced to the truth of the parts. It is also worth noting that there is some evidence for nonlinearity within quantum mechanics,[129] meaning that the idea of movement preceding being in complex systems [and being in part responsible for emergence] is at least a possibility. Finally, the idea that these ideas bear resemblance to event ontology is confirmed by Žižek, who says the behavior of quantum particles is similar to his idea of becoming.[130])

Though I am drawing in part from event ontologists in making my claim about dynamism, there are several problems with how they describe it that must be discussed before the preference for my systems-based ontology can be demonstrated. The outside, as it is used by evental philosophy, is instrumental in explaining where meaning and order originate. Yet, as the outside does not create either on its own, the processes constituting the protostates are integral. Evental theory requires both an outside and a protostate to function. By eschewing the protostate we run into a serious problem, for we cannot reach the outside without it. As long as philosophers hold that there is an external realm they cannot reach, one which is the source of everything they know and experience, it is necessary to posit processes that can grasp it for us. Yet the result of them positing these transcendental processes (i.e., protostates) is that they determine the domain or the form of revolution. Positing an outside from which our knowledge and experience originate thus compels us to once again bind revolution to a state (albeit a much different one than before). This can be demonstrated by looking at how the descriptions evental thinkers give to the outside circumscribe possibilities for change.

Let's take Badiou's example of multiplicity. Badiou's description of the outside as a realm of pure multiplicity indicates that for him the outside is defined by infinite variety and number, for one-ness is always a function of the state. This description means that the outside is permanently characterized by disparity, as it is impossible to have variety and number without that. As a result, change in Badiou's system is permanently subordinated to the condition of disparity. One may object that this does not circumscribe change as it is impossible to have change without disparity. While this is true, change is just as much defined by what it brings together as what it divides. For Badiou, whatever is brought together (and declared a "one") is always properly multiple, for that is its original state. The work that change does in bringing things together is necessarily transitory and derivative, while by contrast divisions are eternal. This theory is valuable in that it preserves the possibility for every "one" to change. But Badiou's insistence that disparity remain permanent calls into question his later concern (discussed in *Conditions*, *The Communist Hypothesis*, and elsewhere) with political fidelity, for by his account there is no connection or common cause I can develop with others that is not artificially created, whereas our differences are natural and permanent. Every unity is capable of breaking apart, but no difference will ever completely disappear (for even if we do not recognize it, it remains in the outside). Badiou's philosophy claims change can only create "simulated" unities while recognizing "real" differences.

In addition to conditioning the manner in which change can occur, and thus attaching revolution to a state, there is another reason why the concept of the outside fails to create a liberated revolution. Since the existence of the outside can be recognized, even if not directly engaged, it is clear that every person in the state has a mediated relationship with it. Within Foucault's system, I relate to the outside through my ability to resist the dominant forms of power in society; as a subject I always have the ability to cut up the world in new ways that oppose those held by academic, economic, and political institutions. Within Kuhn's, I can grasp anomalies by explaining them with a new paradigm that supplants that of "normal science." The fact that I can engage the outside, even in a mediated way, means that evental thought does not just posit relationships between the different parts of the state; it posits that each part of the state has a relationship with the outside as well. This has an important consequence, for it indicates that *the outside is part of the state as well.* Or, to be more specific, it means that evental thinkers—despite their claims otherwise—do not treat the outside as entirely external to the state, but as another level of the state. As they explain it, the outside is not wholly separate from the state but rather an unchanging and permanent part of the state—in short, it is like the permanent figures of the sovereign and history that I critiqued in my respective discussions of social contract theory and Marxism. To explain this in another way, the fact that a relationship exists between the beings of the state and the outside means that they comprise a system. And as a system necessarily presumes the interconnectedness of all the parts such that they are always " 'in motion' " and "exist as responses to one another,"[131] then the outside and the beings of the state must be capable of radically affecting and being affected by each other. The outside must be as open to radical change as every part of the state is. This can also be explained in Foucauldian language as follows: if we admit that a relationship of any sort exists between the parts of the state and the outside, then we must also admit that this relationship has both the attributes of power and resistance. That is, we should be able to resist any determinations given to the outside or the idea that there are any necessary processes (protostates) that must be utilized to reach the outside. Yet if it is open to change in this manner, then it is really not an "outside" in any meaningful way—it certainly fails to meet the definition of outside given earlier in the chapter. We must conclude that the "outsides" of evental thought are just other parts of their states.

My alternative of dynamism does not encounter these problems. Because dynamism equates to pure movement, and pure movement to indeterminacy/nothingness, there is no description to be given to the movement from which the state arises. Even calling it a realm, a plane, or extant is incorrect. Thus, while the idea is inspired by the theories of the outside evental theorists give, it cannot be called an "outside" as such. Demonstrating the truth of this claim requires comparing it to the attributes of the "outside" (namely, that the outside provides meaning when we access it through protostates and that people have a mediated relationship with it). It would be false to claim that we are grasping what exists when we slow the dynamic down, making beings visible and extant. There is no existence, no substance, no graspable entity in the dynamic; there is only movement, understood not as a thing but the absence thereof. To the extent that we "reach" the dynamic in slowing it down, we are engaged in a fabrication rather than a revelation or translation; we are creating ex nihilo instead of uncovering. Second, unlike the outsides described above, people don't have a mediated relationship with pure dynamism, since there is no relationship to be had. One is not interacting with the dynamic in developing a metastate; rather, one is refusing to do so. Inasmuch as it is extreme complexity and perpetual movement that compose the dynamic, we must limit our gaze and pretend some things do not change in order to create a state. The state is created through our inability to relate to the dynamic (and instead relate to a created constant held apart from change), not through a mediated relationship with an outside.

Finally, to those who ask what prevents this theory from allowing anything, anywhere, at anytime (i.e., a simplistic and self-destructive relativism that makes science impossible), or what the metastate engages with when it is undergoing elaboration, I argue the following: complete dynamism is not the same as similitude. Indeterminacy/nothingness is not the same everywhere, just like Being. When a metastate is created, or when the movement of something is ignored for the purpose of understanding, a world is created. This world is composed of beings supposedly unaffected by the movement that is being ignored to create a constant (when in actuality they are), and these entities can be tracked using the measurements the metastate prescribes. But the world is not made predictable and wholly determinate just because we have a metastate. Things still evolve through interaction, and we uncover or create new things by interacting with this world. It is through these interactions that the metastate evolves, and it is the network of relationships created by the metastate that prevents a simplistic relativism.

To sum, dynamism is equivalent to indeterminacy/nothingness, and just as Deleuze freed difference from similitude and Badiou freed multiplicity from the one, so too must dynamism be freed from Being. Just as there is an excess to Being contained in each One, so too is there an excess of movement contained in a system: this is what emergence is and why the Whole is different from the One. If we accept that everything is in movement, and that the being of things is dependent upon their interactions (a fact confirmed by the observation of complex systems, where adaptation and evolution allow for beings to change radically), then "outside" any system there is only indeterminacy/nothingness (understood not in material terms or as absence, but as complete dynamism). This is the best way to understand the realms "outside" comprehension, rather than the descriptions of the Real or multitude and void given by Badiou and Žižek. Similarly, the aleatory and rhizomatic movements Deleuze,

Derrida, and Foucault argue for, where becoming is an outcome of constant interactions and play, are not the foundation upon which Ones are built; they are an inevitable part of every complex and interconnected system. And the movement of the system as a whole can never be reduced to the beings created by the state of the situation (the static system) or the becomings that compose it (the movements the system undergoes independent of the common goal toward which it works). It is the system as a whole that produces both beings and observable movements, just as these things produce the system.

How to Understand Radical Change

With this understanding of systems, states, and dynamism before us, we have the understanding we need to liberate revolution from the state. A revolution that begins with an understanding of pure dynamism won't require rules qua *regulationism* or a trajectory qua *visionary* thinkers. It leaves behind the protostate by describing the transcendental in terms of dynamism, indeterminacy, and nothingness. Now let's look at how radical change is brought about. The existence of complex and interconnected systems shows that we must supplement our account of systems such that in addition to the changes the state recognizes there are also changes that are incommensurable, unpredictable, and indeterminate from the state's perspective. There are two types of unpredictable changes. The first type is catalytic in nature and can revolutionize the state, but—and this is vital—*it results from nothing other than the state itself.* To explain why this is, let us return to the composition of the state itself as a dynamic mixture of agents, objects, and means for change all rendered extant through a metastate. Because we are beginning with the state itself and not with the pieces it resolves into (i.e., a protostate), there is a fundamental interconnectivity that defines the state. Disparate pieces do not come together to form states; rather, the state is constantly dividing, allocating, merging, and transforming itself such that any time a separate piece is identifiable it is shot through and wholly dependent upon everything else in the state. Each piece of the state is so interwoven with the others that a small modification can catalyze a massive effect. The introduction of something new, or the ongoing recurrence of phenomena past what an environment can sustain, can create a sea change in how the system as a whole works. There are numerous illustrations of both of these phenomena. In regard to the former, one example is the radical shift in city planning, culture, and lifestyle that occurred as a result of the introduction of the automobile, not to mention its impact on the environment, economics, and international relations.[132] In regard to the latter, the climate change crisis is an excellent example of how recurrence of phenomena can change a system. The environment is built to absorb carbon dioxide, but not at the level it is being released currently. Unless this stops, scientists predict a worldwide transformation of the climate that will exceed anything humans have ever experienced.[133] Being able to predict phenomena does not mean one is able to predict all their effects. The thoroughly interconnected nature of a system means that everything in the system acts both according to its own plan and in response to others' actions. The most elaborate schematics of systems cannot predict how these actions and reactions will affect the long-term functioning of systems. The behavior of a system in motion is not reducible to the behavior its outline predicts.[134]

The second type of unpredictable change can contribute to a catalytic change, and relates to indeterminacy/nothingness qua absolute dynamism. As we cannot form relationships with that indeterminacy/nothingness, or even detect it as such, we only encounter effects of it in the beings that are part of the state. But—and again this is crucial—to even understand the change as unpredictable, *it must already be in part created by the State.* Only in this way can it be detected or detectable. In other words, the dynamism out of which the state arises can affect all parts of the state, and the state creates those effects as beings. While this means that to some extent the unpredictable movements are always confirming the state, they also have the ability to challenge it as well. They do this by acting as anomalies (as Kuhn describes) or singularities (Badiou) and forming lines of flight (Deleuze) or new discourses (Foucault). The ideas of dark matter and dark energy will help illustrate this point. Neither can be detected, but scientists posit their existence because of observable effects we cannot explain otherwise (e.g., the existence of dark matter is assumed in order to explain why galaxies are rotating as fast as they are without flying apart, while dark energy helps to explain the expansion of the universe).[135] Thus even as dark matter and dark energy challenge our understanding of matter and energy, they also confirm our understanding of galaxies, light, gravity, and other existents. In a sense, what we observe is one part of the state challenging another, which forces us to wrestle with how to resolve that inconsistency.

These two types of unpredictable changes reveal how it is always possible to glimpse other levels of complexity or realize how our metastate is moving in ways we believed were impossible. In such instances, we start to grasp how our state's essential operations are themselves open to change. To show how these changes can produce revolutions, let's examine how they operate in politics. For the purpose of simplicity, I will call the second type of unpredictable change (when absolute dynamism affects parts of the state) a nihil and the first (when small and predictable movements aggregate into something new) an emergent property. Though nihils originally appear from nothing and partially speak for the state, their anomalous nature can be erased by transforming the system to the point where they can be contextualized and explained. This claim begs the question of whether the necessity of incorporating nihils into the system is a limiting factor, given the order of the state. This is an important question as it reveals something about the challenges a revolution faces. Because the order of the state is constantly being produced again and again (rather than the state perpetually being characterized by a particular order), any part of the state is potentially open to change. As a result, the order of the state isn't limiting in the sense of circumscribing change or presenting an impenetrable boundary. However, the order of the state can slow or hold back the speed at which change occurs, and in this sense can limit change (i.e., it can limit the rate of change, not its possibilities). However, as history has shown, attempts by the state to limit change—because of their heavy-handedness—can end up accelerating change. One example of a nihil is the 1999 WTO protests in Seattle colloquially dubbed the "Battle in Seattle." In the lead-up to the protest, no one in the media, political, or economic circles was aware of the political potency of the anti-globalization movement. And while there was significant organizing done prior to the events, as well as a call to action that was distributed widely, even the event's organizers were surprised by the level of turnout received and the impact they had.[136] The events revealed the presence—previously unknown within the political order—of a new political movement with a great amount of power. Note that even as the nihil challenged economic norms, it did so only by being created in a form the state could understand (i.e., a protest reflecting the people's will). Thus it both undermines and confirms the state. Following the events, there was a scramble to understand and situate the anti-globalization movement, and to give it an explanation that would reveal its origin, motives, and goals.

Emergent properties occur when, over time, unexpected outcomes result from fully determinate and understood states. To explain emergent properties, let us observe how systems operate when we work with the assumption that every part of them responds to every other part. First, we see that the movement of states constantly affects how they operate, and so the state is continually open to the possibility of change. When subjects and objects interact they produce outcomes the state responds to. Sometimes these outcomes correspond to predictions about the state, but other times they deviate from them. These deviations are anomalous, but, as they result from fully comprehended systems, they are emergent properties rather than nihils. Only those properties that deviate from expected outcomes count as emergent phenomena, and they should be understood as qualitatively different from outcomes that are predictable. Shifts constantly occur in the state in response to these emergent properties. Some emergent properties produce small shifts (e.g., the presence of protesters leads states to add more police to the streets), but others cause massive disruptions (e.g., the self-immolation of Mohamed Bouazizi led to the Arab Spring). When an emergent property results in the latter, there can be profound consequences for the state. Catalytic change results when, as a result of an emergent property, the state is mobilized against itself. This is why the image of the strong, aggressive revolutionary is not always accurate; sometimes militancy requires withdrawing oneself from the action and letting the state fight itself.

My claim is that a revolution begins in the dysfunction of a state, when the interconnected pieces cease to function as usual. Such dysfunction can result from the catalytic change created by either type of unpredictability. It is important to keep in mind here the distinction I made back in chapter 1 about the two aspects of revolution (anomaly and catalytic change), for by simply saying that catalytic change produces a revolution my argument sounds circular. To reiterate, anomalousness is how revolution appears inasmuch as it indicates the inadequacy of the state, and captures revolution's qualities of exemption from the status quo and deviation from the normal order. Catalytic change is how revolution appears from within the state, and captures the fact that it is a change that changes the changes within the world. And both of these features of revolution are separated from pure dynamism, which is only obliquely indicated through our ability to perceive unpredictability. Nihils and emergent properties are the two types of phenomena a system can encounter that can set a revolution in motion. That is, in appearing they initiate the catalytic change and anomaly of revolution. Nihils and emergent properties are distinguished from the two aspects of revolution because, while their appearance may be unexpected, they do not necessarily lead to revolution. It is possible for nihils and emergent properties to end up intensifying the order of the state rather than undermining it.

This shows that Dynamic Anarchism does not build radical change into the system as the expected result of the proper functioning of determinate processes. *Radical change is an irreducible and foundational feature of systems, just as systems are an irreducible and foundational feature of radical change.* As states arise against a background of pure dynamism (which, again, is different than saying they are conditioned or produced by such), the possibility for radical change is perpetually present. Inasmuch as states are systems characterized by a metastate, they are fully capable of yielding radical change that undermines the order their metastate prescribes. Revolutions can occur when entirely expected and predictable changes in a system cause, by virtue of the complexity and interconnectivity of systems, unexpected and unpredictable changes that fundamentally alter how a system operates. The pure dynamism that exists when there is no metastate present can contribute to radical change as well. Nothing operating behind revolution causes it; rather, revolutions are coincident with and as fundamental as the state (in fact, to the extent that revolutions are radical change, they have more in common with dynamism than the state). More accurately, revolutions are *productions from within the state that indirectly illume the complexity and dynamism from which the State arises,* the effects of which reshape the system such that the old metastate is replaced. The old metastate can be put into motion by holding something else constant, or it may provoke a new metastate by suggesting a "better" position from which to examine something. This theory liberates revolution since it is not based on determinate processes or formalized realms. Revolution is something synchronous with yet irreducible to the state, and indicates how all states are grounded only in themselves. Simultaneously, it obliquely indicates the indeterminacy/nothingness from which states begin.

This last point requires elaboration, for the theory of Dynamic Anarchism insists upon a new basis for understanding radical change. The fact that evental theorists elaborate processes that lead to radical change means that they see such change as the product of specific types of interactions and not as a condition of systematicity. The idea that revolutions are performed by acting in a certain way means that within these theories revolution is always generated by the same mechanism. That mechanism may manifest itself differently in different revolutions, but its basic character remains. Dynamic Anarchism proposes a different concept of radical change, positioning it not as the result of any mechanism, but of the nature of systems and indeterminacy/nothingness. It is part of the character of systems, given their complexity and interconnectivity, to at times yield radical change. Radical change is thus incapable of being described as a product, for the very condition in which things exist is what accounts for it, not any specific process. This is why even the nonmechanistic understanding of Hegelianism is unsatisfactory, for it still presents radical change as something produced through interaction. Radical change can best be described as a system's irreducible tendency to escape its own being.

With the essential theory of Dynamic Anarchism now laid out, I can now finish explaining the topics I introduced at the beginning of this chapter: how systems theory and Dynamic Anarchism are different, and why Dynamic Anarchism is needed. Movement irreducible to Being is an intrinsic part of Dynamic Anarchism. Change is the defining feature of revolution, and stability is its opposite. Systems theory has had to develop new ways of describing change as the mechanistic understanding of change inherited from modern science has proven inadequate in more complex or extreme situations. Thus the ideas of nonlinearity, chaos, and emergence come to play a greater and greater role in systems theory as it expands to embrace new types of systems. But unlike systems theory, Dynamic Anarchism is not beginning its study with conventional notions of Being, change, and so on, intact. It seeks to take the observations of these, developed within systems theory, as a starting point to rework such notions into ones that are in closer alignment with the observations that systems theorists make. For example, systems thinkers often begin by utilizing a previous understanding of what things are and how they work, then examining how that behavior/being can be turned into a rule-following agent. The agent and other forces in the system are modeled together in the same way, and then the outcomes of the interactions are observed. Systems theory doesn't question the basic ontology of the beings that compose systems, though in describing how systems work, it does provide us with the means to do so. Additionally, systems theory is in many ways limited by the tools and resources that technology furnishes us with (i.e., computer modeling is limited by what computers are capable of, and other systems cannot be modeled because we lack the math to describe the behavior of objects we observe, or the ability to observe things that we would like to model). In short, Dynamic Anarchism doesn't just apply systems theory to the problem of revolution. It takes it as a beginning from which a new direction for ontology, metaphysics, and social/political philosophy can be uncovered. For this reason, Dynamic Anarchism should be seen as independent both of systems theory and of previous accounts of Being, structure, and value. It's discussion of the interaction between both yields an innovative philosophy that deserves to be understood as its own thing.

The reason why we need such a philosophy is threefold. First, the world is a complex place that rarely conforms to simple, linear explanations. Beginning with such explanations is helpful for uncovering widespread laws governing being, but these explanations quickly become unhelpful when removed from the isolated environments used in experiments and applied to the world in which we live. For example, it is helpful to know the force of gravity, because it helps us predict how quickly things fall. But when applied to objects in the world, the force must quickly be accompanied by supplements that render its prediction contingent. The shape of an object, temperature, air pressure, and other objects around the one falling all influence its fall. In politics, we can begin with simple axioms, but given how complex the world is, they will only take us a limited way. A theory that incorporates complex systems theory will help us grapple with the nonlinearity we regularly encounter. On a related note, we must understand nonlinearity as rational, not in the sense of reducing it to something expected and predicted (i.e., linear), but in the sense of understanding its origins and operations. Only in this way will we recognize and appropriately respond when it actually occurs. Second, we need the philosophy of Dynamic Anarchism—and its theory of revolution specifically—since we must never imagine revolutions to be contained or controllable. Any fixed set of practices, power relations, sets, signifiers, or ontology—especially one that tries to regulate how change can occur—can be appropriated and misused. The liberation of change promoted by Dynamic Anarchism is advocated specifically as a remedy for any abuse that a positive theory of politics ends up undergoing. Again, an example is instructive here. Political parties in the United States and other countries developed as a way of giving form to particular viewpoints, helping individuals advocate for them in the most effective way. The idea was to promote positions that are popular by facilitating the organization of people who share similar views. Any reasonable observer of the American political system (as well as that in multiple other countries) knows that political parties now play the opposite role. They have amassed enough power to control what counts as legitimate opinion, and consistently eliminate alternative opinions from the public sphere. Often these alternative opinions are popular with large groups of people, sometimes much more so than the policies put forth by the two main political parties. As this clearly shows, the tool of the party, which formed initially to support public opinion, has grown to inhibit its development. Similar dynamics can be seen in the growth of other systems of government (e.g., monarchies, communist states), social movements, daily practices, and more. Dynamic Anarchism promotes a politics that encourages constant renewal and uninhibited change. This will prevent the corruption and misuse. Finally, this philosophy is needed because it is the only one that approaches the concept of revolution with the radical openness that is needed to fully grasp it. This philosophy will enable us to understand revolution as something not trapped by the state, but capable of radical change. It helps us to approach specific revolutions with a productive approach too, such that we don't become dogmatic or staid in our revolutionary practice. Society today needs a revolution that is adaptive and adventurous, or open to trying new things, while at the same time militant in bringing about the whole that its members want. Following a direct line from where society is to where revolutionaries want society to go is not always the best way to get somewhere. Dynamic Anarchism shows us how, through considering the effects of our movement on the systems we are trying to change, we can bring about change in a more productive way by responding to the needs of different parts of the system without forgetting where we want to end up.

As a final note before moving on, I will differentiate my theory from other anarchist theories. Most obviously, my equation of the state and radical change fundamentally challenges the tenet of anarchist thought that the state is always oppressive and must be replaced with a better organization. Mikhail Bakunin, Emma Goldman, and Daniel Guérin represent this tradition. They argue that the statist organization is defined by coercive laws that privilege an elite.[137] It must be replaced with a communal and nonhierarchical system defined by free association and mutual aid. While the systems they describe are preferable to current ones, these arrangements will be as much defined by complexity and interconnectedness as capitalism, representative republicanism, and parliamentary democracy. Were they instituted, these alternative systems would demonstrate the same tendencies that lead to revolution. This is not to say we cannot learn from these thinkers, as their attitude toward authority and mapping of power structures is a key part of how I recommend revolutionaries approach the state (see chapter 6). Nevertheless, I do not believe it possible to replace our flawed systems with perfect ones, and do not separate radical change from the state.

A more contemporary representative of anarchism, James Martel uses the work of Walter Benjamin to argue for adherence to "divine law" rather than "mythical law." His book *The One and Only Law* references the commandment against idolatry as the one rule we must obey. Martel says mythic law is always human-instantiated and flawed, while divine law is unknowable. We must not accept any mythic law as true, for in so doing we mistake our creation for that of God. Neither should we eliminate all law, since doing so leads us to create other idols in the form of our individual goals (if I decide to take someone else's work, that goal becomes my idol). Instead, we must look within ourselves to the "material practices, and those side relationships that occur in the shadow of the laws we make and hold to" for guidance.[138] Martel explicitly associates his anarchism with Kantian-style duty, where we are free to choose that which conforms to the universal. Along with Simon Critchley, who similarly references Benjamin and advocates for anarchism, Martel argues that the best form of anarchism has laws, but ones guided by the divine (Critchley and Martel differ on the character of the divine and its relation to the mythical).[139] The reference to a divine authority distinguishes this Benjamin-inspired version of anarchism from Dynamic Anarchism. Though the pure dynamism I reference is similarly unknowable, it is not outside the state, as the divine is for Martel. Martel uses the divine for guidance and meaning, even if any particular meaning is always inadequate. This conflicts with pure dynamism, where meaning is not just unknowable but always in flux and appears equivalent to indeterminacy/nothingness. Dynamic Anarchism looks to instances of sustainable and resilient systems for clues while recognizing that novelty is a perpetual presence. Martel's take on anarchism, while a valuable study, follows an order irreconcilable with Dynamic Anarchism.

Post-anarchism is very similar to my Dynamic Anarchism and inspired parts of my analysis. Poststructuralism embraces the movement of boundaries, relationships, and meanings in its attempt to find openness in political and social forms. Exploration and novelty are its hallmarks, and connect to the classical anarchist project of challenging coercive structures. As Todd May says, "The theoretical wellspring of anarchism—the refusal of representation by political or conceptual means in order to achieve self-determination along a variety of registers and at different local levels—finds its underpinnings articulated most accurately by the post-structuralist political theorists."[140] These ideas are part of Dynamic Anarchism. The key differences between post-anarchism and Dynamic Anarchism are the description of change and the role of complexity and interconnectivity. My views were described earlier in this chapter and in chapter 4.

The Experience of Revolution

To begin an account of how an event creates change, let's examine the situation that follows the collapse of the state. Lacking a unified system that is well recognized and accepted, agents begin searching for a new order to replace it. The previously cohesive system breaks into many conflicting voices. Some attempt to quell any lingering unrest, and others plea for everyone to come together as a community. Voices of continued militancy call for the criminals of the past to be judged, while remnants of the old regime try to limit any change. To make certain that the ideas they fought for stick, revolutionaries need to continue their work through writing, protest, and organizing. The political arena tends to be fecund after a revolution, with many new political parties forming, ideas being generated, and lifestyles attempted. There are often no permanent rules, meaning that revolution is beginning to understand how dynamism is not a product of states, but has an independent logic. Provisional rules are given by interim rulers, such as the national and state authorities established by the Patriots during and immediately after the American Revolution, or the Supreme Council of the Armed forces established by the Egyptian military following the events of 2011. Beyond the rulers, there are political forces being established throughout the population (such as the Jacobins and Girondists after the French Revolution). During the period of transition following a revolution, there is just as much movement *between* rules as there is movement *within* rules.

Since we cannot actually detect pure dynamism but only see its effects, and because emergent properties can be chaotic and nonlinear, revolutionaries are not provided with an obvious route to a new state. Multiple metastates may need to be tried out, with the goal of both providing tools with which to calculate what was previously unpredictable as well as integrate the new knowledge with other understandings (modifying them as needed). Numerous parts of the old state will need to be interacted with and either kept or discarded as we assess how radical a change is needed to resolve the unpredictable effects that initiated the move to a new metastate. At some point, a new, relatively permanent, metastate will be established. While states can break apart because of revolutions, and the transitional period following a revolution can be excessively long, it is generally true that revolutions end in the creation of a new order. Revolutions are useful tools for creating much needed radical change, but they are poor at securing a newly obtained order from being harmed. With notable exceptions, agents, forces, and objects within a system lean towards the establishment of a new state if for no other purpose than their own protection and longevity. Systems thus exhibit a tendency toward creating a relatively stable and harmonious equilibrium following a massive shift (though, it must be noted, an inherent feature of this equilibrium is that it is always open to radical change). This equilibrium is not teleological in the sense of being the only or the primary goal toward which the system—or the different beings in the system—aim, but, because peoples' desire for change is often accompanied by a pursuit for ways to preserve that change when it arrives, it is often the result. The catalytic change of revolutions is often brought to a halt by the very people and the very forces that brought it about. This is what was meant earlier when I said that revolution leads to the state just as the state leads to revolution. Only in this way will the goals of a revolution be preserved for a substantial length of time.

Thus novelty is followed by a period of provisional orders until the system itself reaches another point of equilibrium. Another way of saying this is that new metastates are experimented with until the catalytic change produced by nihils and emergent properties is minimal. If revolutionaries want to reach their goals, ensuring that this equilibrium is to their liking is as vital a task as instigating the revolution in the first place. The creation of lasting change requires that the equilibrium reached is not equivalent to the one preceding the revolution. Therefore, another way to define revolution is as *a chaotic and nonlinear disruption of a state (understood as a complex, dynamic system) that instigates a catalytic change whose dynamism has the ability to rewrite any and all parts of a state's metastate.*

Finally, what is the relationship of revolution to the state? Because revolution does not come from outside the state and is not assembled upon permanent foundations, the answer must be that each revolution builds a unique relationship to the state. There is no one form that revolution has, for destabilization can occur in many ways. History displays great variety in the strategies, weapons, ideas, technologies, and programs revolutions have used to achieve their goals. For example, radicals have described their relationship to the state in many ways. Some say their movement will raze the entire state to the ground, some see themselves operating on the state as a surgeon operates on malignant growth, and some see their actions as the fulfillment of a promise the state made. The tactics used in revolutions are similarly variable. They range from spectacular shows of nonviolent resistance to hidden guerilla warfare. The specific path of each individual revolution is tailored to the precise nature of that state. No domain names the area within the state to which revolution applies, and no one model captures every relationship between revolution and the state. For those who emphasize the importance of revolutionary fidelity, this discovery should bring pause, for it indicates that there is always an element of presumption that accompanies any revolutionary act (namely, that the alternative system they are proposing will be sustainable and consistent). Because this is impossible to know in advance, revolutionaries must be critical and thoughtful with regard to their propositions. An unthinking and dogmatic revolutionary can be as dangerous in the long term as an unthinking and dogmatic statist.

Revolutions can be described after they happen (though only from the perspective of the state, not absolutely), and the strategies that worked in one place might have currency in another, but no form holds forever. Understood through this lens, the evental theories of Kuhn, Badiou, Foucault, and others are best thought of as strategies that help undermine states. They recast the state in a new light and produce projects that undermine the state's institutions of repression, but they cannot perpetually model how things work. This point is in part meant as a critique of Badiou's truth-procedures, which do a lot of work in justifying how the tactic of militancy can be used to undermine the state. Inasmuch as revolutions often require a great deal of trust, faith, and organizing capacity among revolutionaries, Badiou's idea is an important conceptual tool. But the thing that Badiou claims is external to the state and that justifies his theory, the generic procedures that summon the void into being, are not external to the state but merely another level of the state (they are part of Badiou's protostate). For this reason a transformation of the state has the potential to change the nature and effectiveness of Badiou's truth-procedure model. When a state changes, the theories of evental theorists may not serve the same function. The pieces of the state that evental theorists posit should be seen as devices for the purpose of undermining the state rather than as ontological facts.

Some of the ways the state-revolution relationship has been modeled will be studied in the next chapter, where I will discuss the practical value of Dynamic Anarchism by comparing it to several revolutionary movements. For now, it is enough to close this chapter with the assertion that, by making the state wholly changeable and liberating revolution from it, we also ensure that the two have no definitive relationship. This being the case, it is important for revolutionaries to stay vigilant so as to prevent the state they are opposing from reasserting itself unexpectedly. It may be necessary for them to change their tactics in order to preserve their goals. Revolutionaries must think through the lens of dynamic systems so that they can see the ripple effects their own and other people's actions have, and respond in the most effective way. Militancy must be combined with an openness to change to achieve the best results. Perhaps by thinking about revolution in these terms, revolutionaries will be more cautious about holding too firmly to any particular ground, and less susceptible to repeating the state they just left behind.

6

Changing the World, No Matter the Cost

The Practice of Revolution

The Wisdom of Revolt

Common sense says nothing is more reckless than becoming a revolutionary. It is illegal, immoral, dangerous, and pointless. Moreover, it disrespects society, for why wouldn't someone who cares about its betterment not submit their suggestions for approval? What arrogance that unelected militants claim to know how to best organize others' lives! Every revolutionary, including those now internationally praised as freedom fighters, faces such accusations. The criteria separating a hero from a war criminal is not as stark as is pretended. States prosecute the same actions that created them, claiming that laudable actions can be distinguished from criminal by the campaign they support. But the liberated revolution does not accept the state's judgment regarding which causes are legitimate. No dictates determine its method, and no formulas can say when it is lawful to rebel. The liberated revolution is capable of imagining many possibilities in exchange for its objection to detailed revolutionary programs, though, in order for this theory to be preferable to those built on a state, we must solve two problems. First, how do we make Dynamic Anarchism useful for revolutionaries? Despite its intellectual value, it is functionally useless outside the academy unless it can aid activists. Second, is it possible for Dynamic Anarchism to ward off dangerous revolutions? If Dynamic Anarchism cannot circumnavigate bloody revolutions that produce more disastrous states than the ones overthrown, it may be preferable—even if inauthentic—to stick with a theory of revolution tethered to a state. The purpose of this chapter is to answer these questions by showing that Dynamic Anarchism is not just a curiosity for the intellectual archive, but a powerful weapon for the disenfranchised. Opposing the conventional wisdom, I intend to show that becoming revolutionary is one of the most meaningful actions a person can take.

As I discussed in the last chapter, Dynamic Anarchism utilizes systems theory as a way of illustrating problems within more well-known event ontologies. By observing phenomena like emergence, resilience, interconnectedness, and more; by studying the math and science used to model systems and their outcomes; and by extrapolating from the discoveries made in studies of complex and adaptive systems to an ontology that would best explain them, we reach the conclusions of the last chapter. First, that motion and being must be separate, and pure motion equated with pure nothingness. Second, that accounts of being must not begin with planes, realms, or outsides, but with functions or archetypes. Third, that functions and archetypes do not reach the outside, draw multitudes together, cut up intensities, or otherwise relate themselves to what exists outside understanding. They treat one or a few things as fixed (as opposed to actually fixing them) and, in so doing, create a system that can be interacted with. Finally, radical change is the undermining of an archetype and instituting a new one. The value of this approach was elaborated in the previous chapter, but in short, it helps us to wrestle with complexity, diversity, and interconnectedness in a way other event ontologies do not.

The practical argument in Dynamic Anarchism's favor becomes clear when the phenomena revealed by complexity and interconnectedness are measured against actual revolutions. While revolution doesn't advocate for any particular state, there is nevertheless advice that can be gained from studying revolution using the ideas revealed by systems theory. In addition to answering the question of why Dynamic Anarchism is preferable to the event ontologies of others, engaging this topic is also useful because it contributes to solving perhaps the most pressing dilemma of those involved in revolutions: "What should we do?" For that reason, the final inquiry this project will take up is the question of how one should strategize for revolution. Which approaches are the most effective, and what signs indicate success? To the extent that this constitutes a separate field of study, I call it revolutionary pragmatics to indicate that it is focused on the practical side of revolution. The main insight that comes from our previous investigations into revolution is that revolutions are neither linear nor predictable. They are organic, holistic outcomes of a state in motion, and resist programs or the imposition of boundaries.

The thesis of this chapter is that a successful revolution must efficiently use asymmetry, resilience, emergence, adaptivity, and other features that result from highly complex and interconnected systems. Spelled out in detail, this means that effective revolutions have the following six traits: (1) they function on several levels at the same time, using different tactics for each; (2) they make effective use of speeds, operating slowly or quickly when need be; (3) they are capable of adaptation such that their larger goals are not inhibited by a particular doctrine, being, or tactic when it becomes a hindrance; (4) they are innovative, and in the process force the state to respond in ways the state is unprepared for; (5) they make effective use of the emergent properties of states; and (6) they form a whole that is effective at undermining an archetype. This whole cannot be reduced to any one part or tactic, but has an interconnected character that is capable of rivaling the state in some fundamental way.

These points will be demonstrated by going through each individually and showing how successful historic revolutions exhibited such features.[1] In the process, I will demonstrate how no tactics are universally effective, for the idiomatic nature of revolutions means each one must form a unique relationship with the state and respond to the specific one it confronts.

Before beginning the analysis, I want to address the topic of violence. This is a widely discussed issue in the literature on revolution.[2] The primary topics of concern to theorists of revolution are the issues of whether violence is justified and, if so, what types of violence. Schematically, the debate breaks into the philosophy that violence must be tempered by concern for the oppressed or civilians caught up in it, and the philosophy that any violence necessary to bring a new state into being is justified. Following the arguments of the previous chapters, I argue that we cannot limit revolution with rules about justifiable violence. All such rules would be drawn from the state, including our responsibilities to others, requirements under the law, and relationships with different groups. All are subject to change in a dynamic system. Yet as I indicated in my response to one of regulationism's objections, particular revolutions will operate with limits even if the concept of revolution is unlimited. Particular revolutions are guided by concerns about what it takes to bring its preferred state into being, and must not assume that any violence done to figures of authority will help achieve that goal. As this chapter shows, rarely are events that straightforward. Rather, attacks on authorities can backfire in ways that strengthen the state. The complexity of states and the role of violence in previous revolutions shows that violence is a blunt tool that does not do all the meticulous work of dismantling systems that revolutions require. It is effective for certain purposes, but ineffective for others. For that reason, revolutionaries should be cautious in its use. Think through the potential outcomes in systemic terms (e.g., who are you targeting, and what are their relationships to others? What violence are you using, and who might get hurt?). Be prepared for it to have unanticipated effects. And thoroughly connect the violence to the larger plan for radical change. These guidelines only suggest an approach; they are not absolute rules. As with much about revolution, Dynamic Anarchism asks revolutionaries to attend to their situation when navigating the changing boundaries of appropriate violence.

I will now begin my analysis of how Dynamic Anarchism helps revolutionaries create effective change. Liberating revolution conceptually, while useful for scholars, doesn't bring about radical change. Many systems in the world prevent a healthy society. Neoliberal economics still works for the wealthy, underrepresented groups still face professional difficulties, and international law still has not caught up with the dangers of militarism and online espionage. If liberating revolution is to have worth outside the academy, it should provide normative guidelines to those advocating for change.

Multileveled Revolutions

Every state has levels. They are the planes upon which different operations of the state occur. While they bear a similarity to Marxism's concepts of class, inasmuch as different classes encounter different parts of the state, the levels I describe here are not necessarily part of the typology of the state. Sometimes, levels are outcomes of the state when set into motion, and as such are emergent properties. The idea comes from the fact that one of the core properties of systems is that they are hierarchical. As Ladyman, Lambert, and Wiesner put it, they are "organized into a variety of levels of structure and properties that interact with the level above and below and exhibit lawlike and causal regularities, and various kinds of symmetry, order and periodic behavior."[3] John Holland says hierarchy occurs through the aggregation of agents that create meta-agents (agents that exist on a different level due to the interaction of agents on a lower level).[4] Revolutions should not apply the same tactic to each level, as they do not function in the same way. Each level's processes, beings, and institutions are different, so a tactic that works on one level may not work on another. At the very least the tactic may be ineffective, but at worst it can produce blowback that undermines the chances for a successful revolution.[5] To be effective, a revolution must adapt to the different levels, deploying tactics effective at challenging each.

The tactics of the American and French revolutionaries with regard to the public and British government illustrates this. The tactics addressed to each level were distinct. The public was often targeted with pamphlets and declarations attempting to rally support. Though popular images connected with both revolutions depict people rioting in streets and fighting in fields, each revolution began long before any shots were fired. Revolutionary fervor was first produced through the dissemination of pamphlets outlining positions contra the monarch. The most well-known pamphlet from the American Revolution, Tom Paine's *Common Sense*, has been lauded as "the most incendiary and popular pamphlet of the entire revolutionary era,"[6] though it was supplemented by many others, including James Otis's *Rights of the British Colonies* and Stephen Johnson's *Some Important Observations*. These pamphlets are not dispassionate academic exercises but rabble-rousing treatises. They contain rhetorical flourishes highlighting the populace's grievances and passages meant to kindle peoples' desire for revolt.[7] The French Revolution's pamphlets—such as the *Cahiers de doléances* and Sieyes's *What Is the Third Estate?*—also transmitted revolutionary ideas throughout the country using rhetoric and persuasion. It was just as important that the pamphlets' ideas be available everywhere as it was that they have a convincing message, as it gave the impression that the desire for revolution was not just the agitation of a few insurgents, but reflected the broad feeling of a majority of the population.[8] Even for those who couldn't read the text, the ideas contained in it were passed along verbally.[9] This is important because it shows that the ideas of *Common Sense* were by themselves not what made the pamphlet important, as to some degree those ideas were already present in the colonies.[10] Similarly, many of the *Cahiers* in France were published in order to lend influence and credence to the demands they contained.[11]

These pamphlets made great use of the declaration.[12] By doing this, revolutionary groups claim the right to represent the people, whom they say deserve a voice in policy discussions regarding taxation and the use of public resources.[13] As declarations do not argue for rights, they are not meant to convince people of the nature of man. Rather, they provide an alternative foundation for the state. Whereas the monarch claims that all agency within the state comes from her or him, the declaration provides a semiotic assault on this idea by claiming that agency derives from human nature. Similarly, the documents did not address those committing the violations. They were aimed at the public, who needed to know this alternative foundation. Even as declarations made reference to the king constantly and even, at times, were addressed to him, their primary audience was the people.[14] The idea is that once this new foundation is revealed, it should be considered self-evident. Even if the evidence is debatable, the self-evident nature of the declaration supports the idea that truth does not come from the monarch.

The same actions would have been ineffective at the highest level of British society: the government. The revolutionaries adapted their behavior when engaging the king, Parliament, or other elite representatives of the Crown. In the lead-up to the American Revolution all communication with the king was humble and phrased as a petition.[15] While one may credit common decency for this difference in tone, given the revolutionaries conviction of the importance of truth-telling, this explanation seems inadequate (Franklin says in his testimony that the colonists will resist the Stamp Act at all costs). Similarly, the colonists knew that word of the pamphlets and other protests would reach the king, so they were not hiding their militancy. A better explanation for the difference is that the revolutionaries were adapting their tactics for different levels of the state (in this case, the sovereign's government versus the colonists who didn't represent the British government).

The Chinese Communist revolutionaries were similarly adaptive. They adapted their strategy to the Kuomintang Party and the state it headed. The Kuomintang received support primarily from landed interests[16] and wealthy entrepreneurs who lived in cities. Though the Kuomintang capital was officially located in Beijing (which was at the time called Peiping), there were significant institutions of political power in all China's major cities.[17] The Chinese revolutionaries faced a multileveled system where the Kuomintang elite lived primarily in cities and were often surrounded by industrialists and, to a lesser extent, factory workers. By contrast, the peasants in China were separated from these areas of relative wealth, and often operated independently of what was happening in the city. The tactics Mao and the Red Army took towards peasants differed from the ones they took towards city workers or Kuomintang officials. Many have noted how Mao's base of power came from the peasants, as he originally was one and maintained connections with them throughout his revolutionary career. Among other things, peasants passed along information the Red Army could use and provided sustenance that soldiers needed. Mao encouraged the development of "secret societies" that could carry out covert actions attacking the landowning classes on behalf of the poor.[18] Stuart Schran says that Mao's dependence on the peasants for his rise to power is "an obvious and undisputed fact."[19] Similarly, Philip Huang says that the faith Mao had in the peasants developed when he first encountered the peasants in the Kuomintang's Peasant Department. He quickly formed many unions and found out how strong a desire there was among peasants for social change. Up until that point, the Communists were as skeptical of mass action as the Kuomintang were.[20] Organizing the peasants, and encouraging them to take actions against the Kuomintang, was a central part of the Communist's plan. Yet even among the peasants, Mao mediated his tactics for different groups. Middle peasants (those who wanted a change in society but were not willing to give up everything to achieve it) were often in a better position than the poorest peasants. In order to avoid alienating them, Mao and his supporters advocated a movement that only targeted those whose wealth was considered excessive, rather than attacking wealth as such. This alteration of Marxist doctrine helped form a mass peasant movement.[21] The Communists worked to organize and unify the Chinese peasants to build their revolution.

This was not the attitude that Mao and the Red Army took toward the workers. As a separate group that occupied a different part of the state, collective organization and organizing for revolution was not going to be as effective with the workers as it was with the peasants (especially given how the workers in Chinese society were relatively well-off). When it came to the workers, Mao used a different tactic: emphasizing their role as leaders in a new society. Mao's writings contain many references to the workers as the stewards of a new society, and how the revolution begins with the peasants but is incomplete without the workers.[22] In much of the organizing Mao did in the 1930s, leadership roles were gerrymandered so that the workers would receive proportionally more representation than the peasants.[23] The communes that Mao and others organized throughout the 1930s favored workers over peasants at all levels or organization. The reason for this is because Mao felt that the peasants could not complete a communist revolution without understanding the proletarian mindset, and that they could only get from the workers.[24] Mao and the Communist rebels did more than just tailor their message for their audience (i.e., workers vs. peasants); they developed a strategy that used both groups effectively by having each perform different tasks that, when done together, would interact to attain some of the movement's goals.

Finally, with regard to the top of the Kuomintang state—the leaders and the government—Mao utilized psychological warfare. The enemy needed to be demoralized and disintegrated, such that their old loyalties would be dissolved.[25] Among other things the Red Army did to achieve this mission were to spread myths about the army's size and achievements in order to gain a reputation that preceded them, deceive the Kuomintang into believing that the Reds were committed to fighting the Japanese when they were actually putting significant resources into growing their forces, and creating rumors about the Red's good deeds to convince people on the fence of the Communist's good intentions.[26] Giving the Kuomintang government leadership positions, or mobilizing their desire for change, would not be effective, since they already have the former and are in a position to carry out the latter themselves without help from revolutionaries. The strategies that effectively brought peasants and workers into the movement would not be effective for the Kuomintang. In this case, the difference of tactics was primarily about which aspect of communism to project and which to hide. While there was always an element of truth in what was being said, significant parts of the Communist Party's platform were hidden from each group. The point of doing so was to arrest movement hostile to the long-term goal of creating a communist state while encouraging movement promoting that goal. Each group was played off the other in order to distract from developments that would otherwise concern them. By constraining and producing movement in this way, the Communists were able to effectively oversee the production of a new state using the resources that the various groups provided to them.

While Mao's revolution was effective in its use of multitiered strategies, this practice is not explicitly advocated by Marxists. "Gaining the means of production," as communists encourage, is not described as part of a systemic and complex strategy. Many communist movements have acted programmatically. The idea of behaving with multiple tiers in mind is not a fundamental part of Marxism or any other revolutionary program that is attached to a state. This is why a liberated revolution is necessary. It sees states in their entirety rather than measuring them against the state revolutionaries want to bring into existence. Liberated revolutions look at a state not for its lack in relation to one's ideal, but for the complexity and nuance that is contained within.

Speeds

The importance of utilizing speed effectively is due to the adaptability of systems. States are tailored to their unique situations, and regularly evolve as these change. While there are commonalities between democracies, tyrannies, oligarchies, and other systems of government, each unique formation operates according to unique rules. A revolution must read the circumstances properly to be effective, and this means learning how best to move in order to disrupt the state and prevent it from adapting to the revolution. Models used by advocates of social change are often static, and present the system they are confronting as unchanging or repetitive. While states do have equilibria that they use for purposes of balance, regulation, and control, this does not mean they are incapable of change. States can pass new laws, suspend old ones, grant additional powers, or declare emergency conditions as ways of counteracting threats. Effective revolutions act as quickly or as slowly as is necessary to achieve their goals. This, again, is supported by systems theory, which emphasizes the value dynamism plays in effective engagement with complex systems. Page and Miller say that, "in situations in which equilibria are a possibility, understanding the dynamics is likely to be insightful. In situations where equilibria are nonexistent or transient paths are long, understanding the dynamics is critical."[27] Similarly, Ladyman, Lambert, and Wiesner discuss feedback—or how agents at later times are affected by the behaviors of their neighbors at earlier times—as an intrinsic part of systems.[28] Dynamism is often the result of a large and complex amount of feedback taking place in a system. And a revolution that doesn't prepare for the state's response is in jeopardy.

To illustrate this point, let's begin by demonstrating the value that rushing to achieve an important victory can have. The American revolutionaries illustrate this point as they moved quickly to show to others that their cause was viable. This was especially needed given how the British Empire was the largest one in the world at the time, and had proven itself in multiple battles around the world. One estimate says that the British had upwards of 50,000 troops stationed in North America in 1778, supplemented by 30,000 German mercenaries. Their total population numbered approximately 11 million. By contrast, the Continental Army never numbered more than 5,000 men, supplemented by militias of various sizes. Many of these troops were inexperienced and untrained. The total colonial population was roughly 2.5 million, with one fifth of that consisting of African slaves.[29] The point is that an early, decisive victory would provide the Continental Army with an important strategic position (strategic not just in military terms, but in social, political, and economic ones too) for the rest of the war. Thus, haste was more important to them once fighting broke out.

It is for this reason that the early battles in the American Revolution are so significant. As numerous historians have noted, the fact that many of these battles were either won by the colonial forces, or that more casualties were inflicted upon British forces than people expected, demonstrated that the British were not invincible. Additionally, the victories were important for maintaining the image of American innocence and British guilt. In battles like Lexington, Concord, and Bunker Hill, the message the battles conveyed was just as important as the outcome itself. Historians have noted how, in the aftermath of Lexington and Concord, colonial officials collected sworn testimonies from militia members and British prisoners that confirmed colonial innocence, and the justice of their cause. To beat the official British account of the battles, the colonists sent these depositions upon a quicker boat to London and handed them off to a sympathetic official, who had them printed in newspapers.[30] The colonists attempted to repeat this practice after the Battle of Bunker Hill, but because the British account reached London first, it caused many in the military establishment and royal court to harden their views against the colonists.[31] The point is that throughout the American Revolution, battles sent messages, and control over these messages was a major part of how the revolution was conducted. Whoever was quicker to promote their message achieved the better victory. This point is confirmed by the fact that battles were conducted in full view of the local populations, who spread word of the battle.[32] Though there are some notable differences, a similar dynamic operated in the French Revolution.[33]

By contrast, some revolutions do not benefit from quickness, especially at the beginning. Those conducted using guerrilla warfare often fall into this category. For several reasons, it is dangerous for guerrilla fighters to reveal themselves to the state they oppose, chief among which is that the battle is thoroughly asymmetric (much more so than the American or French Revolutions). Community support is a necessity to achieve victory, but that is not always forthcoming. In many places where revolution occurred via guerrilla warfare, it was far from agreed to that a revolution was needed, and while significant portions of the people were unhappy, this doesn't mean that they trusted the guerrilla forces.[34] More than the contest between the opposing military forces, then, what matters is the contest for the minds of the populace.

This is why many guerrilla warfare manuals emphasize the importance of setting up a propaganda industry. It is important that the message of the war—why it is occurring, what the guerrillas are doing to support it, and the benefits that already liberated areas have reaped—reach the population. In addition, the creation and dissemination of propaganda gives those lacking the constitution to fight yet sympathetic with the cause something to do.[35] The chief goal of propaganda is to convince the indifferent and confused of the virtue of the guerrilla's cause by raising awareness of the state's oppression. Guevara writes that propaganda "ought to create a consciousness of the great national problems, besides offering sections of more lively interest for the reader."[36] Guerrillas reject intentional dishonesty, but they do emphasize that the primary purpose of the news released by the propaganda machine is to promote the guerrilla's cause. The news gathering operation is to be controlled by the guerrilla band itself, without any firewall separating those involved with news gathering from those involved with advocacy.[37] And propagandists are encouraged to only report those facts that are sure to secure support for the cause or that are "directly related to the struggle for liberation."[38] The implicit assumption is that propaganda must act as a countermeasure against the biased media of the state (this is tacitly confirmed by Maj. John Pustay of the US Air Force, who advocates a "psychological-action program" that should be focused on describing government achievements).[39] This is a time-consuming task, but necessary for a successful guerrilla fight.

In effect, guerrilla warfare becomes about sending messages to the people, just like the American Revolution. But why was there a difference in the manner in which the messages were sent (quickly vs. slowly)? The asymmetry of competing forces and new, more destructive weapons are two significant reasons, but the answer goes deeper than that. At stake in guerrilla warfare is a battle over ownership and control that didn't exist in those other revolutions. While the British government wanted to maintain nominal control over the colonies, there was no debate over who maintained effective control on a day to day basis. It was the colonists. In guerrilla warfare, there is a fight over who maintains effective control. In such situations, a quick victory is not an advantage for revolutionaries. Rather, it is more important to gather forces, make connections with the community, and show that one's loyalties lay with the oppressed who suffer under the current rule. Many guerrilla forces started off slowly, and took time to build themselves into a well-organized group. This was necessary to, piece by piece, remove effective control away from the government. In the process, they formed strong relationships with people in the community who trusted the fighters to do the right thing for the country. Nelson Mandela writes that the support of the community was vital for the work of the African National Congress (ANC)[40] and that, as a fugitive, he worked primarily in the night and slept in other peoples' flats.[41] Several times he escaped capture solely because a black policeman sympathetic with the cause of independence refused to bring him in. Mandela concludes, "Black policemen have often been severely criticized during the struggle, but many have played covert roles that have been extremely valuable."[42] The state is aware of this resource, though from its perspective guerrillas are making deceitful and disingenuous appeals to the population. Pustay says that guerrillas are able to achieve their goals by using "character assassination," "psychological warfare," the "covert sponsoring of parties in opposition," and the enlistment of "government officials to serve secretly the revolutionary movement."[43] Accordingly, one of the ways the state can respond is to resettle the population to areas uninhabited by guerrillas, thus "denying [the guerrillas] important sources of logistics and intelligence support."[44] An excellent example of this is the USA's Phoenix program, which consisted of capturing, interrogating, resettling, and, in some cases, torturing and killing the Viet Cong during the Vietnam War.[45] This technique was also used in China in the 1930s and in the Philippines in the 1950s. This, again, is a time-consuming task.

Guerrillas would also continually carry out acts of violence, not for the purpose of gaining a quick victory but so that the government being opposed would have fewer resources and look weaker over time. These highly visible, punctuated acts of sabotage and terrorism must be contrasted with the other form of attack guerrilla's employ: the constant engagement with the state's forces. The point of such exercises is not just to wear away at enemy forces, but to destroy morale.[46] Guerrillas "shoot and scoot," attacking the enemy by surprise at potentially any moment of the day, inflicting maximal casualties, then fleeing before the enemy can mount an effective defense.[47] Because guerrillas spend so much time running away, it is important for them to know the territory they are fighting in and to be able to move quickly over a variety of different terrains.[48] Many guerrilla manuals emphasize the importance of being able to "live the militant life"; that is, being completely sure of the justness of your cause, willing to commit your body and soul to it, and prepared to sacrifice yourself for it. It may be necessary for you to give up your life to ensure that a bombing goes off as planned, or to slow the advance of the enemy so that the rest of the guerrillas get away, and guerrilla manuals emphasize that such fidelity is one way guerrillas can make up for the disadvantages they have compared to their enemy.[49] This sense of commitment, and of aligning your life with a higher purpose, is a resource that—like the support of the locals—can even out the disparity between the state and guerrillas. Like with the previous techniques, the state has recognized this resource and developed countermeasures to it. They recommend using small scale operations instead of large-scale ones, and training troops to be adaptive and semiautonomous.[50] However, because the state's army rarely consists of "people taking a principled stance," but rather paid functionaries, they do not have an easy equivalent to the militant life.

It is clear from this that guerrilla warfare must move slowly, primarily because the goal of wresting effective control away from the government, combined with the asymmetric circumstances, requires slowly undermining the government's forces, and using their resources against them.[51] A guerrilla-led revolution cannot follow the same rules as a regulationist one, for it must view the state differently. The tactics of one revolution aren't necessarily appropriate for another revolution. The virtue of untethering revolution from the state comes from how it frees revolutionaries to act with more attention to their situation.

Adaptation not Hindered by Doctrine

More than a few revolutions have failed because they were not able to adapt in time. They stubbornly persisted in doing the same thing, and believing outdated truths, even after the evidence suggested such an approach to be harmful. At other times, the state was able to surprise the revolutionaries, making their task impossible. Revolutions often throw the unexpected at revolutionaries, so much so that it is perhaps the closest thing one can find to a universal rule in the study of revolution. It is important to go into revolution with an awareness that such events are likely to occur, and prepared to adapt to them as needed. This point is, again, confirmed by the study of complex systems. Adaptive systems have an advantage over nonadaptive ones when their environment changes,[52] and the more resilient a system is (i.e., the better a system is able to maintain its core purpose in the face of changing circumstances), the more likely the system can persist in the midst of unanticipated disruption.[53] The quicker a revolution can adapt, the more likely it will survive and achieve its goals; the longer it takes to recognize and respond to a problem, the more difficult a time it will have.

Revolutions lacking adaptivity keep using the same strategies and ideas again and again, regardless of their efficacy. In the French Revolution's Reign of Terror, the revolutionaries became heavily dogmatic, as evidenced by the ways they regulated culture in educational institutions, libraries, and public spaces. Peter McPhee points out that the number of books published dropped dramatically during the revolutionary war years (from 1,000 to 371, and to only 36 during 1793–94), except for Rousseau's *Social Contract*, which went through thirteen editions between 1792 and 1795. Political songs praising the courage of revolutionaries and mocking royalty were written and spread. From about 116 in 1789 the number jumped to 325 in 1792, 590 in 1793, and finally 701 in 1794.[54] Numerous other practices changed during this time to reflect the revolution's adoration of republicanism, equality, and the Enlightenment, as well as their hatred of monarchy, hierarchy, and medievalism. Plays, cartoons, and paintings castigated symbols of the ancien régime like the church. Symbols of royalty were burned in public during festivals, followed by the release of doves carrying signs saying "We are free! Imitate us!" The word *vous* was exorcised from the language and replaced with *tu*, as the former was a symbol of elitism and the latter an indication of brotherhood. Lastly, multiple neologisms (e.g., *robespierriste, pittiste, maratiste*), place names, and birth names were created to reflect a revolutionary, non-Christian culture.[55]

While experimentation occurs in every revolution, the diversity of such experimentation during the Terror was limited because it was being exterminated by the Jacobins. McPhee writes that "the civil wars of 1793 had also served to underline the dangers of local autonomy, just as the *armées révolutionnaires*, the surge of radical women's demands, and dechristianization highlighted the challenge of local initiatives."[56] Much of the exploration being done on the local level was seen as a threat to the homogeneous unity the Jacobins desired. They cracked down on the speaking of other languages and signs of minority culture, exacerbating peoples' mistrust of Paris.[57] In addition, they saw the revolutionary culture of the *sans-culottes* (as well as other "extremists" and "indulgents") as an impediment to the creation of the "single will" Rousseau advocated. To confront this threat, the Jacobins shut down many popular societies and enacted economic, political, and social controls.[58]

In sum, during the Reign of Terror a Rousseauian-inspired ideology came to dominate the Convention in Paris. Because the Jacobins had extinguished other practices of revolution, they lacked the resources needed to adapt when their circumstances changed. Additionally, their centralized and imperious system of authority meant other revolutionary groups lacked an easy means to steer the revolution away from disaster. I argue that the problem with the Terror is not that it was too militant, too unethical, or unfortunate for encountering extreme circumstances; it is that, in the name of unity, they forgot to cultivate an adaptive capacity by encouraging other revolutionary practices. When they felt that the public was threatened, they returned again and again to the same practices (e.g., imprisonment, censorship, and guillotines). The end of the Reign of Terror was not just an end to one ruling group, but an end to this way of *doing* the revolution.[59]

To see how revolutions can avoid the danger of dogmatism, let's look at the organization of guerrilla fighters and the tactics of the Russian Revolution between the February and October revolutions. Beginning with the former, one of the reason guerrilla bands are often effective is because they can adapt quickly. When guerrillas can rely on the locals they do not need to worry as much about setting up defenses, developing supply lines, and protecting captured land. They can live hidden, their location protected, until it is time to strike. After the strike, they can just as easily disappear into the social milieu. Mao Zedong says a guerrilla force will fail "if its political objectives do not coincide with the aspirations of the people and their sympathy, co-operation, and assistance cannot be gained,"[60] while Carlos Marighella claims a guerrilla "must know how to live among the people, and he must be careful not to appear strange and different."[61] Because the forces guerrillas have traditionally fought are more privileged, making direct and open confrontation futile (i.e., the state's control is so complete that it is impossible to rally any sort of collective resistance), the best approach is to organize groups so that they can carry out their work without having to consult a centralized planner for every action. Though the general goals of the resistance are known by all, groups are given independence within the borders of their area as to how to achieve those goals, and information about specific tactics and how to carry them out is shared. Hoang Van Thai's manual for Vietnamese guerrillas claims that once peasants are recruited to the cause, they should not join an army but "stick to the people and to their locality, forming the core of the guerrilla forces in the villages."[62] The goal is not to destroy the enemy quickly and thoroughly, but to "exhaust him on a large scale" by striving to "annihilate enemy forces in small operations." This goal will only be achieved through "initiative of action," "flexibility," "secrecy," and "surprise."[63] Though this flexibility allows "the guerrilla fighter [to invent] his own tactics at every minute of the fight,"[64] the decentralization of guerrilla bands does not imply a lack of order. Guerrilla bands have strong hierarchies,[65] but the commands issued from the top are open enough to allow for innovation by the fighters.

The success of the Bolsheviks following the February Revolution is similarly due to an ability to adapt. They would go out in the street, write op-eds, give speeches, and use violence as needed to gain an advantage, and were willing to alter course when one tactic became harmful. Following the success of the February Revolution, there was a tentative agreement between the liberal democrats and soviets, both of whom opposed the tsar. They decided to share power while the Constituent Assembly worked on a new constitution.[66] This "dual-power" pact was supposed to create an inclusive Provisional Government, which in turn would create buy-in from all major political groups. For a time, the Soviets were willing to make alliances with many political groups, which in turn helped them come to and maintain power (this is not something that was actively pursued by those involved in the Reign of Terror, which helps explain the different outcomes). While perhaps a worthwhile ideal, the difficulty of reaching common ground pushed the socialists further to the left and the liberal democrats into a more conservative stance. This led to infighting between the liberal democrats, Mensheviks, and other enfranchised groups as the tsarist forces marshaled their troops on the outskirts of civil society. In the midst of this, the Bolsheviks used the outcome of the Kornilov rebellion—when a former general tried and failed to overthrow the provisional government and install a military dictatorship—to achieve victory.[67] The Bolsheviks received significant support following the attempted coup, as many recognized both the importance of protecting the revolution and the inadequacy of the moderates' attempts to do so.[68] Documents show that the Bolsheviks radically changed their tactics because of this development. Prior to this level of support, violent insurrection was anathema for most Bolshevik leaders, and its primary supporter, Lenin, had gone into hiding in Finland. Afterwards, several on the Bolshevik Central Committee changed their tactics, seeing an opportunity to bring about their program.[69] Ultimately this group, aided by the attempt of Russia's leader at the time, Kerensky, to shut down the Bolshevik press, won out.[70] The Bolsheviks were highly adaptable in the strategies and tactics they employed during the time between the February and October Revolutions, which helped them to achieve their objectives.[71]

These examples show the importance of building *dynamic and reactive networks*. By this I mean an arrangement of relationships capable of responding quickly to incidents. All the pieces of such revolutionary networks already exist in the state; the task of revolutionaries is to create an awareness of the network among its parts. This act slightly alters the role the individual agents, and the network as a whole, play in the state, giving it a more revolutionary purpose. The network can be cemented by building new relationships between the parts while reinforcing those that already exist. The production of these fluid, militant, and—most important—conscious networks creates new agents within the state capable of more efficiently pushing a state to a moment of disruption. Revolutions stand or fail by how quickly allies can be mobilized and how firm the relationships within the network are. Networks that can react quickly to actions by the state or reproduce disruptive forms of behavior throughout the state are more effective at achieving their goals and more resilient to attack. Building connections across age groups, geographic locations, and even color lines provides more resources to draw upon in times of social upheaval and a greater degree of agency in producing a situation amenable to revolution. The question is how to frame your network so that it is flexible and resilient without being so lax that it cannot pull together when needed. Every network must have a compelling center that keeps people organized and mobilized, but that center cannot be too rigid—or the network too inflexible—without becoming elitist and alienating allies. The most effective network is one that is itself centered around an ideal or a goal, but in which no part of the network is itself the center. The network must be allowed to evolve, while the center itself must be reexamined and critiqued periodically to ensure that it is still represents the goal people are interested in pursuing. No network should see itself as permanently necessary, as there may come a time when circumstances and the good of the cause require a network to disband. This means of organizing revolutionary movements works well because it takes advantage of the inherent dynamism and complexity of systems. Rather than trying to create another static and determinate system to replace the current one, this method of organizing draws from one of the benefits revolutionaries always have on their side—that every system is by its nature dynamic. By using adaptive and reactive networks revolutionaries can maintain their presence even as the state changes in response to them, updating their allies and practices as needed to confront new challenges. Only in this way will a revolutionary network be both dynamic and durable.

Ultimately, the importance of adaptability comes down to one final point: radicals must shift their perception of their enemy from one that is static to one that is variable. Radicals should resist the belief that if they just find the right formula of resistance, the state they oppose can be put to an end. Given the behavior of systems, states should be understood as highly mobile, fluid, and resilient. They have no central core, only a variety of manifestations. As such, there is no best strategy for challenging them, nor does the fact that one strategy failed mean it was wrong. States evolve in response to resistance, and the best approach to combat them is to be open to the development of new tactics and unfazed when they fail. Violence is not necessarily a misstep, as some say, but neither will it be permanently effective. Collaboration with different groups, and experimentation with alternate practices of resistance, do not inevitably destroy a movement. Though there is a need for collaborative and well-organized action—thus my argument that action should be organized via adaptive networks and take place on several levels—diversity should not be seen as a weakness. Movements should think about developing an adaptive capacity so that if one tactic fails, they have others to fall back on. In sum, resistance itself must become a site of creative struggle.

Creativity would flounder if a revolution were too determinate. Deciding the form of revolution in advance and fixing its relationship to the state inhibits imagination. Revolutions thrive when advocates use their knowledge to develop a movement tailored to the needs of the situation they are in. Liberating revolution encourages imagination and shows the importance of embracing adaptation for success.

Use of Emergent Properties

The world is a complicated place, composed of many agents and relationships constantly interacting in novel ways. There is always more being produced than went into a system. These emergent properties display "downward causation" (they can't easily be traced back to physical phenomena),[72] the persistence of patterns, and multifunctionality.[73] They also occur in systems with higher and lower level order, such that the cause of higher level order cannot be found in the lower level.[74] In other words, they are not reducible to things that happen on a smaller scale, and while their presence can sometimes be predicted, how they insert themselves into any particular situation cannot. They should be considered opportunities, for while a state may be prepared to handle emergent properties as such, emergent properties can always be repurposed in ways that require a state to adapt. In doing so, resources are taken away from other areas, leaving the state with a diminished ability to confront a revolutionary force. Revolutions that strategize how to use emergent properties to their advantage will be more likely to succeed than those that don't. As long as a revolution doesn't itself get overwhelmed by emergence, it can be a valuable tool for revolutionaries.

A good example of such an emergent property that was well utilized by a revolution is *fidelismo*, the cult of personality surrounding Fidel Castro. It is predictable that populations will want something to unite them, and it is not uncommon for a revolutionary leader to play such a role. Yet it is not possible, purely from examining the pieces of a revolution, to know whether your leader will inspire a cult of personality (i.e., the higher level order is not reducible to the lower level). It is unpredictable whether the character of the leader will be inspirational both before and after the revolution. Fidel Castro was by many accounts a compelling and charismatic leader. He gave regular talks and radio broadcasts where he explained his policies, attacked his enemies, spoke of socialism's value, and of the philosophies that inspired him. In doing so, he brought many people to the revolutionary cause (which was already a popular one).[75] After the revolution ended, his charisma influenced many people to stay with the cause even when there were significant problems setting up a government, resisting American intervention, and serving the needs of the people.[76] By contrast, the role Ahmed Ben Bella played in the Algerian Revolution and afterwards was markedly different. By most accounts, Ben Bella was a good soldier who was an excellent planner with an inspiring vision for Algeria. His work with the FLN helped achieve victory, and he was instrumental in producing the agreement that got France to withdrawal. Yet he was not considered charismatic, and spent most of his life prior to taking power out of the public eye (first in Cairo, and then in a French Algerian prison).[77] Phillip Naylor describes Ben Bella as a "romantic politician . . . and egotist . . . who attempted to personify [his] state . . . and to pursue international prestige"[78] and as a "mercurial and quixotic leader."[79] There was nowhere near the level of adoration for Ben Bella that there was for Castro, so when Ben Bella began eliminating enemies and making more unilateral decisions, fewer were willing to follow him.[80] A few years after his election, his government was overthrown.[81] Unlike Castro, there was no emergent property—in the form of a cult of personality—surrounding Ben Bella.

Another emergent property that can play good or bad effects in revolution is that of peoples' reactions to war. It is predictable that people will feel strongly about war, but how they will feel is not. Some wars encourage patriotic feelings and nationalism, while others produce anger or frustration. It is easier to convince a population of the need for revolution when the latter occurs. During wars, states often enact coercive measures meant to discipline the population and procure the materials necessary for battle. The population is conscripted, food rationed, and laws to surveil potential threats passed. In states where the government is already unpopular, these measures are seen as further examples of oppression. The French and Indian War, the American Revolutionary War, and World War I contributed to the American Revolution, French Revolution, and Russian Revolution, respectively. Following the French and Indian War, the British government levied new taxes to pay for the war.[82] The king felt them justified by the resources he spent defending the colonists, but the colonists felt his insistence on money for doing his job—especially when they had no representation—was unjust. Similarly, the American Revolutionary War cost the royal bank in France over one billion livres. Attempts by the royalty to reform the economic system (by instituting a land tax) were met with hostility by the nobles and peasants, who were demanding more representation and autonomy.[83] The royalty resisted these requests, exacerbating the conflict between these groups. World War I led to a series of harsh measures from the tsar, who took control of the army in an attempt to prevent further defeats. The losses that followed were directly traced back to the tsar, who was also blamed for corruption and the severe lack of resources found throughout the population.[84] While in all three cases there are other important causes, the fact of war, operating in the background, helped revolutionaries make the case for change.

Yet like the phenomena of leaders, while war can make revolution more achievable in the short term, it is not clear how else it will affect a revolution. The parallel drawn among the three revolutions mentioned earlier diverges once one begins to examine the other effects war had on society. Most notably, the French and Indian War was over by the time of the American Revolution, as was the war that influenced the French Revolution, while World War I continued throughout the Russian Revolution. The Russian revolutionaries thus faced a choice not given to the French and Americans: whether to continue the war. The debate between the Bolsheviks, who wanted to withdraw, and the other factions, who felt that by 1917 the war had become necessary, created an urgency to finalize the revolution, as many felt the integrity of the country hinged on which group held power.[85] And while the French Revolution did not begin while fighting a war, several insurrections and wars occurred during the process,[86] which raised nationalist and existential concerns in the minds of French citizens. America, by contrast, was relatively free of such concerns. Except for some minor clashes with Native Americans, pirates, and other powers that had a presence at sea, they were at peace.

Emergent properties—such as the cult of personality surrounding leaders and the reactions to war, in the examples given earlier—can help or harm the goals of revolution. They provoke strong feelings that turn people for or against the goal of radical change. The question revolutionaries must ask is how they should respond to emergent properties. The best way to understand what these emergent properties do is to think of them as opening pathways. When all paths are owned and operated by the state, it is difficult to challenge established systems of power. Emergent properties are predictable in some respects, but are not part of the state as it is designed. While states prepare for them, there is a limited amount they can do. The possible outcomes of introducing an emergent property are too numerous, and dependent upon so many other interactions, so complete prediction is impossible. Revolutionaries can step into this space by utilizing an emergent property in a way the state is unprepared for. Yet to make sure a revolution benefits from, rather than being harmed by, an emergent property, there are several pieces of advice worth following.

First, *seek useful emergent properties in places where a state is resisting something*. The value of emergent properties for revolutionaries being in the way they illumine alternative pathways, the state is always trying to head off possibilities by which such a pathway becomes clear. This does not mean that anytime the state resists something there is a readymade emergent property to be found, only that it is at such times that the possibility of one exists. Most of the times a state is resisting something there will likely be no emergent property, but on rare occasions one will exist. To use the example of Cuba, *fidelismo* started when the state resisted Castro's attempt to seize the Moncada barracks on July 26, 1953. Castro was well-known at the time, but hardly an icon. It was only during his trial and afterwards, when Castro's speech "History Will Absolve Me" was given and then spread around the island, that the cult of personality gained a foothold.[87] The inspirational speech, combined with the way the attempted seizure of the barracks was seen as a powerful symbol of opposition to government corruption, gave rise to a movement to free those imprisoned, and in May 1955 Batista, in an effort to sympathize with the desires of the people, signed a general amnesty. The point here is that emergent properties that the revolutionary can use will create orders on the higher level that the state tries to dominate. Their prevention is one of the key aims of a state, and so watching where a state tries to resist changes to the higher order is where one will find useful emergent properties.

Second, *use the emergent property to shine a light on an alternative pathway*. Though there is no formula for creating an emergent property, to play their role for revolution they must show the value of the revolution to those who will make the difference between success and failure. This means illuminating how things could be different or revealing a hidden power whose existence society was unaware of. Emergent properties of the type revolutionaries must use need to make something visible that was not visible before. In the examples of the American, French, and Russian Revolutions, the ire felt at the government revealed a weakness in the reigning government and a resolve in the people capable of confronting the leaders. More than that, though, one sees in the reactions to wars a germ of the society that the revolution was going to try to create. In the Russian Revolution, for example, the frustration the people felt was accompanied by a lack of industrial capacity compared to the Germans.[88] The goal of material development—for example, by modernizing the areas where peasants lived—thus accompanied discussions about the trajectory the revolution should take.[89] The French Revolution, by contrast, was impelled forward by the aristocratic forms of power and order operating in society.[90] Discussions during the revolution focused much more on overcoming these functions/operations than on development as such. Finally, while the American revolutionaries also wrestled with an autocratic system, freedom and autonomy were much more important than challenging royalty as such. For this reason, liberty and choice often trumped equality.[91] In each case, the reaction to war revealed a flaw in the higher level order governing society and suggested potential remedies to it. Revolutionaries took up the banner and ran with it, elaborating upon the suggestions in order to draw people to the vision of another society.

As a final point, emergent properties and revolutionaries maintain a codependent relationship. Revolutionaries utilize them, as discussed earlier, but are also created by them. The emergent property generates the pathway the revolution will follow just as revolutionaries adopt the properties for their own purpose. For this reason, it is dangerous for a revolution to force an emergent property to fit a premade doctrine. To do so is to ignore how adaptable emergent properties are, and how minor shifts can cause them to change their character or collapse. Forcing emergent properties to fit the pathway you or your doctrine insist on means labeling the factors producing the property as unimportant. If you don't care for these factors, the emergent property may not remain, or it may revert to the original path you were trying to move it from. The Russian Revolution's experience with organized religion exemplifies this. Both before and after the revolution, the Bolsheviks argued against such religion regularly. Lenin said that religion should be a private affair and that as economic oppression disappeared, so would religious ideology.[92] A textbook on communism written by Bakunin and Preobrazhensky in 1920 said that now was the time to fight religious dogma.[93] And official decrees from the Soviet government banned religious organizations from owning property, having legal rights, and carrying out religious performances that undermined public order.[94] While they did succeed in removing the Russian Orthodox church from its position of power, the Bolsheviks failed to erase religion, as an estimated sixty to seventy million remained religious practitioners (a significant portion of the population).[95] Many of the anti-religious campaigns ended in failure or a significant revision of policy such that the faithful were recognized.[96] Part of the reason for this is that the emergent property the Bolsheviks relied on was partially the product of Christians and similar believers who felt the Orthodox church and similar establishments were failing to uphold Christian values, and that socialism was the solution.[97] Emergent properties are dynamic, not doctrinal. Without being thoughtful about one's relationship to them, grave outcomes are possible.

Innovation and Novelty

Thus far we have talked about how make a revolutionary movement effective, and focused specifically on approaches that prevent one's movement from being misled or inhibited. This is important for maintaining a revolutionary movement, but it doesn't address how to make it successful. At some point, a revolution must overthrow what it opposes and enact a new order. The next two pieces of advice discuss how to do that. The first, being innovative in ways the state is unprepared for, means that a revolution must put forth a challenge that confronts the state in an unexpected way. States thrive when people and forces do what they are supposed to do, and they build in contingency procedures to prevent their downfall. A revolution won't succeed if either of these are effective. This doesn't mean a revolution must be stronger than the state, for few revolutions are. What revolutionaries have going for them is a lack of obligations equal to those of the state and the fact that disrupting control is easier than maintaining it. Revolutions can use their relative lack of size and responsibility to short-circuit the state, disrupting the patterns upon which the state relies to function. The particular trait of systems theory being drawn on for this is nonlinearity.[98]

The Cuban Revolution illustrates this point well. The Batista government in power prior to the installation of a communist regime operated as a military dictatorship and included the canceling of elections, brutal police tactics, suspensions of rights, killings, and significant inequality.[99] In addition, a major—and archetypal—part of the Batista government was its support from the USA. The dynamics of power in Cuba during the Batista years heavily depended on what the USA provided, so this relationship was essential to the Batista regime. The cost of living in Cuba was heavily underwritten by the USA, as the imports from the USA increased from $515 million to $777 million between 1950 and 1958. As Luis Perez, Jr., concludes, "Cuba was integrated directly into the larger United States economic system and the concomitant consumption patterns."[100] In addition, the mafia in Cuba during the Batista years was largely supported by the American mob and sanctioned by Batista himself.[101] In exchange for profiting from the island's resources, the mafia helped keep Batista in power. Upsetting this foundational relationship at the heart of the Batista regime would destabilize the state in a way that would be difficult to counteract. Thus halting the production of goods the USA desired from Cuba was an effective means of separating Bastista from both foreign and domestic elites.[102] Over time, these actions were so disruptive that Batista's supporters couldn't envision an end to the counterinsurgency without first having Batista leave. It was this abdication of support for Batista that demoralized the army and produced desertions en masse, allowing the communist rebels to take charge.[103] The rebels were able to challenge a necessary and fundamental part of the state, and in doing so disrupt it's functioning enough that they could take over.

Struggles for African and African-American liberation prove this point as well. Colonial Algeria operated under the thesis that Algeria was part of France, as France was a world power. Indeed, the whole concept of Algeria as a nation was a product of colonization, though there were communities that approximated the concept in practice prior to the arrival of the French.[104] The first sense of an Algeria independent of France came during the process of colonization, when Emir Abd al-Qadir tried to develop an area free from European control in what is now western Algeria. That attempt failed, and the concept of Algeria that took hold was of a country inextricably linked to imperial France.[105] This ideology was expressed and transmitted through books, education, official documents, and a host of social, political, and economic practices that produced, according to Frantz Fanon, a "massive psychoexistential complex."[106] It wasn't until the 1930s that this concept of Algeria began to be replaced with one that was independent of France, and it wasn't until the 1950s that this concept took hold in francophone literature. Algerian writers developed an identity separate from that provided by colonial France, and resisted the characterizations of Algerians given by European "others."[107] The Front Liberation Nationale (FLN) developed as an organization aimed at eradicating French colonization and producing an authentic Algerian identity.[108] They were clear that this program was not just about throwing off the yoke of oppression, but also the creation of a new society, and while they disagreed about the form that new society should take, there were many in the movement who spoke about the revolution they sought as the fabrication of a new life.[109] As Naylor writes, "The FLN's primary postcolonial objective was to conceive and construct a state."[110] The point is that the revolution introduced a novelty into society that challenged the archetype of the state. Algeria was reconceived as independent, and France as a postimperial power.[111]

The novel identities utilized among African-American liberation movements helped disrupt racial hierarchies in the USA. Throughout the history of black radical thought, there have been debates over how to conceive of the struggle for liberation, including who to unite with and how to bring the unity into being. The goal has always been to introduce a new concept of community to supplant the racist one inherited from the past. Those who argue for a qualified support with whites argue that the best results will come when blacks and whites communicate with each other about the goals of society and take responsibility for enfranchising blacks. Booker T. Washington and the early W. E. B. Du Bois emphasize the importance of racial harmony for different races to solve the race problem effectively.[112] Others—like Frederick Douglass, Martin Luther King, Jr., the Student Nonviolent Coordinating Committee, and the Southern Christian Leadership Conference—insist that nothing will be given blacks without a movement compelling whites to change, for it is not simply ignorance but prejudice, avarice, and privilege that entrench racial disparity.[113] Opposing this belief that whites and blacks must unify is the claim that uniting blacks around the world actually increases one's strength. Pan-Africanists like the later W. E. B. Du Bois, Back-to-Africa advocates like Marcus Garvey, and Black Power activists like the Black Panthers all call for the creation of an international body that can promote the interests of blacks. Given the significant numbers of blacks throughout the world, a unified struggle of all peoples of African descent is said to be more effective than fighting colonialism and racism independently in every country in which it exists. In addition, results will come quicker as more pressure can be brought to bear with greater expediency.[114] Yet some claim even this tactic is limiting and dangerous. As any coalition excludes some and includes others, we must be careful about how we define our community. An overly rigid concept of blackness—even one that includes blacks worldwide—can entrench a certain concept of blackness while subordinating other concerns (such as gender and class discrimination) to this one conception. Without including a critique of black identity within the coalition building that one does, one risks perpetuating dangerous systems of power and alienating potential allies.[115] This final approach concludes that the importance of solidarity comes more from the practice of it than who one unifies with. Because racism can change form, black radicals must vary their partners in order to respond to the new challenges it poses.

While these examples from Cuba, Algeria, and America illustrate how revolutions incorporate a novelty that undermines an essential part of the state, we must also show how the movements introduced this novelty effectively. Revolutions will fail unless they insert the novelty that spreads quickly and successfully challenges the preexisting state. In Cuba, for instance, the government was essentially a client state for the USA, though the Mafia had a significant amount of power on the island. Showing the impotence of the Cuban government apart from the USA and its Mafia backers would spread the idea that another government can more efficiently serve the needs of the people. Thus the Cuban revolutionaries conducted attacks not just to harm the enemy, but to send a message to the public. The guerrillas needed anonymity to organize and move effectively, but, because their purpose was political, needed to attract attention with spectacles. In addition, they needed to choose targets that would incapacitate the enemy state. Che Guevara's book on guerrilla warfare claims that sabotage targets should be chosen for how effectively they paralyze society. For him, it is pointless to attack a soft-drink company, because "a certain number of workers are put out of a job but nothing is done to modify the rhythm of industrial life," yet it's perfectly justified to attack a power plant because, though workers will be displaced, it leads to "the paralysis of the life of the region."[116] Guevara also says that loss of life is acceptable if "it is used to put to death some noted leader of the oppressing forces well known for his cruelty, his efficiency in repression, or other quality that makes his elimination useful."[117] While sabotage and executions are valuable for guerrilla warfare inasmuch as they destroy the enemy's capacities, they also instill fear in the elites being targeted.[118]

In Algeria, power was directly applied by the French government to the local populace, and supported by the French citizens living in the country. As the revolution hinged on convincing the people that the French and Algerians deserved separation, the rebels' tactics needed to emphasize the difference between French and Algerian identities. Ironically, it was the French government that did most of this work, as the regime of torture inflicted upon the Algerians (but not the French) emphasized the division. Between 140,000 and 250,000 Algerians were killed, while probably millions of others were adversely affected,[119] and the images or stories of these people spread the idea that the French were not in Algeria to help. The image of the tortured Muslim fighting for national rights became a rallying cry for resistance and a founding idea of Algeria.[120] Torture methods included electrodes, suffocation, water torture, sexual humiliation, and being tied for long periods of time.[121] Alistair Horne cites people who claim the torture was brutal enough divide much of the unity that existed between the two peoples. French citizens turned against each other, and Algerians saw the government's ugly face. It was communist newspaper editor Henri Alleg's book *The Question* that first revealed the systematic torture of Algerians, causing an uproar when it was released.[122] While torture may have worked in the short term, there is good reason to think that it was a major reason the French lost Algeria in the long term.[123] Adding to impressions of the French government's bad faith was how the torture was revealed through a communist newspaper and how the French tried to hide it from the populace.

Black radicals used the tactic of solidarity, as it was, and is, universally agreed to be a precondition for liberation. Blacks tried to communicate effectively and organize themselves into groups capable of responding to threats. Such solidarity is more intimate than being added to an email listserve or joining the Rotary, as members of black radical groups often protected each other and encouraged the development of personal connections within the black community, in some circumstances going so far as to operate with the same close-knit practices found in a military unit. Malcolm X emphasizes the danger of factionalism, saying that black groups are "usually . . . divided and spend a lot of time . . . being suspicious of each other,"[124] and highlighting the importance of blacks recognizing "their humanity, . . . their own worth, and . . . their heritage."[125] The Black Panthers, in order to advance their agenda of—among other things—full education, security, and human rights for all blacks, organized themselves into the "Black Liberation Army," complete with military titles, a weapons program, and mandatory education classes on first aid, politics, and revolutionary ideology.[126] Some groups focused on local problems within a particular nation while others tried to unite all black people.[127] These tactics cultivated communal identities needed for combatting racism. Angela Davis says that "it is important to recognize the various forms of agency with which identities can be and are constructed, in order not to get stuck in them," concluding that "ideological affinity is not essential to coalition work" and that it is more important to work on issues and raise questions than focus on achieving purity within one's coalition.[128] Manning Marable agrees, emphasizing that community itself is a site of struggle and that only through building partnerships across identities can we reach our goals.[129] Spreading these tactics required speeches and writings, one powerful type of which is autobiography. The telling of personal stories illustrative of the problems of racism conveys its harm far more powerfully than a purely abstract account would. By narrating their individual experiences of being excluded, degraded, objectified, or worse, black radicals made the often-unseen practices of racism tangible. Autobiography became a tactic of resistance by making racism real while building relationships of responsibility and solidarity that can combat it.[130] This practice had a profound effect on whites as well.[131] This recapturing of agency, and reframing of commonly held "truths," is something George Yancy speaks about in his discussion of Frederick Douglass's autobiography, saying, "Through the process of narrating his existence, Douglass challenged the racist assumption that Black people have no perspective on the world . . . [and] he defied and challenged the caricatured myths and normativity of whiteness."[132] Many black radicals have used this strategy,[133] for it rehabilitates a power racism has long denied them: the ability to decide who they are.

Creating novelty and inserting it effectively are crucial steps in a successful revolution. Doing so produces point(s) of disruption out of which one's alternative political order can arise and thrive. While predicting the point of disruption is near impossible, given all the factors that go into the state and the difficulty of modeling how they all interact, revolutionaries should push forth in trying to manufacture one. The point of disruption is the place and time where the changes that often go into constructing a state can become undermining instead. Given the diversity of revolutions, the point of disruption is not always a brief moment in time or a small physical location, as sometimes revolutions take place gradually over a long period of time and across great distances. Putting the state in conflict with itself, short-circuiting its functioning, or illustrating weaknesses generally kept hidden, are all effective ways of creating such moments, opening a space for novelty to arise. We can see here why the approach of Dynamic Anarchism is valuable for revolutionaries. It resists any necessary foundation and allows for novelty that statist groundings would prohibit.

Whole That Undermines an Archetype

The final piece of advice summarizes how the revolution as a whole must operate in order to be successful. The previous piece of advice, innovation and novelty, describes how to begin creating a new state, but this piece of advice is about how to make that new state, and the movement confronting the old state, successful. One of the core messages—discussed in the last chapter—of Dynamic Anarchism is that we must understand the complex phenomenon we observe as organic wholes. This is true both of the state you challenge and the state you are creating. Without mapping the complex networks that compose the state, the ways forces are distributed throughout it, and the ways phenomena like resilience, emergence, hierarchy, and more play a role, the revolution will encounter trouble. As Ladyman, Lambert, and Wiesner put it, complex systems are characterized by spontaneous order and a lack of centralized control.[134] Specifically, the order "arises from the aggregate of a very large number of uncoordinated interactions between elements,"[135] where the elements are spread throughout the system and not regulated from one central place. In order for a revolution to be successful, this property of systems must be challenged and overcome. And the state that the revolution sets up must also incorporate these properties, or it will very likely fall prey to a host of other possible problems.

Proving this point requires three things. First, showing the highly interconnected and decentralized nature of states revolutions confronted. Second, examining how revolutions disrupted those features. Third, how the states revolutions set up after a successful revolution either had those features too or failed to create a healthy society. Beginning with the first, it is necessary to show how multiple agents were both capable of and did make decisions to adapt to their surroundings, which affected decisions made on multiple other levels. The first criteria, capability, is obviously true, as any human with basic decision-making traits is capable of adapting to their surroundings. But we see that the British government and its colonial administrators did make such decisions as well in the lead-up to the American Revolution. Richard Johnson makes this point in his description of the British Empire's formation in the 1700s, saying it was "many-handed" and "shaped by forces as much centripetal as centrifugal."[136] There is also evidence for a decentralized and interconnected view of colonial politics in the writings of Alan Tully, who, summarizing Bernard Bailyn, says that "political rivalries and alliances among provincials—personal, regional, economic, social, and issue-related—produced a bewildering vista of 'milling factionalism,' an 'almost unchartable chaos of competing groups.' "[137] The point is that even though there was a hierarchy (the king, constrained by the British Parliament, appointment governors and councils, who in turn appointed tax collectors and other representatives of the Crown), decisions were made at multiple levels and through a variety of relationships that influenced all other levels. This pattern is found in other states. Perez describes a complex state in Cuba during the late 1930s and 1940s, with Batista collaborating with many former opponents, liberal reformers skeptical of both sides, and the US government operating independently in ways that affected the economy for good and ill.[138] There were multiple political parties, citizens involved in voting, and other interests regularly intervening in political affairs.

The American revolutionaries were able to undermine this elaborate system by taking over large amounts of the British government's operations using excess capabilities existing in the colonies. For example, women played a pivotal role in maintaining basic services the army needed while the revolution was being carried out,[139] while resources and technologies supplemented and expanded upon the economy that used to be run by British hands.[140] A similar dynamic occurred—though not without some notable differences—as several African countries fought for independence. European countries extracted great amounts of material wealth from their colonies, and did so through a variety of social, legal, economic, and military means. To give one example, Pierre Bourdieu describes the colonial agrarian system in Algeria as a "true example of social vivisection" that "tended to transform jointly owned lands into private property" and concentrated "the best properties in the hands of the Europeans."[141] He goes on to describe how similar procedures alienated native Algerians from other resources like health, cars, agricultural products, jobs, and more. When the Algerian Revolution broke out many people started incorporating new practices into their lives. Some of these practices came from traditional society, some came from European society, and some were relatively new, but they all had the same goal: to create an independent system of care and justice focused on the native Algerians. The FLN, as part of their war of liberation, issued many dictates to the population about how Algerians were supposed to live.[142] The point of these was to undermine the French system by replacing it with another. There also existed the practice of recombining parts to form new wholes. Julius Nyerere did this many times both during and after Tanganika's struggle for liberation. Giving voice to Pan-Africanism, forming the Organization of African States, and building relationships with Jamaica, New Zealand, China, and the USSR, among other actions, are examples of this practice. Nyerere was also known for confronting what he perceived to be harmful operations, practices, and relationships, such as the British's selling of weapons to countries in Africa whose governments were genocidal. The point here is that, when building new capacities with already extant resources is not possible, then one creates a new whole that has the relationships, resources, and so on, that one needs.[143] This means developing an interconnected system whose parts work together and interact to produce outcomes that are unexpected and unpredictable when looking at the parts by themselves. Nyerere worked along several avenues to try and produce such an interconnected system, and while his success is a matter of debate, it is clear he was thinking about how multiple institutions and hierarchies could be incorporated into a network that provided for Africa's wellbeing. This happens through the production and spread of new ideologies, exchanges that establish persistent relationships, and encounters that change traditional dynamics.

Guerrilla manuals are full of ideas for how to disrupt the state's self-ordering. Guerrillas are encouraged to think creatively about how to disrupt the state and to be, in essence, bricoleurs of revolution. They are to use whatever means available, be it hillsides, nighttime, or abandoned weaponry, to push for the state's overthrow. They must be careful of the propensity for disordering effects to become ordering effects (and vice versa), for any action can have either effect given the right context. Sabotage can end up promoting the state if it inconveniences too many people, while terrorism can repel sympathizers if it targets innocents in large numbers. Because all undermining activities are immanent to the state, the role they play is dependent upon the broader context of the state and its movements. Revolutionaries must be canny about deploying them even as they are militant in trying to bring the state to a moment of crisis. It is this danger of hypermilitancy that has made guerrilla warfare risky, and at times harmful to the cause of revolution. Because it is conducted so much from the shadows, its methods are rarely subject to scrutiny.[144] This can lead to the development of spontaneous orders harmful to the long-term goals of the revolutionary movement. The revolutionary movement ceases to be ordered for the purpose of creating sustainable change, and becomes one aimed at the maintenance of the revolutionary movement itself. While a revolutionary movement does need to incorporate actions aimed at its own sustainability, this change in emphasis becomes the difference between a revolutionary movement as a whole that undermines an archetype and one that is satisfied existing alongside the archetype—or recreates the archetype.

This can be seen in the outcomes of several guerrilla movements, especially those that form a dogmatic or permanent vanguard. Such vanguards fail to take into account the interconnectedness and the movements of the system as a whole, focusing instead on their own band while protecting themselves with the claim that anything done in the name of the revolution is justified. Highly undemocratic and brutal policies are enacted by this self-appointed vanguard of the revolution, which often undermine the very principles of the revolution. Following his victory, Fidel Castro tasked Committees for the Defense of the Revolution with monitoring the population and reporting any signs of dissent, among other things. These committees have been responsible for numerous violations of human rights during their existence.[145] Similarly, Mao's Cultural Revolution led to the persecution of many dissidents and ethnic minorities in the name of preserving the legacy of the revolution.[146] Though such historical events are clearly not the result of one isolated factor, they could not have occurred without those in power claiming to be guarding the revolution and justifying their authoritarianism as an extension of the revolution's legacy. Such practices are a misuse of guerrilla warfare's tactics of invisibility and violence, which, while perhaps justified as a way of disordering the state and creating a point of disruption, cannot be justified as means of governance. This dogmatism about how to be militant enshrines one specific approach toward the state as the paragon of revolution, and justifies its hold on power by claiming this approach is a necessary precondition to rule. When guerrilla warriors refuse to see their movement as an evolving and fluid affair, the vanguard they establish in the state following their revolution ends up conducting guerrilla warfare on their own population.

Finally, we see that the revolutionary societies that were the best at achieving their goals came from those that were best at building highly interconnected and decentralized systems. It is true that doing this means walking a tight line for revolutionaries, for events after a revolution are in flux, as the traditional equilibrium has been undermined. Finding a new equilibrium is tricky and can take time. While the new equilibrium is being reached, those in power don't want the revolution's enemies to regain control. This is why harsh measures have often been used after a revolution's success. Yet it is also true that the harsh measures themselves can undermine a revolution's goals, or can even become the new equilibrium. Russia is perhaps the best example of this latter point, although Cuba and China illustrate it as well. The goal of the Soviets, as stated in Lenin's writings, was the creation of a social democracy. Until the workers were ready for this, the practice of governing would be handled by a constituent assembly and provisional revolutionary government.[147] Following the October Revolution, when the Constituent Assembly met and refused to recognize the Bolshevik government as legitimate, Lenin disbanded it.[148] Not long afterwards, the Social Democrats (who made up a plurality of the Constituent Assembly) were targeted by the Red Terror for their terrorist activities. Many were killed as "class enemies," even when there was a lack of evidence, and freedom of expression was curtailed.[149] After Lenin's death, the Politburo decided to rule as a group, even as they fought each other in private, until ultimately Stalin prevailed.[150] To preserve the gains of revolution, and to keep those with the "right" vision in control, the goal of democracy and worker representation was cut back again and again. Similarly, China and Cuba were ruled by Mao and Castro, respectively, for their entire lives, and at times antidemocratic and harmful measures were enacted in order to "preserve" the revolution. China had the Cultural Revolution, where innocent people were regularly punished as subversive,[151] while Cuba had UMAP camps to reeducate "problem" Cubans who did not identify with the collective struggle.[152] By contrast, the American government had a federated system that left many decisions in the hands of the states,[153] African countries like Ghana and Tanzania made a point of seeking out the opinions of the various tribes that comprised their country's populace,[154] and African American radicals regularly rethought which voices should be included (e.g., the poor, women, youth, etc.) as the movement developed.[155]

In sum, there are *ordering and disordering effects* that are present in every state. These effects are the products of the movement of the state, and in particular the interactions of the agents, objects, and processes found at any particular moment. *Ordering effects* are those that go toward the promotion of the state, while *disordering effects* are those that go toward its dissolution. It is necessary for a successful movement to consider these effects as an organic whole, and to measure them against what is needed to undermine the archetype of the state it confronts. Only then can a revolution start to draw a path from where it is now to where it seeks to end up.

The guidelines laid out in this chapter are not guarantees. Revolutions often combat states that are complex, adaptive, and well-equipped. No plan contains a foolproof method for successful revolution. What the guidelines above can do is give revolutionaries an approach that is more effective than the approaches informed by the state. This approach does not advocate for a particular state or obscure parts of the state revolutionaries are confronting by focusing on what is wrong. Effective revolutions will appreciate complexity and recognize the resilience states display. Viewing the state through the lens of the liberated revolution will provide a more effective way of uncovering effective tactics and strategies for radical change.

Notes

Chapter 1

1. I am thinking here of the Arab Spring and its beginning with the death of Tunisian Mohamed Bouazizi via self-immolation.

2. Here I am thinking of how Occupy Wall Street began with a call to action in *Adbusters*.

3. "Black Lives Matter: What We Believe," accessed August 19, 2019, https://blacklivesmatter.com/about/what-we-believe/.

4. Amy Goodman, host, "Live from Cairo: Democracy Now!'s Sharif Abdel Kouddous and Anjali Kamat on Egypt's 'Farewell Friday,' " *Democracy Now!*, February 11, 2011, http://www.democracynow.org/2011/2/11/live_from_cairo_sharif_abdel_kouddous.

5. Amy Goodman, host, " 'Occupy Wall Street': Thousands March in NYC Financial District, Set Up Protest Encampment," *Democracy Now!*, September 19, 2011, www.democracynow.org/2011/9/19/occupy_wall_street_thousands_march_in.

6. Meighan Stone, "Five Questions with Denise Ho: From the Front Lines of the Hong Kong Protests," blog post, Council on Foreign Relations, June 13, 2019, https://www.cfr.org/blog/five-questions-denise-ho-front-lines-hong-kong-protests.

7. Jacob Heilbrunn, "Interview with Konstantin Remchukov: Moscow Election Protests Reflect a 'Stark' Generational Shift," *National Interest*, July 29, 2019, https://nationalinterest.org/feature/interview-konstantin-remchukov-moscow-election-protests-reflect-%E2%80%9Cstark%E2%80%9D-generational-shift.

8. *France 24*, "Venezuelans take to the streets again in anti-Maduro protests," 24, January 30, 2019, https://www.france24.com/en/20190130-venezuela-anti-maduro-protests-guaido-us-sanctions.

9. Me Too, "#MeToo Masculinity, Male Privilege and Consent Discussion Guide," February 2020, https://metoomvmt.org/toolkit/metoo-masculinity-male-privilege-consent-discussion-guide/.

10. "Inside Occupy Wall Street: A Tour of Activist Encampment at the Heart of Growing Protest," hosted by Juan Gonzalez, *Democracy Now!*, September 30, 2011, http://www.democracynow.org/2011/9/30/inside_occupy_wall_st_a_tour.

11. Mitt Romney, quoted in Amy Bingham, "Romney Says Occupy Wall Street Protests Are the 'Wrong Way to Go,'" *ABC News*, October 10, 2011, http://abcnews.go.com/blogs/politics/2011/10/romney-says-occupy-wall-street-protests-are-the-wrong-way-to-go/.

12. John Paulson, quoted in Shira Ovide, "Billionaire Tells Occupy Wall Street to Get Off His Lawn," *Wall Street Journal*, October 11, 2011, https://www.wsj.com/articles/BL-DLB-35047.

13. On the Umbrella Movement, see Jonathan Kaiman, "Hong Kong's Umbrella Revolution," *Guardian*, September 30, 2014, https://www.theguardian.com/world/2014/sep/30/-sp-hong-kong-umbrella-revolution-pro-democracy-protests.

14. See Jake Cigainero, "Who Are France's Yellow Vest Protesters, and What Do They Want?" *NPR*, December 3, 2018, https://www.npr.org/2018/12/03/672862353/who-are-frances-yellow-vest-protesters-and-what-do-they-want.

15. Ralph Waldo Emerson, "Concord Hymn," https://www.poetryfoundation.org/poems/45870/concord-hymn.

16. Jeff Goodwin and Theda Skocpol, "Explaining Revolutions in the Contemporary Third World," in *Social Revolutions in the Modern World*, by Theda Skocpol (Cambridge: Cambridge University Press, 1994), 260.

17. Alexander Anievas and Kerem Nişancıoğlu, *How the West Came to Rule: The Geopolitical Origins of Capitalism* (London: Pluto, 2015), 175.

18. François Furet. *Interpreting the French Revolution* (Cambridge: Cambridge University Press, 1981) 51.

19. Hannah Arendt. *On Revolution* (New York: Penguin, 1963), 58.

20. Thomas Hobbes, *Leviathan* (Harmondsworth, UK: Penguin, 1968), 370.

21. Ibid., 370–71.

22. Karl Marx and Friedrich Engels, *Manifesto of the Communist Party*, in *The Marx-Engels Reader*, ed. Robert C. Tucker (New York: Norton, 1978), 483.

23. Ibid., 484.

24. Ibid., 491.

25. Michael Hardt and Antonio Negri, *Empire* (Cambridge, MA: Harvard University Press, 2000), 133.

26. Michel Foucault, "On Popular Justice: A Discussion with Maoists," in *Power/Knowledge: Selected Interviews and Other Writings 1972–1977*, ed. Colin Gordon (New York: Pantheon, 1980), 27.

27. Howard Zinn, "The Spirit of Rebellion," in *The Zinn Reader* (New York: Seven Stories Press, 1997), 688. Appeared originally as "The Brooklyn Bridge and the Spirit of the Fourth," *Boston Globe*, July 4, 1975.

28. Germaine Greer, *The Female Eunuch* (New York: Harper Perennial, 1970) 353–72.

29. Yevgeny Zamyatin, "On Literature, Revolution, Entropy, and Other Matters," in *Soviet Heretic: Essays*, trans. Mirra Ginsburg (Chicago: University of Chicago Press, 1974), 103–12.

30. Eric Hobsbawm, *Primitive Rebels* (New York: Norton, 1959), 57–74.

31. Fred Hampton, from the speech "You Can Kill a Revolutionary, but You Can Never Kill the Revolution," on the album *Power to the People: The Black Panther Speeches*, Fred Hampton, 2012, MP3 from Amazon Music.

32. Both the French and Cuban revolutions fell far short of the goals revolutionaries espoused. Human Rights Watch claims that following Fidel Castro's takeover he instituted a highly effective machinery of repression, while Amnesty International charges the Cuban government with carrying out 216 political executions between 1959 and 1987 (other estimates place the number significantly higher). Human Rights Watch, *Cuba's Repressive Machinery* (New York: Human Rights Watch, 1999); Amnesty International, *When the State Kills: The Death Penalty v. Human Rights* (London: Amnesty International Publications, 1989). The French Revolution's Reign of Terror led to the guillotining of at least 16,594, while another 40,000 were summarily executed or died awaiting trial. Hugh Gough, *The Terror in the French Revolution* (Basingstoke, UK: Palgrave Macmillan, 2010), 77.

33. Wendy Brown, "Resisting Left Melancholy," *boundary 2* 26, no. 3 (1999): 20.

34. Rosalyn Deutsche, "Hiroshima after Iraq: A Study in Art and War," *October*, no. 131 (2010): 3.

35. Eric Canter and Mitt Romney in Bingham, "Romney Says."

36. See "List of Wars and Anthropogenic Disasters by Death Toll," Wikipedia, accessed May 2019, http://en.wikipedia.org/wiki/List_of_wars_and_anthropogenic_disasters_by_death_toll; Polynational War Memorial, "Cuban Revolution," updated August 10, 2014, http://www.war-memorial.net/Cuban-revolution-3.115; Emerson Kent.com, "The Russion Revolution of 1917," http://www.emersonkent.com/wars_and_battles_in_history/russian_revolution_of_1917.htm. It is important to note that the several thousands who died in the Russian Revolution of 1917 does not include those killed in the Russian Civil War following the revolution.

37. John Markcoff makes this point in his work, saying, in one example, seigneurial rights "were a continual bone of contention between rural communities who found the early enactments of the legislators to be thoroughly inadequate and legislators faced with continuing rural turbulence." John Markoff, *The Abolition of Feudalism: Peasants, Lords, and Legislators in the French Revolution* (University Park: Pennsylvania State University Press, 1996), 3.

38. Vladimir Ilyich Lenin, *State and Revolution* (Peking: Foreign Language Press, 1970), 116.

39. The principles of Taylorism are laid out in Frederick Winslow Taylor, *The Principles of Scientific Management* (New York: Harper, 1915).

40. The appropriation of Taylor's system by the Soviets is detailed in Thomas P. Hughes, *American Genesis: A Century of Invention and Technological Enthusiasm, 1870–1970* (Chicago: University of Chicago Press, 1989), 255–61.

41. Vladimir Ilyich Lenin, "The Taylor System: Man's Enslavement by the Machine," trans. Bernard Isaacs and Joe Fineberg, in *Collected Works* (Moscow: Progress, 1972), 20:152–54, https://www.marxists.org/archive/lenin/works/cw/volume20.htm.

42. Daniel A. Wren and Arthur G. Bedeian, "The Taylorization of Lenin: Rhetoric or Reality?," *International Journal of Social Economics* 31, no. 3 (2004): 287–88.

43. Lenin, *State and Revolution*, 121.

44. Joseph V. Stalin, "Results of the First Five-Year Plan," in *Works*, vol. 13 (Moscow: Foreign Language Publishing House, 1954), http://www.marxists.org/reference/archive/stalin/works/1933/01/07.htm.

45. Stalin executed nearly 700,000 people between 1937 and 1938. Barry McLoughlin, "Mass Operations of the NKVD, 1937–1938: A Survey," in *Stalin's Terror: High Politics and Mass Repression in the Soviet Union*, ed. Barry McLoughlin, and Kevin McDermott (Basingstoke, UK: Palgrave Macmillan, 2002), 141.

46. The Gulag had fourteen-hour workdays and overcrowded, underheated barracks. See Roy Rosenzweig Center for History and New Media, *Gulag: Many Days, Many Lives*, accessed May 13, 2021, https://gulaghistory.org/nps/onlineexhibit/stalin/work.php.

47. Joseph V. Stalin, "The Bolshevik Party in the Struggle for the Collectivization of Agriculture (1930–1934)," in *History of the Communist Party of the Soviet Union (Bolsheviks)* (New York: International Publishers, 1939), http://www.marxists.org/reference/archive/stalin/works/1939/x01/ch11.htm#4.

48. Marx, "German Ideology," in *The Marx-Engels Reader*, ed. Robert C. Tucker (New York: Norton, 1978), 162.

49. Arendt, *On Revolution*, 165.

50. Ibid., 135.

51. Jennifer Gaffney, "Memories of Exclusion: Hannah Arendt and the Haitian Revolution," *Philosophy and Social Criticism* 44, no. 6 (2018): 715.

52. There are many explanations of set theory and the need for axioms, but for one, see Felix Nagel, *Set Theory and Topology*, http://www.felixnagel.org/publications/nagel_set_theory_and_topology_part_ii.pdf.

53. For the basics of Chaos Theory, see the seminal paper by Edward N. Lorenz, "Deterministic Nonperiodic Flow," *Journal of the Atmospheric Sciences* 20, no. 2 (1963): 130.

54. Jacques Derrida, "Signature Event Context", in *Limited Inc.* (Evanston, IL: Northwestern University Press, 1977), 21.

55. Jacques Derrida, "Différance," in *Margins of Philosophy* (Chicago: University of Chicago Press, 1982), 10–11.

56. As an example to explain this concept, which Derrida terms "différance," Derrida chooses the opposition of "present" with "past" and "future" ("Différance," 13).

57. Hardt and Negri, *Empire*, 75.

58. Ibid., 75.

59. Ibid., 71.

60. Maurice Merleau-Ponty, *Phenomenology of Perception* (London: Routledge, 1958), 385.

61. Georg Wilhelm Friedrich Hegel, *Elements of the Philosophy of Right*, ed. Allen W. Wood, trans. H. B. Nisbet (Cambridge: Cambridge University Press, 1991), 23.

Chapter 2

1. M. J. Mavidal and M. E. Laurent, eds., *Archives parlementaires de 1787 à 1860*, première série (1787–99), 82 vols. (Paris: Dupont, 1879–1913), 53–56:390–93.

2. Ibid., 53–56:324–26.

3. Thomas Paine, *Common Sense*, in *Collected Writings*, ed. Eric Foner (New York: Library of America, 1955), 20.

4. Mintz, Samuel I., *The Hunting of Leviathan: Seventeenth Century Reactions to the Materialism and Moral Philosophy of Thomas Hobbes* (Cambridge: Cambridge University Press, 1962), 34–35; and Israel, Jonathan, *Revolution of the Mind: Radical Enlightenment and the Intellectual Origins of Modern Democracy* (Princeton, NJ: Princeton University Press, 2010), viii.

5. John Locke, *Second Treatise of Government*, ed. C. B. Macpherson (Indianapolis: Hackett, 1980), 5.

6. Thomas Hobbes, *Leviathan* (Harmondsworth, UK: Penguin, 1968), 183.

7. Jean-Jacques Rousseau, *The Social Contract*, trans. Maurice Cranston (London: Penguin, 1968), 95.

8. Mintz, *Hunting of Leviathan*, 29.

9. Israel, *Revolution of the Mind*, 205.

10. Hobbes, *Leviathan*, 190.

11. Locke, *Second Treatise*, 18.

12. Ibid., 52.

13. Hobbes, *Leviathan*, 192.

14. Israel, *Revolution of the Mind*, 3–6.

15. Mary Wollstonecraft, *Vindication of the Rights of Men* (Oxford: Oxford University Press, 1993), 12–13. Israel, *Revolution of the Mind*, 1–2, 21.

16. F. P. Lock, *Edmund Burke*, vol. 1, *1730–1784* (Oxford: Clarendon Press, 1998), 155.

17. David Hume, *Moral Philosophy* (Indianapolis: Hackett, Indianapolis, 2006), 202.

18. Adam Smith, *An Inquiry into the Nature and Causes of the Wealth of Nations* (Indianapolis: Liberty Classics, 1976), 26.

19. Ibid., 56.

20. Ibid., 61.

21. Rousseau, *Social Contract*, 134.

22. Ibid., 131.

23. Ibid., 135.

24. Brian Singer, "Montesquieu on Power: Beyond Checks and Balances," in *Montequieu and His Legacy*, ed. Rebecca Kingston (Albany: State University of New York Press, 2009), 97–100. Israel, *Revolution of the Mind*, 62.

25. Israel, *Revolution of the Mind*, 39.

26. Ibid., 92–93.

27. Ibid., 186.

28. Locke, *Second Treatise*, 8.

29. Baruch Spinoza, *Theological-Political Treatise*, ed. Jonathan Israel (Cambridge: Cambridge University Press, 2007), 197. As Spinoza later rejects social contract theory in his *Political Treatise*, my inclusion of Spinoza focuses on the social contract framework developed specifically within the *Theologico-Political Treatise*.

30. Hobbes, *Leviathan*, 188.

31. Ibid., 190.

32. Locke, *Second Treatise*, 9.

33. Rousseau, *Social Contract*, 58.

34. Ibid., 53.

35. Ibid., 10.

36. David Hume, *Political Essays* (Cambridge: Cambridge University Press, 1994), 21.

37. Montesquieu, *The Spirit of the Laws*, trans. and ed. Anne M. Cohler, Basia Carolyn Miller, and Harold Samuel Stone (Cambridge: Cambridge University Press,1989), 7.

38. Edmund Burke, *Reflections on the Revolution in France* (New York: Dutton, 1951), 93.

39. Hugo Grotius, *The Rights of War and Peace*, ed. Richard Tuck (Indianapolis: Liberty Fund, 2005), 1:65.

40. Hobbes, *Leviathan*, 185.

41. Spinoza, *Theological-Political Treatise*, 203.

42. Locke, *Second Treatise*, 37.

43. Rousseau, *Social Contract*, 50.

44. Hume, "On the Origin of Government," in *Political Essays*, 20.

45. Hume, *Moral Philosophy*, 210.

46. Burke, *Reflections*, 32.

47. Frank O'Gorman, *Edmund Burke*, vol. 2 of *Political Thinkers* (London: Routledge, 1973), 132.

48. Montesquieu, *Spirit of the Laws*, 6.

49. Hobbes, *Leviathan*, 223.
50. Rousseau, *Social Contract*, 59.
51. Hobbes, *Leviathan*, 118–30.
52. Grotius, *War and Peace*, 2:20.
53. Rousseau, *Social Contract*, 50.
54. Spinoza, *Theological-Political Treatise*, 198.
55. Ibid., 198.
56. Ibid., 199.
57. Grotius, *War and Peace*, 2:8.
58. Burke, *Reflections*, 94.
59. Wollstonecraft, *Rights of Men*, 30–31.
60. Hume, *Moral Philosophy*, 202.
61. Hume, *Political Essays*, 20.
62. Ibid., 22.
63. Ibid., 150.
64. Ibid., 159.
65. Ibid., 161.
66. Ibid., 161.
67. Ibid., 180.
68. Ibid., 139.
69. Ibid., 189.
70. Ibid., 162.
71. Ibid., 258.
72. Ibid., 259.
73. Hobbes, *Leviathan*, 185–86.
74. Ibid., 188.
75. Ibid., 112.
76. Ibid., 190.
77. Ibid., 227.
78. Ibid., 189.
79. Spinoza, *Theological-Political Treatise*, 195–96.
80. Ibid., 196.
81. Ibid., 252.
82. Montesquieu, *Spirit of the Laws*, 6–7.
83. Locke, *Second Treatise*, 19.
84. Rousseau, *Social Contract*, 50.
85. Locke, *Second Treatise*, 14.
86. Ibid., 8.
87. Ibid., 31.
88. Ibid., 56.
89. Rousseau, *Social Contract*, 50.
90. Ibid., 51.

91. Ibid., 51.

92. Locke, *Second Treatise*, 46.

93. Ibid., 52; Rousseau, *Social Contract*, 60.

94. Burke, *Reflections*, 94.

95. Wollstonecraft, *Rights of Men*, 15, 21, 49, 357–79.

96. Tom Paine, *The Rights of Man*, in *Collected Writings*, ed. Eric Foner (New York: Library of America, 1955), 463.

97. Paine, *Rights of Man* (pt. 1), 548.

98. Ibid., 551–52.

99. Locke, *Second Treatise*, 8; Rousseau, *Social Contract*, 65.

100. Paine, *Rights of Man* (pt. 1), 566.

101. Hobbes, *Leviathan*, 285.

102. Hume, *Political Essays*, 18, 31.

103. Ibid., 271.

104. Locke, *Second Treatise*, 18, 111.

105. Ibid., 110.

106. Hume, *Moral Philosophy*, 217.

107. Spinoza, *Theological-Political Treatise*, 258.

108. Hume, *Political Essays*, 18, 31.

109. Aimee Bearbeau, *Theorizing the Nation: The French Revolution and the Social Contract* (PhD diss., Georgetown University, 2014).

110. Locke, *Second Treatise*, 53.

111. Ibid., 52.

112. Hobbes, *Leviathan*, 191.

113. Ibid., 197.

114. Rousseau, *Social Contract*, 59.

115. Jeffrey R. Collins, *The Allegiance of Thomas Hobbes* (Oxford: Oxford University Press, Oxford, 2005), 4.

116. Grotius, *War and Peace*, 1:259.

117. Hobbes, *Leviathan*, 227.

118. Ibid., 243.

119. Ibid., 236; Grotius, *War and Peace*, 1:63.

120. Grotius, *War and Peace*, 1:276; Hobbes, *Leviathan*, 231.

121. Burke, *Reflections*, 93.

122. Burke, *Reflections*, 32.

123. Burke, *Reflections*, 27.

124. Rousseau, *Social Contract*, 112–14.

125. Ibid., 82–83.

126. Hume, *Moral Philosophy*, 205.

127. Wollstonecraft, *Rights of Men*, 51.

128. Montesquieu, *Spirit of the Laws*, 10, 18–19.

129. Knud Haakonssen, introduction to Hume, *Political Essays*, xx–xxi; Wollstonecraft, *Rights of Men*, 365; Montesquieu, *Spirit of the Laws*, 10–11, 15–21.

130. Locke, *Second Treatise*, 69; Rousseau, *Social Contract*, 72–74; Maurice Cranston, introduction to Rousseau, *Social Contract*, 36.

131. Hume, *Moral Philosophy*, 217.

132. Wollstonecraft, *Rights of Men*, 66.

133. Montesquieu, *Spirit of the Laws*, 21–28.

134. Locke, *Second Treatise*, 76.

135. Ibid., 69.

136. Rousseau, *Social Contract*, 130.

137. Ibid., 123.

138. Hume, *Philosophical Essays*, 22–34; Hume, *Moral Philosophy*, 214–15.

139. Montesquieu, *Spirit of the Laws*, 52.

140. Mary Wollstonecraft, *An Historical and Moral View of the French Revolution* (Oxford: Oxford University Press, 1993), 364–65.

141. Spinoza, *Theological-Political Treatise*, 200; Paine, *Rights of Man* (pt. 1), 551.

142. Spinoza, *Theological-Political Treatise*, 200.

143. Paine, *Rights of Man* (pt. 1), 567.

144. Spinoza, *Theological-Political Treatise*, 202.

145. William Large, "Spinoza for our Time: Politics and Modernity," *Contemporary Political Theory* 16 (2017): 161–64.

146. Paine, *Rights of Man* (pt. 1), 567.

147. Spinoza, *Theological-Political Treatise*, 258.

148. Paine, *Rights of Man* (pt. 1), 506.

149. Spinoza, *Theological-Political Treatise*, 200.

150. Paine, *Rights of Man* (pt. 1), 536.

151. Spinoza, *Theological-Political Treatise*, 220; Paine, *Rights of Man* (pt. 1), 438.

152. Grotius, *War and Peace*, 1:94–95; Hobbes, *Leviathan*, 363–68.

153. Grotius, *War and Peace*, 2:504.

154. Hobbes, *Leviathan*, 369.

155. Mark Hartman, "Hobbes's Concept of Political Revolution," *Journal of the History of Ideas* 47, no. 3 (1986): 492.

156. Grotius, *War and Peace*, 2:894; Hobbes, *Leviathan*, 268.

157. Burke, *Reflections*, 93.

158. Locke, *Second Treatise*, 31; Rousseau, *Social Contract*, 52–53; Hume, *Moral Philosophy*, 202–3; Wollstonecraft, *Rights of Men*, 12, 22; Montesquieu, *Spirit of the Laws*, 83, 99.

159. Locke, *Second Treatise*, 114.

160. Ibid., 113.

161. Elizabeth Frazer and Kimberly Hutchings, "Politics, Violence, and Revolutionary Virtue: Reflections on Locke and Sorel," *Thesis Eleven* 97, no. 1 (2009): 57.

162. Locke, *Second Treatise*, 111.

163. Rousseau, *Social Contract*, 89.

164. Ibid., 126.

165. Ibid., 147.

166. Locke, *Second Treatise*, 113; Rousseau, *Social Contract*, 89.

167. Wollstonecraft, *Rights of Men*, 333–38, 355.

168. Wollstonecraft, *View of French Revolution*, 288, 319.

169. Hume, *Political Essays*, 18.

170. Ibid., 31.

171. Specifically, Montesquieu says revolution can remove corruption, but that revolution won't necessarily fix problems (especially when the people conducting it are corrupt). Montesquieu, *Spirit of the Laws*, 119–21.

172. Ibid., 132.

173. Spinoza, *Theological-Political Treatise*, 200; Paine, *Rights of Man* (pt. 1), 445.

174. Spinoza, *Theological-Political Treatise*, 258.

175. Paine, *Rights of Man* (pt. 1), 513.

176. Spinoza, *Theological-Political Treatise*, 200, 258.

177. Paine, *Rights of Man* (pt. 1), 443–45.

178. Locke, *Second Treatise*, 114.

179. Rousseau, *Social Contract*, 136.

180. Tom Paine, *Rights of Man*, in *The Complete Writings of Thomas Paine* (New York: Citadel, 1945), 341–42.

181. Mintz, *Hunting of Leviathan*, 34; Israel, *Revolution of the Mind*, 90–91.

182. Mintz, *Hunting of Leviathan*, 34; Israel, *Revolution of the Mind*, 63–65.

183. Locke, *Second Treatise*, 69–70.

184. Hobbes, *Leviathan*, 234.

185. Ibid., 263–64.

186. Ibid., 227, 272.

187. Rousseau, *Social Contract*, 50–51; Spinoza, *Theological-Political Treatise*, 6–7.

188. Paine, *Rights of Man* (pt. 2), 342–44.

189. Ernst Cassirer, *The Philosophy of Enlightenment* (Princeton, NJ: Princeton University Press, 2009), 22–23.

190. Fred J. Evans, *Multivoiced Body* (New York: Columbia University Press, 2008), 24.

191. Hobbes, *Leviathan*, 118–30.

192. Charles Mills, *The Racial Contract* (Ithaca, NY: Cornell University Press, 1997), 43.

193. Carole Pateman, *The Sexual Contract* (Stanford, CA: Stanford University Press, 1988), 2.

194. Mills, *Racial Contract*, 72; Pateman, *Sexual Contract*, 41.

195. Mills, *Racial Contract*, 6.

196. Ibid., 53.

197. Hobbes, *Leviathan*, 187; Locke, *Second Treatise*, 13.

198. Pateman, *Sexual Contract*, 120.

199. Locke, *Second Treatise*, 44.

200. Rousseau, *Social Contract*, 50.

201. Carole Pateman, *The Disorder of Women* (Standford, CA: Stanford University Press, 1989), 213.

202. Ibid., 213.

203. Hobbes, *Leviathan*, 253.

204. Mills, *Racial Contract*, 84–85.

205. Pateman, *Disorder of Women*, 74.

206. Mills, *Racial Contract*, 59.

207. Ibid., 59.

208. Pateman, *Sexual Contract*, 50.

209. Ibid., 52.

210. Hobbes, *Leviathan*, 255.

211. Locke, *Second Treatise*, 17.

212. Rousseau, *Social Contract*, 58.

213. Ibid., 79.

214. Pateman, *Sexual Contract*, 65.

215. Richard Dinnon, *Rebel in Paradise: A Biography of Emma Goldman* (Chicago: University of Chicago Press, 1961), 215.

216. Mills, *Racial Contract*, 85.

217. Pateman, *Sexual Contract*, 159.

218. Ibid., 165.

219. John Rawls, *A Theory of Justice* (Cambridge, MA: Harvard University Press, 1971), 124–25.

220. Ibid., 125.

221. Ibid., 128.

222. Ibid., 129.

223. Ibid., 119.

224. Ibid., 309–10.

225. John Rawls, *Political Liberalism* (New York: Columbia University Press, 1993), 50–51.

226. Ibid., 36.

227. Rawls, *Theory of Justice*, 3–4.

228. Rawls, *Political Liberalism*, 36.

229. Ibid., 55.

230. Ronald Dworkin, *Taking Rights Seriously* (Cambrdige, MA: Harvard University Press, 1977), 91.

231. Ibid., 88.

232. Ibid., 91.

233. Ibid., 92–93.

234. Ibid., 211.

235. Ibid., 214–15.

236. Robert Nozick, *Anarchy, State, and Utopia* (Oxford: Blackwell, 1974), 12.

237. Ibid., 13–14.

238. Ibid., 22–23.

239. Ibid., 17.

240. Ibid., 101–2.

241. Ibid., 133–36.

242. Habermas, *Theory of Communicative Action*, vol. 2, *Lifeworld and System: A Critique of Functionalist Reason* (Beacon Press: Boston, 1981), 125–26.

243. Ibid., 139.

244. Ibid., 131.

245. Habermas, *Between Facts and Norms* (Cambridge, MA: MIT Press, 1996), 103.

246. Ibid., 388–89, 488–89.

247. Grotius, *War and Peace*, 2:191.

248. Tom Paine, *Common Sense*, in *The Complete Writings of Thomas Paine*, ed. Eric Foner (New York: Citadel, 1945), 30.

Chapter 3

1. Georg Wilhelm Friedrich Hegel, *Phenomenology of Spirit*, trans. Arnold V. Miller (Oxford: Oxford University Press, 1976), 10.

2. Ibid., 11.

3. Ibid., 12.

4. Ibid., 14.

5. Georg Wilhelm Friedrich Hegel, *Political Writings*, ed. Laurence Dickey and H. B. Nisbet. Trans. H. B. Nisbet (Cambridge: Cambridge University Press, 2004), 217.

6. Ibid., 216–17.

7. Ibid., 21.

8. Croce, Benedetto. *Logic as Science of Pure Concept* (London: Macmillan, 1917), 542–44; Giovanni Gentile, *The Theory of Mind as Pure Act* (London: Macmillan, 1922), 54.

9. Gentile, *Theory of Mind*, around 44.

10. Ibid., 51.

11. Ibid., 56.

12. Only Gentile identified as a fascist (it is widely believed he wrote part of "The Doctrine of Fascism" with Benito Mussolini). Croce's politics are not widely known, but he expressed a number of liberalism's commitments. That said, his philosophy inspired Gentile, among other fascists.

13. Karl Marx, "The Possibility of Non-violent Revolution," in *The Marx-Engels Reader*, ed. Robert C. Tucker (New York: Norton, 1978), 523.

14. Karl Marx, *The German Ideology* (New York: Prometheus, 1998), 41–42; "Theses on Feuerbach," in *The German Ideology*, 570.

15. Marx, *German Ideology*, 160–61; Karl Marx, *Grundrisse: Foundations of the Critique of Political Economy*, trans. Martin Nicolaus (New York: Vintage, 1973), 495–97.

16. Marx, *German Ideology*, 66.

17. Karl Marx, "Critique of the Gotha Program," in *Karl Marx: Selected Writings*, ed. David McLellan (Oxford: Oxford University Press, 1977), 615.

18. For one example, see Terry Eagleton, "Introduction, Part 1," in *Marxist Literary Theory: A Reader* (Cambridge, MA: Blackwell, 1996), 1.

19. Karl Marx, *Economic and Philosophic Manuscripts of 1844*, trans. Martin Milligan (New York: Prometheus, 1988), 155, 167.

20. Marx, *German Ideology*, 49–50.

21. Karl Marx, "On the Jewish Question," in *The Marx-Engels Reader*, 45–46.

22. Marx, *Manuscripts of 1844*, 75.

23. Ibid., 150–51.

24. Ibid., 75, 155.

25. Leszek Kołakowski, *The Founders*, vol. 1 of *Main Currents of Marxism: Its Rise, Growth, and Dissolution*, trans. P. S. Falla (Oxford: Clarendon Press, 1978), 156.

26. Marx, *German Ideology*, 50.

27. See Karl Marx, "Capital, Volume Three," in *The Marx-Engels Reader*, 439–42, for discussion of classes that informs this.

28. Karl Marx and Friedrich Engels, *Manifesto of the Communist Party*, in *Economic and Philosophic Manuscripts of 1844*, by Karl Marx (New York: Prometheus, 1988), 209.

29. Karl Marx, "Society and Economy in History," in *The Marx-Engels Reader*, 138–39.

30. Marx, *German Ideology*, 82.

31. Marx and Engels, *Manifesto*, 209.

32. Marx, *German Ideology*, 45.

33. Peter Osborne, *How to Read Marx* (New York: Norton, 2005), 44.

34. Marx, *Manuscripts of 1844*, 117–18.

35. Marx, "Jewish Question," 46.

36. Marx, *Manuscripts of 1844*, 154.

37. Karl Marx, *Capital*, vol. 1 (London: Penguin, 1976), 138.

38. Ibid., 131.

39. Erich Fromm, *Marx's Concept of Man*, trans. T. Bottomore (New York: Continuum, 2004), 14.

40. Marx, *German Ideology*, 59–60.

41. Marx, *Capital*, 547.

42. Ibid., 918.

43. Marx and Engels, *Manifesto*, 211.

44. Karl Marx, "After the Revolution: Marx Debates Bakunin," in *The Marx-Engels Reader*, 543.

45. Marx and Engels, *Manifesto*, 210–11.

46. See Marx, *Capital*, 683–91; Engels, "Socialism: Utopian and Scientific," in *Marx-Engels Reader*, 704–5; "Jewish Question," 44–45; Marx and Engels, *Manifesto*, 213.

47. Marx, *German Ideology*, 81.

48. Engels, "Socialism: Utopian and Scientific," 697.

49. Marx, *German Ideology*, 58.

50. Ibid., 58–59.

51. Ibid., 60–61.

52. Kołakowski, *Founders*, 382.

53. Marx and Engels, *Manifesto*, 221–22.

54. Marx, *Capital*, 104.

55. Marx, *German Ideology*, 46.

56. Marx and Engels, *Manifesto*, 239.

57. Marx, *Capital*, 103.

58. Francis Wheen, *Marx: A Life* (New York: Norton, 1999), 119.

59. Marx, *Manuscripts of 1844*, 104–6.

60. Marx and Engels, *Manifesto*, 211, 223–24.

61. Friedrich Engels, "The Tactics of Social Democracy," in *The Marx Engels Reader*, 560–61.

62. Marx, *German Ideology*, 66.

63. Karl Marx, "Speech at the Anniversary of the *People's Paper*," in *The Marx Engels Reader*, 577.

64. Marx, *German Ideology*, 92.

65. Kołakowski, *Founders*, 409–10.

66. Marx, "Jewish Question," 46.

67. Marx, *German Ideology*, 60.

68. Marx, "Jewish Question," 45.

69. Marx, *German Ideology*, 62.

70. Karl Marx, "The Coming Upheaval," in *The Marx Engels Reader*, 218–19.

71. Marx, *German Ideology*, 86–88.

72. Marx, "Marx Debates Bakunin," 543.

73. Ibid., 544.

74. Ibid., 545–46.

75. Bernard Yack, *The Longing for Total Revolution* (Princeton, NJ: Princeton University Press, 1986), 286.

76. Marx and Engels, *Manifesto*, 221.

77. Kołakowski, *Founders*, 286.

78. Marx, *German Ideology*, 38–43.

79. Marx and Engels, *Manifesto*, 211–12.

80. Marx, *Manuscripts of 1844*, 76.

81. Ibid., 139–40.

82. Marx and Engels, *Manifesto*, 229.

83. Marx, *German Ideology*, 47–49.

84. Marx, *Capital*, 544.

85. Marx, "Eighteenth Brumaire of Louis Bonaparte," in *The Marx Engels Reader*, 606.

86. Marx, *Capital*, 590–91.

87. Yack, *Total Revolution*, 298.

88. See Karl Marx, *The Letters of Karl Marx*, trans. Saul K. Padover (Engewood Cliffs, NJ: Prentice Hall, 1979) 68–69, 128; Friedrich Engels, "Socialism: Utopian and Scientific," in *The Marx-Engels Reader*, 717; Georg Lukács, "Critical Observations on Rosa Luxembourg's 'Critique of the Russian Revolution,' " in *History and Class Consciousness*, trans. Rodney Livingstone (London: Merlin, 1971), 281–83; Antonio Gramsci, "The Soviet Union on the Path to Communism," in *Pre-prison Writings*, trans. Virginia Cox (Cambridge: Cambridge University Press, 1994), 303–4.

89. Alice Echols, *Daring to Be Bad: Radical Feminism in America, 1967–1975* (Minneapolis, University of Minnesota Press, 1989), 135–37.

90. Tim Wise, "F.A.Q.s," accessed January 2014, timwise.org; Judith Butler, *Gender Trouble* (New York: Routledge, 1990), 196.

91. Amnesty International, When the State Kills: The Death Penalty v. Human Rights (London: Amnesty International Publications, 1989); Human Rights Watch, *Cuba's Repressive Machinery* (New York: Human Rights Watch, 1999).

92. Aleksandr Solzhenitsyn, *The Gulag Archipelago, 1918–1956* (New York: Harper and Row, 1973).

93. Wheen, *Marx: A Life*, 362.

94. Vladimir Ilyich Lenin, *State and Revolution* (New York: International Publishers, 1932), 7.

95. Ibid., 20.

96. Ibid., 23.

97. Mao Zedong, "Be a Revolutionary," in *Selected Works of Mao Tse-tung* (Peking: Foreign Language Press, 1965), 5:39.

98. Mao Zedong, "On Practice," in *Selected Works of Mao Tse-tung* (Peking: Foreign Language Press, 1965), 1:305.

99. Slavoj Žižek, *In Defense of Lost Causes* (New York: Verso, 2008), 230.

It is notable that Žižek criticizes Lenin for his claim to objective knowledge, saying, "What this position overlooks is how this 'objective' meaning is already subjectively mediated" (230).

100. Lenin, *State and Revolution*, 26–28.

101. Mao Zedong, "On Contradiction," in *Selected works of Mao Tse-tung* (Peking: Foreign Language Press, 1965), 1:313.

102. Ibid., 319–20.

103. Ibid., 332–33.

104. Lenin, *State and Revolution*, 77.

105. Ibid., 79.

106. Mao Zedong, *On New Democracy* (Peking: Foreign Language Press, 1940), 41.

107. Marx, "Non-violent Revolution," 523.

108. Marx and Engels, *Manifesto*, 500.

109. Ibid., 490.

110. See Marx's thoughts on the Paris Commune. Karl Marx, "The Civil War in France," in *The Marx-Engels Reader*, 635–36.

111. Lea Ypi, "On Revolution in Kant and Marx," *Political Theory* 42, no. 3 (2014): 280.

112. Louis Althusser, *For Marx*, trans. Ben Brewster (New York: Penguin, 1969), 13.

113. For Althusser, see *For Marx*, 28–30, 193. Lenin discusses Marxism's scientific approach to the external world in Vladimir Ilyich Lenin, "Karl Marx," in *Collected Works* (Moscow: Progress Publishers, 1960) 21:52–53. Mao discusses Marxism's scientific approach in Mao, "On Practice," 296–97.

114. Althusser, *For Marx*, 170.

115. Ibid., 183.

116. Ibid., 183–84.

117. Ibid., 191.

118. Ibid., 228.

119. Ibid., 223.

120. While Althusser, Mao, and Lenin all discuss Marxism as science, it is worth noting that there are theological dimensions to their philosophies discussed in secondary literature. See Roland Boer, *The Criticism of Heaven and Earth* (Boston: Brill, 2007).

121. Alexandre Kojève, *Introduction to the Reading of Hegel* (Ithaca, NY: Cornell University Press, 1969), 171.

122. Ibid., 174.

123. Ibid., 212–15.

124. Jean-Paul Sartre, *Being and Nothingness*, trans. Hazel Barnes (New York: Washington Square Press, 1956), 5.

125. Maurice Merleau-Ponty, *Phenomenology of Perception* (New York: Routledge, 1968), 9.

126. Ibid., 10.

127. Jean Paul Sartre, *Critique of Dialectical Reason*, trans. Alan Sheridan-Smith (New York: Verso, 2004), 36–37.

128. Maurice Merleau-Ponty, *Adventures of the Dialectic*, trans. Joseph Bien (Evanston, IL: Northwestern University Press, 1973), 60.

129. Sartre, *Critique of Dialectical Reason*, 31.

130. Ibid., 33–34.

131. Ibid., 20.

132. Martin Jay, *Marxism and Totality: The Adventures of a Concept from Lucács to Habermas* (Berkeley: University of California Press, 1984), 375.

133. Jay, *Marxism and Totality*, 380–81.

134. Merleau-Ponty, *Adventures*, 203–4.

135. Ibid., 204–5.

136. Ibid., 206–7.

137. Merleau-Ponty, *Phenomenology of Perception*, 198–200.

138. Theodor Adorno, *Negative Dialectics*, trans. E. B. Ashton (London: Routledge, 1973), 6.

139. Ibid., 5.

140. Ibid., 11.

141. Ibid., 15–16.

142. Ibid., 6.

143. Ibid., 28.

144. Jay, *Marxism and Totality*, 267.

145. Ibid., 374.

146. Ibid., 375.

147. A. T. Nuyen, "Adorno and the French Post-structuralists on the Other of Reason," *Journal of Speculative Philosophy*, n.s., 4, no. 4 (1990): 316.

148. Herbert G. Reid, "Critical Phenomenology and the Dialectical Foundations of Social Change," *Dialectical Anthropology* 2, no. 2 (1977): 117.

149. Adorno, *Negative Dialectics*, 137–40.

150. Ibid., 149.

151. Lenin, *State and Revolution*, 42.

152. Lenin, *What Is to Be Done?* (New York: International Publishers, 1929) 28.

153. Louis Althusser, "Lenin before Hegel," in *Lenin and Philosophy, and Other Essays*, trans. Ben Brewster (New York: Monthly Review Press, 1971), 123.

154. Louis Althusser, "Lenin and Philosophy," in *Lenin and Philosophy, and Other Essays*, trans. Ben Brewster (New York: Monthly Review Press, 1971), 65.

155. Mao, "On Contradiction," 340.

156. Kojève, *Introduction*, 212–15; Sartre, *Being and Nothingness*, lvii; Merleau-Ponty, *Phenomenology of Perception*, xxii.

157. Merleau-Ponty, *Phenomenology of Perception*, xiv.

158. Sartre, *Critique of Dialectical Reason*, 25–26.

159. Ibid., 31.

160. Merleau-Ponty, *Phenomenology of Perception*, 198–200.

161. Kojève, *Introduction*, 177.

162. Sartre, *Critique of Dialectical Reason*, 57.

163. Ibid., 47–48.

164. Merleau-Ponty, *Adventures*, 204.

165. Ibid., 204–5.

166. Ibid., 205–6.

167. Althusser, *For Marx*, 100, 201–2.

168. Jay, *Marxism and Totality*, 406.

169. Althusser, *For Marx*, 198–99.

170. Ibid., 232.

171. Ibid., 233.

172. Ibid., 243–44.

173. Ibid., 246–47.

174. Althusser, "Ideology and Ideological State Apparatuses," in *Lenin and Philosophy, and Other Essays*, trans. Ben Brewster (New York: Monthly Review Press, 1971), 173–74.

175. Ibid., 175.

176. Ibid., 181.

177. Althusser, *For Marx*, 245.

178. Max Horkheimer, "Traditional and Critical Theory," in *Critical Theory: The Essential Readings*, ed. David Ingram and Julia Simon-Ingram (St. Paul, MN: Paragon House, 1992), 241–42.

179. Ibid., 241.

180. Jay, *Marxism and Totality*, 214.

181. Merleau-Ponty, *Phenomenology of Perception*, 419.

182. Ibid., 151.

183. Ibid., 102.

184. Horkheimer, "Traditional and Critical," 246–47.

185. Max Horkheimer, "Materialism and Metaphysics," in *Critical Theory: Selected Essays*, trans. Matthew O'Connell (New York: Continuum, 2002), 27–28.

186. Merleau-Ponty, *Phenomenology of Perception*, 169.

187. Horkheimer, "Materialism and Metaphysics," 28.

188. Max Horkheimer, "Means and Ends," in *Critical Theory: The Essential Readings*, ed. David Ingram and Julia Simon-Ingram (St. Paul, MN: Paragon House, 1992), 35.

189. Ibid., 40–41, 45.

190. Ibid., 38.

191. Ibid., 47.

192. David Bloor, *Knowledge and Social Imagery* (London: Routledge, 1976), 36.

193. Althusser, *For Marx*, 245.

194. Ibid., 245.

195. Horkheimer, "Traditional and Critical," 241.

196. Ibid., 244–45.

197. Ibid., 247.

198. Lenin, *What Is to Be Done?*, 112.

199. Ibid., 114.

200. Mao, *On New Democracy*, 24–25.

201. Ed Pluth, *Alain Badiou* (Cambridge, UK: Polity, 2010), 20.

202. Mao Zedong, "Win the Masses in Their Millions," in *Selected Works of Mao Tse-tung* (Peking: Foreign Language Press, 1965), 1:290.

203. Merleau-Ponty, *Adventures*, 60; Sartre, *Critique of Dialectical Reason*, 23.

204. Merleau-Ponty, *Adventures*, 209.

205. Ibid., 221.

206. Ibid., 219.

207. Ibid., 222.

208. Ibid., 222–23.

209. Maurice Merleau-Ponty, "Indirect Language and the Voices of Silence," in *Signs*, trans. Richard C. McCleary (Evanston, IL: Northwestern University Press, 1964), 70.

210. Maurice Merleau-Ponty, *The Visible and the Invisible*, trans. Alphonso Lingis (Evanston, IL: Northwestern University Press, 1968), 94–95.

211. Sartre, *Critique of Dialectical Reason*, 349.

212. Ibid., 549.

213. Kojève, *Introduction*, 64–65.

214. Ibid., 52–53.

215. Ibid., 57.

216. Kojève insists the dialectic is a "method of philosophical research and exposition" and that a reality composed of absolute truth is "an abstraction.". Kojève, *Imagination*, 181, 177. Similarly, he emphasizes that work can transform falsehoods (revealed by Nature) into truths (189), demonstrating that the dialectic is not a passive unfolding but an active creating—including the stages of history.

217. Martin Jay, *The Dialectical Imagination* (Berkeley: University of California Press, 1973), 14, 28.

218. Ibid., 36.

219. Jay, *Marxism and Totality*, 218.

220. Louis Althusser, "Philosophy as a Revolutionary Weapon," in *Lenin and Philosophy, and Other Essays* (New York: Monthly Review Press, 1971), 13.

221. Althusser, *For Marx*, 99.
222. Ibid., 100.
223. Ibid., 101.
224. Ibid., 95.
225. Althusser, "Philosophy as a Revolutionary Weapon," 22.
226. Sartre, *Critique of Dialectical Reason*, 86.
227. Adorno, *Negative Dialectics*, 52.
228. Marx, *German Ideology*, 74–77.
229. Lenin, *State and Revolution*, 110–11.
230. Sartre, *Critique of Dialectical Reason*, 52.

Chapter 4

1. Althusser writes that one of the innovations of Marx's philosophy is the development of new forms with which to "think the new object." See Louis Althusser, *For Marx*, trans. Ben Brewster (New York: Penguin, 1969), 85. Numerous Althusser inspired political philosophers have since taken up this project, such as Jacques Rancière, Antonio Negri, and Étienne Balibar. See Jacques Rancière and Peter Hallward, "Only in the Form of Rupture: An Interview with Jacques Rancière," in *Concept and Form*, vol. 2, *Interviews and Essays on the Cahiers pour l'Analyse*, ed. Peter Hallward and Knox Peden (London: Verso, 2012); Michael Hardt and Antonio Negri, *Commonwealth* (Cambridge, MA: Harvard University Press, 2009); Étienne Balibar, *Masses, Classes, Idea: Studies on Politics and Philosophy before and after Marx*, trans. James Swenson (New York: Routledge, 1994).

2. Michel Foucault, *History of Madness*, trans. Jonathan Murphy and Jean Khalfa (London: Routledge, 2006) 47–48.

3. Edward Said, *Orientalism* (New York: Vintage, 1978), 222–24.

4. Alain Badiou, *Being and Event*, trans. Oliver Feltham (New York: Continuum, 2005), 23.

5. Alain Badiou, *Logic of Worlds*, trans. Alberto Toscano (New York: Continuum, 2009), 122.

6. Badiou, *Being and Event*, 29.

7. Oliver Marchart, *Post-foundational Political Thought: Political Difference in Nancy, Lefort, Badiou, and Laclau* (Edinburgh; Edinburgh University Press, 2007), 114.

8. Marguerite La Caze, "At the Intersection: Kant, Derrida, and the Relation between Ethics and Politics," *Political Theory* 35, no. 6 (2007): 781–805.

9. Jacques Derrida, *Of Grammatology*, trans. Gayatari Spivak (Baltimore: Johns Hopkins University Press, 1974), 70. Also Jacques Derrida, "Différance," in *Margins of Philosophy*, trans. Alan Bass (Brighton, UK: Harvester, 1982), 9–11.

10. Derrida, "Structure, Sign, and Play in the Discourse of the Human Sciences," in *Writing and Difference*, trans. Alan Bass (London: Routledge, 1978), 354.

11. Hardt and Negri, *Commonwealth*, 43.

12. Ibid., 338.

13. Michel Foucault, "So Is It Important to Think?," in *Power*, ed. James Faubion, vol. 3 of *Essential Works* (New York: New Press, 2001), 548.

14. Michel Foucault, *Discipline and Punish*, trans. Alan Sheridan (New York: Vintage, 1995), 47.

15. Michel Foucault, *Society Must Be Defended: Lectures at the Collège de France, 1975–76*, ed. Mauro Bertani and Allesandro Fontana, trans. David Macey (New York: Picador, 1997), 243–56.

16. Deleuze and Guattari refer to "matter" as the plane of consistency and the "organic" as an example of strata when talking about biology, and indirect discourse as the plane of consistency and grammar as a strata when talking about linguistics. Gilles Deleuze and Félix Guattari, *A Thousand Plateaus*, trans. Brian Massumi (Minneapolis: University of Minnesota Press, 1987), 41, 45, 75–77.

17. Michel Foucault, *The History of Sexuality*, vol. 1, *An Introduction*, trans. Robert Hurley (New York: Vintage, 1978), 82.

18. Derrida, *Of Grammatology*, 61.

19. Rancière, *Dissensus: Politics and Aesthetics*, ed. and trans. Steven Corcoran (New York: Continuum, 2010), 38.

20. Badiou, *Being and Event*, 181.

21. Ibid., 190.

22. Ibid., 176.

23. Ibid., 181.

24. Badiou, *Logic of Worlds*, 577.

25. Badiou, *Being and Event*, 23.

26. Ibid., 66–67.

27. Ibid., 236.

28. Marchart, *Post-foundational Thought*, 123–24.

29. Michel Foucault, "Useless to Revolt," in *Power*, ed. James Faubion, vol. 3 of *Essential Works* (New York: New Press, 2001), 449.

30. Hardt and Negri, *Commonwealth*, 242–43.

31. Michel Foucault, *Archaeology of Knowledge*, trans. Sheridan Smith (New York: Routledge, 2002), 193.

32. Ibid., 195.

33. Ibid., 94.

34. Ibid., 111–12.

35. Thomas Nail, "Deleuze, Occupy, and the Actuality of Revolution," *Theory and Event* 16, no. 1 (2013): 7.

36. Ibid., 168–68.

37. Hardt and Negri, *Commonwealth*, 240.

38. Ibid., 23–24.

39. Thomas Kuhn, *The Structure of Scientific Revolutions* (Chicago: University of Chicago Press, 1962), 85.

40. Ibid., 204.

41. Fred Evans, *The Multivoiced Body* (New York: Columbia University Press, 2008), 186.

42. Kuhn, *Scientific Revolutions*, 169.

43. Ibid., 62.

44. Rancière, *Dissensus*, 39, 139.

45. Ibid., 86.

46. Ian Hacking, "Working in a New World," in *World Changes: Thomas Kuhn and the Nature of Science*, ed. Paul Horwich (Cambridge; MIT Press, 1993), 276.

47. Alain Badiou, *Metapolitics*, trans. Jason Barker (New York: Verso, 2005), 144.

48. Ibid., 145.

49. Badiou, *Logic of Worlds*, 596.

50. Badiou, *Being and Event*, 522.

51. Ibid., 105.

52. Ibid., 106.

53. Alain Badiou, *Metapolitics*, 145.

54. Adrian Johnston, *Badiou, Žižek, and Political Transformations* (Evanston, IL: Northwestern University Press, 2009), 39.

55. Bruno Bosteels, *Badiou and Politics* (Durham, NC: Duke University Press, 2011), 236.

56. Rancière, *Dissensus*, 36.

57. Rancière, *Dissensus*, 31–33.

58. Rancière, *Dissensus*, 42–44.

59. Foucault, *Discipline and Punish*, 194.

60. Ibid., 48–49.

61. Ibid., 307.

62. Ibid., 296–97.

63. Judith Butler, Ernesto Laclau, and Slavoj Žižek, *Contingency, Hegemony, Universality* (New York: Verso, 2000), 11.

64. Ibid., 101.

65. Badiou, *Logic of Worlds*, 374.

66. Ibid., 359.

67. Ibid., 377.

68. Ibid., 378.

69. Bosteels, *Badiou and Politics*, 244.

70. Badiou, *Logic of Worlds*, 50–60.

71. Badiou, *Being and Event*, 53.

72. Kuhn, *Scientific Revolutions*, 10.

73. Ibid., 116.

74. Paul Hoyningen-Huene, *Reconstructing Scientific Revolutions: Thomas S. Kuhn's Philosophy of Science* trans. Alexander T. Levine (Chicago: University of Chicago Press, 1993), 100–101.

75. Kuhn, *Scientific Revolutions*, 11, 126.

76. Ibid., 170–71.

77. Badiou, *Being and Event*, 29.

78. Kuhn, *Scientific Revolutions*, 52–53.

79. Ibid., 52–53.

80. Badiou, *Logic of Worlds*, 376.

81. Ibid., 378.

82. Kuhn, *Scientific Revolutions*, 82–83.

83. Deleuze and Guattari, *A Thousand Plateaus*, 366–67.

84. Ibid., 367–68.

85. Ibid., 423.

86. Nail, "Deleuze, Occupy," 7.

87. Hardt and Negri, *Commonwealth*, 175.

88. Ibid., 115–18.

89. Ibid., 334.

90. Badiou, *The Communist Hypothesis*, trans David Macey and Steve Corcoran (London: Verso, 2010), 230–35; Deleuze and Guattari, *What Is Philosophy*, trans. Hugh Tomlinson and Graham Burchell (New York: Columbia University Press, 1994), 68.

91. Badiou, *Being and Event*, 183.

92. Badiou, *Logic of Worlds*, 69.

93. Badiou, *Metapolitics*, 145; *Logic of Worlds*, 596; *Being and Event*, 522.

94. Yiju Huang, "On Transference: Badiou and the Chinese Cultural Revolution," *Comparative Literature Studies* 52, no. 1 (2015): 36.

95. Foucault, *History of Sexuality*, 1:98.

96. Foucault, "The Subject and Power," in *Power*, ed. James Faubion, vol. 3 of *Essential Works* (New York: New Press, 2000), 329.

97. Ibid., 342.

98. Ibid., 344.

99. Janet Arfay and Kevin B. Anderson, *Foucault and the Iranian Revolution: Gender and the Seductions of Islam* (Chicago: University of Chicago Press, 2005), 89.

100. Michel Foucault, *The Courage of Truth (Government of the Self and Others II)*, trans. Graham Burchell, Lectures at the Collège de France 1983–1984 (Palgrave Macmillan; New York, 2011), 186. In this passage Foucault does not mean cynicism in the conventional sense of the term, but in relation to the set of philosophers collectively known as the Cynics.

Chapter 5

1. Jay Forrester describes systems as "a grouping of parts that operate together for a common purpose." Jay Forrester, *Principles of Systems* (Cambridge, MA: Wright Allen, 1968), 1-1.

2. Melanie Mitchell, *Complexity: A Guided Tour* (Oxford: Oxford University Press, 2009), 297.

3. Alain Badiou, *Being and Event*, trans. Oliver Feltham (New York: Continuum, 2005), 90.

4. Ibid., 24.

5. Alain Badiou, *Logic of Worlds*, trans. Alberto Toscano (New York: Continuum, 2009), 119.

6. Badiou, *Being and Event*, 24–25.

7. Ibid., 84.

8. Ibid., 95.

9. Ibid., 96–97.

10. Gilles Deleuze and Félix Guattari, *A Thousand Plateaus*, trans. Brian Massumi (Minneapolis: University of Minnesota Press, 1987). 8.

11. Ibid., 21.

12. Ibid., 502.

13. Ibid., 505.

14. Ibid., 508–9.

15. Badiou, *Being and Event*, 24; Deleuze and Guattari, *Thousand Plateaus*, 9.

16. Deleuze and Guattari, *Thousand Plateaus*, 506–7.

17. Ralph Abraham and Christopher Shaw, *Dynamics: The Geometry of Behavior* (Redwood City, CA: Addison-Wesley, 1992), 13.

18. Abraham and Shaw, *Dynamics*, 22.

19. Ibid., 22.

20. Ibid., 22–27.

21. Badiou, *Being and Event*, 90.

22. Ibid., 524–55.

23. For one example, see John H. Holland, *Adaptation in Natural and Artificial Systems* (Cambridge, MA: MIT Press, 1992), 188–96. There he shows how the classification scheme can't predict the behavior of the agents, and in particular the emergence of new or autocatalytic structures (195).

24. Edward N. Lorenz, "Deterministic Nonperiodic Flow," *Journal of the Atmospheric Sciences* 20, no. 2 (1963): 140–41.

25. Strogatz, *Nonlinear Dynamics and Chaos* (Reading, MA: Perseus, 1994), 319–20. A system that crosses itself in a 2D plane doesn't in a 3D plane. What presents itself as a geometric structure that merges actually cannot merge if you study the math closely.

26. See, for example, Abraham and Shaw, *Dynamics*, 148–57. It is the type of object and the fact that its movement can be represented as a circle that prescribes the torus as the shape of the space upon which the system is shown.

27. String theory, for instance, implies that space has twenty-one dimensions.

28. Newton himself describes the project of the *Principia Mathematica* as the application of geometric principles to moving bodies. Isaac Newton, *Principia Mathematica* (New York, 1846), lxvii–lxviii. And A. P. French says that Newton's great accomplishment in mechanics was to deduce laws of motion and force from everyday observations. A. P. French, *Principles of Newtonian Mechanics* (London: Nelson, 1975, 7).

29. J. M. Knudsen and P. G. Hjorth write that a precondition of Newtonian mechanics is Gallileo's method of seeking "pure" motion by "disregarding features of . . . motion that need separate analysis," as those features are "not . . . fundamental feature[s] of the motion." J. M. Knudsen and P. G. Hjorth, *Elements of Newtonian Mechanics: Including Nonlinear Dynamics* (Heidelberg: Springer, 1995), 2. In short, Newton succeeded by ignoring complexity.

30. James Ladyman, James Lambert, and Karoline Wiesner, "What Is a Complex System?," *European Journal for Philosophy of Science* 3, no. 1 (2013): 30.

31. Yaneer Bar-Yam, *Dynamics of Complex Systems* (Reading, MA: Addison-Wesley, 1997), 1.

32. Lorenz, "Deterministic Nonperiodic Flow," 140–41.

33. Strogatz, *Nonlinear Dynamics and Chaos*, 3–4.

34. Bar-Yam. *Dyanmics of Complex Systems*, 5.

35. Forrester, *Principles of Systems*, 1–5.

36. John H. Holland, *Emergence* (Cambrdige, MA: Perseus, 1998), 225.

37. Scott E. Page, *Diversity and Complexity* (Princeton, NJ: Princeton University Press, 2011), 38.

38. Ibid., 43.

39. John H. Holland, *Hidden Order* (Reading, MA: Helix, 1995), 25.

40. Ibid., 26.

41. For one example, see Joshua M. Epstein, *Agent Zero: Toward Neurocognitive Foundations for Generative Social Science* (Princeton, NJ: Princeton University Press, 2014), which looks at complex systems through the lens of social science, discovering similar principles at work.

42. Fred Evans, *The Multivoiced Body* (New York: Columbia University Press, 2008), 8.

43. Ibid., 75.

44. Georg Wilhelm Friedrich Hegel, *Phenomenology of Spirit*, trans. Arnold V. Miller (Oxford: Oxford University Press, 1976), 13.

45. Ibid., 491.

46. Ibid., 493.

47. Michel Foucault, "The Discourse on Language," in *The Archaeology of Knowledge, and The Discourse on Language*, trans. Sheridan Smith (New York: Pantheon, 1972), 235.

48. Foucault, "Theatricum Philosophicum," in *Aesthetics, Method, Epistemology*, ed. James Faubion, vol. 2 of *Essential Works* (New York: New Press, 1998), 358.

49. Friedrich Nietzsche, *Twilight of the Idols*, ed. Aaron Ridley and Judith Norman (Cambridge University Press; Cambridge, 2005), 159.

50. Slavoj Žižek, *Less Than Nothing* (London: Verso, 2012), 195, 199.

51. Ibid., 201.

52. Theodor Adorno, *Negative Dialectics*, trans. E. B. Ashton (London: Routledge, 1973), 21–22.

53. Foucault, "Interview with Michel Foucault," in *Power*, ed. James Faubion, vol. 3 of *Essential Works* (New York: New Press, 1998), 291.

54. Jacques Derrida, *Writing and Difference*, trans. Alan Bass (London: Routledge, 1978), 19.

55. Michel Foucault, *The History of Sexuality*, vol. 1, *An Introduction*, trans. Robert Hurley (New York: Vintage, 1978), 86.

56. C. M. Newman and D. L. Stein, "Spatial Inhomogeneity and Thermodynamic Chaos," *Physical Review Letters* 76, no. 25 (1996): 4281.

57. C. M. Newman and D. L. Stein, "The Metastate Approach to Thermodynamic Chaos," *Physical Review E* 55, no. 5 (1997): 1.

58. I am indebted to Stephen Eubank and Madhav Marathe for this insight.

59. Henri Poincaré, *Science and Hypothesis* (London: Cosimo, 1914), 111–12.

60. Henri Poincaré, *The Value of Science* (New York: Dover, 1958), 136.

61. In reality, they tend to move toward those with power and influence. But that's beside the point.

62. Thomas Hobbes, *Leviathan* (Harmondsworth, UK: Penguin, 1968), 206–7.

63. Buckminster Fuller's *Synergetics* states that any model of the world cannot be portrayed except as plural, as to see it as a "one" is to miss its movement. Buckminster Fuller, *Synergetics: Explorations in the Geometry of Thinking* (New York: Macmillan, 1975), 87).

64. As in the last chapter, contingency plays a big role here. Things in the state are contingent upon the rest of the system—in particular the relations and movements that comprise and maintain it. The state itself is contingent upon the continuous reproduction of it by the system. And because the way in which systems are interconnected and dynamic is so open to change, both states and the things within them are also open to significant change.

65. Holland, *Emergence*, 45.

66. Gilles Deleuze *Difference and Repetition*, trans. Paul Patton (New York: Columbia University Press, 1994), 265.

67. Ibid., 265–69.

68. Badiou, *Being and Event*, 93.

69. Ibid., 105.

70. Judith Butler, Ernesto Laclau, and Savoj Žižek, *Contingency, Hegemony, Universality* (New York: Verso, 2000), 110.

71. Peter Hallward, "Order and Event," *New Left Review*, no. 53 (2008): 115.

72. See Deleuze and Guattari, *Thousand Plateaus*, 141–42, 486–88, 502, 510, for their discussion of how the plane of consistency exists as an amorphous becoming without articulation, and upon which abstract machines function to produce content and expression on the plane of organization.

73. Ibid., 486–88.

74. Mitchell, *Complexity*, 105–8.

75. Strogatz, *Nonlinear Dynamics and Chaos*, 2.

76. For one example of how movement is connected to beings, and how the study of dynamics changes when that happens, see Bar-Yam, *Dynamics of Complex Systems*. He lays out how movement, and our modeling of it, changes when we move from one type of object to another (e.g., neurons to proteins, or ecosystems to human development).

77. Quentin Meillassoux, *After Finitude: An Essay on the Necessity of Contingency* (London: Continuum, 2009), 23.

78. Ibid., 11.

79. Ibid., 10.

80. Graham Harman, *Quentin Meillassoux: Philosophy in the Making* (Edinburgh: Edinburgh University Press, 2011), 94.

81. Meillassoux, *After Finitude*, 47.

82. Ibid., 105.

83. Ibid., 130–31.

84. Ibid., 130.

85. Ibid., 170.

86. Karen Barad, *Meeting the Universe Halfway: Quantum Physics and the Entanglement of Matter and Meaning* (Durham, NC: Duke University Press, 2007, 139.

87. Ibid., 65, 151.

88. Ibid., 151.

89. Ibid., 170.

90. Ibid., 163–65 for description of experiment, 167 for quote.

91. Ibid., 178, 180.

92. Ibid., 182.

93. Ibid., 120–21.

94. Ibid., 100.

95. Matt Austern, "What Is the Mass of a Photon?," https://www.desy.de/user/projects/Physics/ParticleAndNuclear/photon_mass.html.

96. Barad, *Meeting the Universe Halfway*, 176.

97. Ibid., 177.

98. Ibid., 178.

99. Ibid., 148.

100. Ibid., 170.

101. Ibid., 33.

102. Ibid., 178.

103. Stacey Moran, "Quantum Decoherence," *Philosophy Today* 63, no. 4 (2019): 1054–55.

104. Meillassoux, *After Finitude*, 66–67.

105. Eric W. Weisstein, "Indeterminate," *MathWorld: A Wolfram Web Resource*, https://mathworld.wolfram.com/Indeterminate.html.

106. There is also a debate in set theory about how it can incorporate the continuum hypothesis. ZF Axioms fail to do so, and there are several alternative versions of set theory that attempt to do so. Peter Koellner, "The Continuum Hypothesis," in *Stanford Encyclopedia of Philosophy*, Spring 2019 ed., ed. Edward N. Zalta, https://plato.stanford.edu/archives/spr2019/entries/continuum-hypothesis/.

107. Ricardo L. Nirenberg and David Nirenberg, "Badiou's Number: A Critique of Mathematics as Ontology," *Critical Inquiry* 37, no. 4 (2011): 606.

108. See Kevin Hartnett, "With Category Theory, Mathematics Escapes from Equality," *Quanta Magazine*, October 10, 2019, https://www.quantamagazine.org/with-category-theory-mathematics-escapes-from-equality-20191010/; "Will Computers Redefine the Roots of Math?," *Quanta Magazine*, May 19, 2015, https://www.quantamagazine.org/univalent-foundations-redefines-mathematics-20150519/.

109. For some examples, see Thierry Coquand, "Type Theory," in *Stanford Encyclopedia of Philosophy*, Fall 2018 ed., ed. Edward N. Zalta, https://plato.stanford.edu/archives/fall2018/entries/type-theory/.

110. Meillassoux, *After Finitude*, 102–3.

111. Arthur Schopenhauer, *World as Will and Representation* (Cambridge: Cambridge University Press, 2010), 1:125.

112. Schopenhauer, *World as Will and Representation*, 1:124.

113. Friedrich Nietzsche, *Beyond Good and Evil: Prelude to a Philosophy of the Future* (Cambridge: Cambridge University Press, 2002), 19.

114. Friedrich Nietzsche, *Writings from the Late Notebooks* (Cambridge: Cambridge University Press, 2003), 50–51.

115. Foucault, *History of Sexuality* 1:94.

116. Michel Foucault, *Discipline and Punish*, trans. Alan Sheridan (New York: Vintage, 1995), 28.

117. Michel Foucault, "Thought of the Outside," in *Aesthetics, Method, Epistemology*, ed. James Faubion, vol. 2 of *Essential Works* (New York: New Press, 1998), 150.

118. Michel Foucault, "Nietzsche, Genealogy, History," in *Aesthetics, Method, Epistemology*, ed. James Faubion, vol. 2 of *Essential Works* (New York: New Press, 1998), 371.

119. Michel Foucault, "Theatrum Philosophicum," in *Aesthetics, Method, Epistemology*, ed. James Faubion, vol. 2 of *Essential Writings* (New York: New Press, 1998), 353.

120. Deleuze and Guattari, *Thousand Plateaus*, 506.

121. Badiou, *Being and Event*, 39.

122. Thomas Kuhn, *The Structure of Scientific Revolutions* (Chicago: University of Chicago Press, 1962), 112.

123. Jacques Derrida, "Différence," in *Margins of Philosophy*, trans. Alan Bass (Brighton, UK: Harvester, 1982), 21.

124. Slavoj Žižek, *The Parallax View* (Cambridge, MA: MIT Press, 2005), 37.

125. This is something event ontologists do. For example, Foucault claims that the subject and object exist as multiple, and our perceptions of motion are connected to these multiple states. Žižek relates the Real to a "Thing," and Deleuze and Badiou connect motion to intensities/becomings and multiplicities.

126. Mitchell, *Complexity*, 13.

127. Ibid., 189.

128. Peter J. Lewis, *Quantum Ontology: A Guide to the Metaphysics of Quantum Mechanics* (Oxford: Oxford University Press, 2016), 173.

129. Robert McKay, "Many Body Quantum Mechanics," in *Nonlinear Dynamics and Chaos: Where Do We Go from Here?*, ed. John Hogan et al. (Bristol: Institute of Physics Publishing, 2003), 21–54.

130. Slavoj Žižek, *The Indivisible Remainder* (London: Verso, 1998), 225.

131. Evans, *Multivoiced Body*, 75.

132. For one analysis of the automobile's impact, see Jane Holtz Kay, *Asphalt Nation* (Oakland: University of California Press, 1997).

133. For more, see Bill McKibben, ed., *The Global Warming Reader* (New York: Penguin, 2012).

134. Within revolutionary theory, the development of Marxism serves as an example of this type of unpredictability. Marxists Nicos Poulantzas, Ross Abbinett, and Terry Eagleton have all questioned whether core parts of Marxist doctrine still hold after significant events. Nicos Poulantzas, "Is There a Crisis in Marxism," in *The Poulantzas Reader* (London: Verso, 2008), 381; Terry Eagleton, "Introduction, Part 1," in *Marxist Literary Theory: A Reader*, ed. Terry Eagleton and Drew Milne (Cambridge, MA: Blackwell, 1996), 3. See Ross Abbinett, *Marxism after Modernity: Politics, Technology, and Social Transformation* (New York: Palgrave, 2007), 3.

135. CERN, "Dark Matter," https://home.cern/science/physics/dark-matter.

136. David Solnit, "The Battle of the Story of the Battle of Seattle," in *The Battle of the Story of the Battle of Seattle* (Edinburgh: AK Press, 2009), 19, 24.

137. See Mikhail Bakunin, "The Organization of the International," in *Writings* (Indore: Modern, 1947), 6–7; Emma Goldman, "Anarchism: What It Really Stands For," in *Anarchism, and Other Essays* (New York: Mother Earth Publishing,

1911); Daniel Guérin, *Anarchism* (New York: Monthly Review Press, 1989), 14–15.

138. James Martel, *The One and Only Law: Walter Benjamin and the Second Commandment* (Ann Arbor: University of Michigan Press, 2014), 42–43.

139. See Martel, *The One and Only Law*, 182; Simon Critchley, *The Faith of the Faithless: Experiments in Political Theology* (New York: Verso, 2012).

140. Todd May, "Is Post-structuralist Political Theory Anarchist?," *Philosophy and Social Criticism* 15, no. 2 (1989): 167–82.

Chapter 6

1. Some revolutions were successful at some goals but failed at others. When that is the case, I will show how their success was due, at least in part, to following the advice laid out previously, and their failure due to their inability to do so.

2. See Holger Hoock, *Scars of Independence: America's Violent Birth* (New York: Crown, 2017); Glenn A. Moots and Phillip Hamilton, *Justifying Revolution: Law, Virtue, and Violence in the American War of Independence* (Norman: University of Oklahoma Press, 2018); Bedross Der Matossian, *Shattered Dreams of Revolution: From Liberty to Violence in the Late Ottoman Empire* (Palo Alto, CA: Stanford University Press, 2014); Larry J. Reynolds, *Righteous Violence: Revolution, Slavery, and the American Renaissance* (Athens: University of Georgia Press, 2011); Mary Ashburn Miller, *A Natural History of Revolution: Violence and Nature in the French Revolutionary Imagination, 1789–1794* (Ithaca, NY: Cornell University Press, 2011); Howard G. Brown, *Ending the French Revolution: Violence, Justice, and Repression from the Terror to Napoleon* (Charlottesville: University of Virginia Press, 2006).

3. James Ladyman, James Lambert, and Karoline Wiesner, "What Is a Complex System?," *European Journal for Philosophy of Science* 3, no. 1 (2013): 10.

4. John H. Holland, *Hidden Order* (Reading, MA: Helix, 1995), 11–12.

5. Examples of this can be seen in other studies. The means used to study physics at the visual level is different than the means used to study the quantum level, while the phenomenon encountered by physics, chemistry, and biology are quite different because of how added layers of complexity interact.

6. Gordon S. Wood (2002), *The American Revolution: A History* (New York: Modern Library, 2002), 55.

7. Paine says that "the sun never shone on a cause of greater worth" than the American Revolution, while James Otis inveighs that "if a man is not his *own assessor*" then "his liberty is gone or lays entirely at the mercy of others." Thomas Paine, *Common Sense*, in *Collected Writings*, ed. Eric Foner (New York: Library of America, 1955), 17; James Otis, as quoted in David Burg, *The American Revolution: An Eyewitness History* (New York: Facts on File, 2007), 44.

8. Paine's pamphlet, which had an initial printing of 1,000 copies, eventually sold about 150,000 copies throughout the colonies and later on made it to Europe and Latin America. Eric Foner, *Tom Paine and Revolutionary America* (New York: Oxford University Press, 1976), 79.

9. Alfred Aldridge, *Man of Reason: The Life of Thomas Paine* (London: Cresset, 1959), 43.

10. Ibid., 35.

11. Gilbert Shapiro and John Markoff, *Revolutionary Demands: A Content Analysis of the Cahiers de Doléances* (Stanford, CA: Stanford University Press, 1998), 131.

12. Both the American and French revolutionaries are known for candidly stating what powers the king possesses and which belong to the people, such as in the Declaration of Independence and the Declaration of the Rights of Man.

13. Georges Lefebvre, *The French Revolution*, trans. Elizabeth Moss Evanson (London: Routledge, 1962), 108. For example, the Declaration of Rights and Grievances, published by the First Congress of the American Colonies in 1765, opposed the actions of the crown with a formal declaration that, for all Englishmen, "no taxes should be imposed on them, but with their own consent, given personally, or by their representatives" and that every man has the right to choose who represents them. First Congress of the American Colonies, Declaration of Rights and Grievances, http://en.wikisource.org/wiki/Declaration_of_Rights_and_Grievances.

14. Pamphlets like Paine's and Otis's were addressed to the colonists specifically. The Declaration of Rights and Grievances and Declaration of Independence were written in an open manner for anyone to read, and addressed the king as "his majesty" rather than "your majesty"—indicating they wanted many to read the document.

15. The Albany Plan for Union in 1754 begins, "It is proposed that humble application be made for an act of Parliament of Great Britain," while the Massachusetts Assembly's protest of the Stamp Act (1765) begins with "May it please your Excellency," references "Our duty to the king," and "begs that your Excellency would consider the people of this province as having the strongest affection for his Majesty." "The Albany Plan for Union (1754)," Alpha History, https://alphahistory.com/americanrevolution/albany-plan-for-union-1754/; "Massachusetts' Assembly Protests the Stamp Act (1765)," Alpha History, https://alphahistory.com/americanrevolution/massachusetts-assembly-protests-stamp-act-1765/. Even Benjamin Franklin's testimony in front of Parliament in 1766 mentions how colonists believed Great Britain to be "the best in the world" and how "they submitted willingly to the government of the Crown, and paid, in all their courts, obedience to acts of Parliament." "Benjamin Franklin's Testimony to Parliament (1766)," Alpha History, https://alphahistory.com/americanrevolution/benjamin-franklins-testimony-parliament-1766/. While at none of these times had revolutionary fervor reached a fever pitch, both Johnson's and Otis's pamphlets, containing numerous declarations, had been published by the time Franklin testified.

16. Philip Huang, "Mao Tse-tung and the Middle Peasants, 1925–1928," in *Mao Zedong and the Chinese Revolution*, vol. 1, ed. Gregor Benton (London: Routledge, 2008), 41.

17. Michael Lynch, *The Chinese Civil War 1945–49* (Osprey: Oxford, 2010), pg 20–21.

18. Stuart Schram, "Mao Tse-tung and Secret Societies," in *Mao Zedong and the Chinese Revolution*, vol. 1, ed. Gregor Benton (London: Routledge, 2008), 28–29, 32.

19. Schram, "Mao Tse-tung and Secret Societies," 25.

20. Huang, "Mao Tse-tung and the Middle Peasants, 1925–1928," 40–41, 44–45.

21. Ibid., 54–55.

22. Nick Knight, "Mao Zedong and the Peasants: Class and Power in the Formation of a Revolutionary Strategy," in *Mao Zedong and the Chinese Revolution*, vol. 1, ed. Gregor Benton (London: Routledge, 2008), 64–65.

23. Ibid., 74–75.

24. Ibid., 70–71.

25. Francis Fuller, "Mao Tse-tung: Military Thinker," in *Mao Zedong and the Chinese Revolution*, vol. 1, ed. Gregor Benton (London: Routledge, 2008), 122.

26. Ibid., 122–25.

27. John H. Miller and Scott E. Page, *Complex Adaptive Systems: An Introduction to Computational Models of Social Life* (Princeton, NJ: Princeton University Press, 2007), 84.

28. Ladyman, Lambert, and Wiesner, "What Is a Complex System?," 6.

29. Wood, *American Revolution*, 76.

30. Examples of the depositions, and a letter to Benjamin Franklin, who was charged with publishing them, can be found in the *Journals of the Continental Congress, 1774–1789* (Washington, DC: USGPO, 1904–1937), 2:26–44, https://memory.loc.gov/ammem/amlaw/lwjclink.html. Also, "Battles of Lexington and Concord," Wikipedia, at "Aftermath," accessed May 27, 2021, https://en.wikipedia.org/wiki/Battles_of_Lexington_and_Concord#Aftermath.

31. See Stephen C. Bullock, *The American Revolution: A History in Documents* (Oxford: Oxford University Press, 2003), 46; Wood, *American Revolution*, 51. The casualty counts were higher than expected. The British elite believed that the colonists were thus unlikely to truly desire reconciliation, and that a harsh line was needed to bring the colonies to heel. As a result, the British government rejected the Olive Branch Petition that was sent to Great Britain shortly thereafter (the last appeal to end the fighting).

32. Tony Horwitz, "The True Story of the Battle of Bunker Hill," *Smithsonian Magazine*, May 2013, https://www.smithsonianmag.com/history/the-true-story-of-the-battle-of-bunker-hill-36721984/. Also, Denis Collins, "Summer Soldiers, Spectators Rejoice at Yorktown Battle," *Washington Post*, October 18, 1981, https://

www.washingtonpost.com/archive/politics/1981/10/18/summer-soldiers-spectators-rejoice-at-yorktown-battle/a29c30f9-f633-4209-bb8a-90f0979aabf9/?utm_term=.00122d97a01e.

33. The Third Estate, via the National Assembly, was constantly hurrying to counter Louis's attempts to subvert their authority, and vice versa. When Louis locked the doors to the National Assembly's meeting place, they met on a local tennis court and drafted the Tennis Court Oath, which spurred other representatives from the other estates to confront Louis and the royal court. After Louis dismissed Jacques Necker, his one non-noble minister, rumors swirled of a potential attack on the Third Estate and its representatives. To ward off that threat, the Third Estate seized guns and laid siege to the Bastille. According to Peter McPhee, the quick action taken in storming the Bastille, "saved the National Assembly" by institutionalizing the Third Estate's control of Paris. Peter McPhee, *The French Revolution, 1789–1799* (Oxford: Oxford University Press, 2002), 52–55.

34. For example, peasants in the Chinese Revolution did not automatically support the Communists. Nick Knight, "Mao Zedong and the Peasants," 58.

35. Alberto Bayo, "One Hundred Fifty Questions to a Guerrilla," in *Strategy for Conquest: Communist Documents on Guerrilla Warfare*, ed. Jay Mallin (Coral Gables, FL: University of Miami Press, 1970), 325.

36. Guevara, *Guerrilla Warfare*, trans. Brian Loveman and Thomas M. Davies, Jr. (Wilmington, DE: SR Books, 1997), 121.

37. Carlos Marighella, "Armed Propaganda," in *Minimanual of the Urban Guerrilla*, https://www.marxists.org/archive/marighella-carlos/1969/06/minimanual-urban-guerrilla/ch31.htm.

38. Guevara, *Guerrilla Warfare*, 121.

39. John Pustay, *Counterinsurgency Warfare* (New York: Free Press, 1965), 96–97.

40. Nelson Mandela, *Long Walk to Freedom* (Boston: Little, Brown, 1994), 147.

41. Ibid., 232.

42. Ibid., 234.

43. Pustay *Counterinsurgency Warfare*, 57.

44. Ibid., 100.

45. For two sources on the Phoenix program, see Colonel Andrew R. Finlayson, "A Retrospective on Counterinsurgency Operations," https://www.cia.gov/static/df2d35f5993e5d6c2bd43922f308952d/tay-ninh-provincial-reconnaissance.pdf; and the CIA's 1968 declassified document, Reports Branch of the Central Phoenix Directorate in Saigon, "Phoenix Fact Sheet," nsarchive.files.wordpress.com/2010/11/phoenix.pdf.

46. Bayo, "One Hundred Fifty," 351.

47. Mao Zedong, "The Strategy of Guerrilla Resistance against Japan," in *On Guerrilla Warfare*, https://www.marxists.org/reference/archive/mao/works/1937/guerrilla-warfare/ch07.htm.

48. Bayo, "One Hundred Fifty," 347.

49. See Guevara, *Guerrilla Warfare*, 56; Vo Nguyen Giap "The Big Victory; the Great Task," in *Strategy for Conquest: Communist Documents on Guerrilla Warfare*, ed. Jay Mallin (Coral Gables, FL: University of Miami Press, 1970), 199.

50. Pustay, *Counterinsurgency Warfare*, 113–15.

51. For example, Levy's book discusses how, after ambushes, guerrillas should use the enemy's equipment or documents as they see fit. "Yank" Bert Levy, *Guerrilla Warfare* (Boulder, CO: Paladin, 1964), 74–75; Guevara, *Guerrilla Warfare*, 13. There is a concerted effort by guerrilla warfare fighters to feel at home in their country, or feel comfortable exercising authority over others.

52. Miller and Page, *Complex Adaptive Systems*, 241–42.

53. Andrew Zolli and Ann Marie Healy, *Resilience: Why Things Bounce Back* (New York: Simon and Schuster, 2012), 7.

54. McPhee, *French Revolution*, 134–35.

55. Ibid., 135–39.

56. Ibid., 143.

57. Ibid., 143.

58. Ibid., 144–45.

59. McPhee says that "It was also the end of a regime which had had the twin aims of saving the Revolution and creating a new society. It had achieved the former, at great cost, but the vision of the virtuous, self-abnegating civic warrior embodying the new society had palled." Ibid., 151–52.

60. Mao Zedong, "What Is Guerrilla Warfare," in *On Guerrilla Warfare*, https://www.marxists.org/reference/archive/mao/works/1937/guerrilla-warfare/ch07.htm.

61. Carlos Marighella, "How the Urban Guerrilla Lives," *Minimanual of the Urban Guerrilla*, http://www.marxists.org/archive/marighella-carlos/1969/06/minimanual-urban-guerrilla/ch03.htm.

62. Hoang Van Thai, "Some Aspects of Guerrilla Warfare in Vietnam," in *Strategy for Conquest: Communist Documents on Guerrilla Warfare*, ed. Jay Mallin (Coral Gables; University of Miami Press, 1970), 245.

63. Ibid., 246.

64. Guevara, *Guerrilla Warfare*, 59–60.

65. For examples, see ibid., 125–26; Mao, *On Guerrilla Warfare*, the chapter on organization of guerrilla fighters.

66. Sheila Fitzpatrick, *The Russian Revolution* (Oxford: Oxford University Press, 1994), 40.

67. Fitzpatrick, *Russian Revolution*, 42–43.

68. Michael Hickey, "July 1917–October 1917," in *Competing Voices from the Russian Revolution*, ed. Michael Hickey (Santa Barbara, CA: Greenwood, 2011), 265–66, 272–73.

69. Hickey, "July 1917–October 1917," 274–76; also, Michael Hickey, "The Bolshevik Party Central Committee Session of 16 October 1917," in *Competing Voices*, 224–39.

70. Michael Hickey, "The First Four Months of Soviet Rule," in *Competing Voices*, 449.

71. This is not to say that the Soviets were not dogmatic at times, and in ways that hurt them or their movement. After taking power and dissolving the Provisional Government, the Soviets at times pursued a formulaic and doctrinaire means to bring about communism, which occasionally hurt their cause. For a discussion of how the Bolsheviks changed their strategies between the February and October Revolutions, and then again after taking power, see Fitzpatrick, *Russian Revolution*, 55, 60–63, 96–99.

72. Ladyman, Lambert, and Wiesner, "What Is a Complex System?," 8–9.

73. John H. Holland, *Emergence* (Cambridge, MA: Perseus, 1998), 226–27.

74. Ladyman, Lambert, and Wiesner, "What Is a Complex System?," 9.

75. Luis Perez, Jr., *Cuba: Between Reform and Revolution* (Oxford: Oxford University Press, 2006), 238–39.

76. Ibid., 252–53.

77. Joseph Gregory, "Ahmed Ben Bella, Revolutionary Who Led Algeria after Revolution, Dies at 93," *New York Times*, April 11, 2012, https://www.nytimes.com/2012/04/12/world/africa/ahmed-ben-bella-algerias-first-president-dies-at-93.html.

78. Phillip Naylor, *France and Algeria: A History of Decolonization and Transformation* (Gainesville: University of Florida Press, 2000), 70.

79. Ibid., 73.

80. Lawrence Joffe, "Ahmed Ben Bella Obituary," *Guardian*, April 11, 2012, https://www.theguardian.com/world/2012/apr/11/ahmed-ben-bella. Accessed 5/31/2019.

81. Naylor, *France and Algeria*, 72.

82. Bullock, *American Revolution*, 13.

83. McPhee, *French Revolution*, 35.

84. Hickey, "The Context of World War 1," in *Competing Voices*, 12–13.

85. Fitzpatrick, *Russian Revolution*, 37.

86. McPhee, *French Revolution*, 105–6.

87. Sebastian Balfour, *Castro* (London: Longman, 1990), 41.

88. Leon Trotsky, *History of the Russian Revolution*, ed. Chris Russell (Marxists Internet Archive, 2000), 13.

89. Hickey, "Chapter Four: What the Revolution Means to Me, Part I: Soldiers, Workers, Professionals, Industrialists, and Students," in *Competing Voices*, 133–35; "What the Revolution Means to Me, Part II: Clergy, Peasants, Aristocratic Landowners, Women, and National and Religious Minorities," in *Competing Voices*, 153–57.

90. McPhee, *French Revolution*, 35.

91. Bullock, *American Revolution*, 107, 116–18. The latter document makes clear that equality was seen as a means to liberty.

92. Vladimir Ilyich Lenin, "Socialism and Religion," in *Collected Works* (Moscow: Progress, 1960), 10:83–87.

93. Nikolai Bukharin and Evgenii Preobrazhensky, *The ABC of Communism* (Harmondsworth, UK: Penguin, 1969), ch. 11, sec. 89, https://www.marxists.org/archive/bukharin/works/1920/abc/11.htm.

94. Sovnarkom, "Decree on Separation of Church and State," https://www.marxists.org/history/ussr/events/revolution/documents/1918/02/5.htm.

95. Theodore Weeks, *Across the Revolutionary Divide: Russia and the USSR 1861–1945* (Chichester, UK: Wiley-Blackwell, 2011), 163.

96. Ibid., 164–71.

97. Sonia Calista, "Religion and the Russian Revolution," Hampton Institute, February 26, 2016, https://www.hamptonthink.org/read/religion-and-the-russian-revolution.

98. Specifically, the way nonlinearity exists in complex systems, since nonlinearity itself is diverse. Ladyman, Lambert, and Wiesner, "What Is a Complex System?," 4.

99. Perez, *Cuba between Reform and Revolution*, 221–24; *New York Times*, "Batista, Ex-Cuban Dictator, Dies in Spain," August 7, 1973, https://www.nytimes.com/1973/08/07/archives/batista-excuban-dictator-dies-in-spain-unending-exile-succession-of.html; "Fulgencio Batista (1901–1973)," American Experience, https://www.pbs.org/wgbh/americanexperience/features/castro-fulgencio-batista-1901-1973/.

100. Perez, 225.

101. Belen Fernandez, "The US in Cuba: A History of Organised Crime," Al Jazeera, July 20, 2015, https://www.aljazeera.com/indepth/opinion/2015/07/cuba-history-organised-crime-united-states-neoliberalism-150719090821297.html.

102. Perez, 233–34.

103. Perez, 234–35.

104. Naylor, *France and Algeria*, 6.

105. Naylor, *France and Algeria*, 7–9.

106. Frantz Fanon, *Black Skin, White Masks*, trans. Richard Philcox (New York: Grove, 1967), 12.

107. Naylor, *France and Algeria*, 9–10.

108. Ibid.10–11.

109. Ibid., 12.

110. Ibid., 1.

111. Ibid., 2.

112. Booker T. Washington, "The Negro and the Signs of Civilization," in *African American Political Thought, 1890–1930*, ed. Cary Wintz (New York: Sharpe,

1996), 42; W. E. B. Du Bois, "My Evolving Program for Negro Freedom," in *What the Negro Wants*, ed. Rayford Whittingham Logan (New York: Agathon, 1944), 49.

113. Frederick Douglass, "An address on West India Emancipation (3 August 1857)," in *Frederick Douglass: Selected Speeches and Writings*, ed. Philip Foner (Chicago: Lawrence Hill, 1950), 367; Southern Christian Leadership Conference, *Constitution and Bylaws of the Southern Christian Leadership Conference*, pp. 4–5, http://www.crmvet.org/docs/sclc_const.pdf; "Recommendations of the Findings and Recommendations Committee," Youth Leadership Conference, Shaw College, Raleigh, NC, April 1960, p. 2, http://www.crmvet.org/docs/6004_shaw_recommendations.pdf; Richard S. Reddie, *Martin Luther King Jr: History Maker* (Oxford, UK: Lion, 2011), 154; Carl Rowan, "Martin Luther King's Tragic Decision," *Reader's Digest* 91, no. 545 (1967), 42.

114. LeRoi Jones, "The Last Days of the American Empire," in *Home: Social Essays* (New York: Morrow, 1966), 203.

115. Angela Davis, "Coalition Building among People of Color," in *The Angela Y. Davis Reader*, ed. Joy James (Malden, MA: Blackwell, 1998), 300–301; Manning Marable, *Black Liberation in Conservative America* (Boston: South End Press, 1997), 9.

116. Guevara, *Guerrilla Warfare*, 61.

117. Ibid., 60.

118. Ibid., 118.

119. Naylor, *France and Algeria*, 274.

120. Martin S. Alexander, Martin Evans, and J. F. V. Keiger, *The Algerian War and the French Army, 1954–62* (New York: Palgrave MacMillan, 2002), 3, 6.

121. Alistair Horne, *A Savage War of Peace: Algeria, 1954–1962* (New York: New York Review of Books, 1977), 197.

122. Ibid., 199; Henri Alleg, *The Question* (New York: Calder, 1958).

123. Horne, *Savage War of Peace*, 204, Battle for Algiers chapter. It should not be ignored that the FLN violence produced a wave of opposition that, while not making people feel close association with the French, nevertheless made them feel that the French were safer than the alternative. Alexander, Evans, and Kieger, *The Algerian War and the French Army*, 124–25. While at no point was the whole population of either side unified behind any one vision for Algeria, producing a situation where the French, in order to defend themselves, were required to increase the levels of brutality exercised upon the populace encouraged the spread of the Afro-Muslim identity that the FLN desired.

124. Malcolm X, *Malcolm X Speaks* (New York: Grove, 1965), 206.

125. Ibid., 198.

126. John Brown Society, *An Introduction to the Black Panther Party*, 21–23, http://archive.lib.msu.edu/DMC/AmRad/introblackpanther.pdf 21–23.

127. The Southern Christian Leadership Conference focused on organizing blacks in the south, while the Student Nonviolent Coordinating Committee only

organized students in the USA. *Constitution and Bylaws of the Southern Christian Leadership Conference*, 4–5; *Recommendations of the Findings and Recommendations Committee*. Garvey's Universal Negro Improvement Association tried to emancipate blacks everywhere while the Black Panthers spoke of uniting all colonized peoples. Marcus Garvey, "Address to the Second UNIA Convention, New York, August 31, 1921," in *African American Political Thought, 1890–1930*, ed. Cary Wintz (New York: Sharpe, 1996), 219; Stokely Carmichael and Charles Hamilton, *Black power: The Politics of Liberation in America* (New York: Vintage, 1967), xi.

128. Davis, "Coalition Building among People of Color," 300–301.

129. Marable, *Black Liberation in Conservative America*, 9.

130. For one example, see Alex Haley, epilogue to *The Autobiography of Malcolm X* (New York: Ballantine, 1999), 393.

131. Attallah Shabazz, forward to *The Autobiography of Malcolm X* (New York: Ballantine, 1999), xiii, xix–xxi.

132. Yancy, *Black Bodies, White Gazes* (Lanham, MD: Rowman and Littlefield, 2008), 157.

133. Many black radicals have used this technique. In addition to Malcolm X, they include Frederick Douglass, LeRoi Jones (Amiri Baraka), Booker T. Washington, W. E. B. Du Bois, Shirley Chisholm, and bell hooks.

134. Ladyman, Lambert, and Wiesner, "What Is a Complex System?," 7.

135. Ibid.

136. Richard Johnson, "Empire," in *A Companion to Colonial America*, ed. Daniel Vickers (Malden, MA: Blackwell, 2006), 106.

137. Alan Tully, "Colonial Politics," in *A Companion to Colonial America*, ed. Daniel Vickers (Malden, MA: Blackwell, 2006), 292.

138. Perez, 211–12.

139. Bullock, *American Revolution*, 93–95; Kendall F. Haven, *Voices of the American Revolution: Stories of Men, Women, and Children Who Forged Our Nation* (Englewood, CO: Libraries Unlimited, 2000), 113.

140. Bullock, American Revolution, 108. Wood, *American Revolution*, 116.

141. Bourdieu, *The Algerians*, 121.

142. Bourdieu, *The Algerians*, 163.

143. Horace Campbell, "Julius Nyerere: between statecentred and people-centred Pan-Africanism," in *Africa's Liberation: The Legacy of Julius Nyerere*, ed. Chambi Chachage and Annar Cassam (Cape Town: Pambazuka, 2010), 47–48; Chief Emeka Anyaoku and Annar Cassam, "Nyerere and the Commonwealth," in *Africa's Liberation: The Legacy of Julius Nyerere*, ed. Chambi Chachage and Annar Cassam (Cape Town: Pambazuka, 2010), 67–70.

144. For instance, guerrilla groups in Laos who opposed the Communist forces of Southeast Asia trafficked in heroin, relying upon material support from the CIA. See Alfred McCoy, *The Politics of Heroin in Southeast Asia* (New York: Harper and Row, 1972), 247–48. Evidence of this, as well as numerous other crimes carried out by US supported militants, was hidden from the US Congress and the

American people for years through manipulation of the news media. See Fred Branfman, "Presidential War in Laos, 1964–1970," in *Laos: War and Revolution*, ed. Nina Adams and Alfred McCoy (New York: Harper and Row, 1970), 268.

145. One good personal account that describes how these committees work can be found in Luis Garcia's *Child of the Revolution: Growing up in Castro's Cuba* (St Leonards: Allen & Unwin, 2007), while Amnesty International and Human Rights Watch have been keeping track of the human rights violations committed in Cuba. See, for instance, Daniel Wilkinson and Nik Steinberg, "Cuba—A Way Forward," in *New York Review of Books*, May 27, 2010, republished by Human Rights Watch at https://www.hrw.org/news/2010/04/28/cuba-way-forward.

146. See Roderick MacFarquhar and Michael Schoenhals, *Mao's Last Revolution* (Cambrdige, MA: Harvard University Press, 2005).

147. Vladimir Ilyich Lenin, "Two Tactics of Social-Democracy in the Democratic Revolution," in *Collected Works* (Moscow: Progress, 1960), 9:21–24. For Lenin's discussion of the dictatorship of the proletariat, see Lenin, "State and Revolution," *Collected Works*, 25:465–67.

148. Weeks, *Across the Revolutionary Divide*, 35.

149. Ibid., 37.

150. Ibid., 41.

151. Tom Phillips, "The Cultural Revolution: all you need to know about China's political convulsion," *Guardian*, May 11, 2016, https://www.theguardian.com/world/2016/may/11/the-cultural-revolution-50-years-on-all-you-need-to-know-about-chinas-political-convulsion.

152. Antoni Kapcia, *Cuba in Revolution: A history since the Fifties* (Chicago: Reaktion, 2008), 134–35.

153. See "Federalist-Antifederalist Debate," in Wood, *The American Revolution*, 158–67. Even though the system was federalist, in practice many decisions remained in the hands of the states, which is still true today.

154. Julius Nyerere and Nawal El Saadawi, "Nyerere talks to *El Mussawar*," in *Africa's Liberation: The Legacy of Nyerere*, ed. Chambi Chachage and Annar Cassam (Cape Town: Pambazuka, 2010), 12–13, 17; see also 82, 84–85. Nyerere here talks about the importance of dissent and a plurality of opinions for true unity, and a commentator discusses why getting many views is important. Also, Kwame Botwe-Asamoah, *Kwame Nkrumah's Politico-Cultural Thoughts and Policies* (New York: Routledge, 2005), 93–94. It is worth noting that later in his presidency, Nkrumah did institute some harsh, oppressive measures, which were a factor in his overthrow in 1966.

155. Marcus Garvey, "Motive of the NAACP Exposed," in *African American Political Thought, 1890–1930*, ed. Cary Wintz (New York: Sharpe, 1996), 226; LeRoi Jones, "What Does Nonviolence Mean?," in *Home: Social Essays* (New York: Morrow, 1966), 76; Angela Davis, "Reflections on the Black Woman's Role in the Community of Slaves," in *The Angela Y. Davis Reader*, ed. Joy James (Malden, MA: Blackwell, 1998), 126–27.

Bibliography

Abbinett, Ross. *Marxism after Modernity: Politics, Technology, and Social Transformation*. New York: Palgrave, 2007.

Abraham, Ralph, and Christopher Shaw. *Dynamics: The Geometry of Behavior*. Redwood City, CA: Addison-Wesley, 1992.

Adorno, Theodor. *Negative Dialectics*. Translated by E. B. Ashton. London: Routledge, 1973.

Afary, Janet, and Kevin Anderson. *Foucault and the Iranian Revolution: Gender and the Seductions of Islam*. Chicago: University of Chicago Press: Chicago, 2005.

"The Albany Plan for Union (1754)." Alpha History. https://alphahistory.com/americanrevolution/albany-plan-for-union-1754/.

Aldridge, Alfred. *Man of Reason: The Life of Thomas Paine*. London: Cresset, 1959.

Alexander, Martin S., Martin Evans, and J. F. V. Keiger. *The Algerian War and the French Army, 1954–62*. New York: Palgrave MacMillan, 2002.

Alleg, Henri. *The Question*, New York: Calder, 1958.

Althusser, Louis. *For Marx*. Translated by Ben Brewster. New York: Penguin, 1969.

———. "Ideology and Ideological State Apparatuses." In *Lenin and Philosophy, and Other Essays*, translated by Ben Brewster, 127–86. New York: Monthly Review Press, 1971.

———. "Lenin and Philosophy." In *Lenin and Philosophy, and Other Essays*, translated by Ben Brewster, 23–67. New York: Monthly Review Press, 1971.

———. "Lenin before Hegel." In *Lenin and Philosophy, and Other Essays*, translated by Ben Brewster, 107–26. New York: Monthly Review Press, 1971.

———. "Philosophy as a Revolutionary Weapon." In *Lenin and Philosophy, and Other Essays*, translated by Ben Brewster, 11–22. New York: Monthly Review Press, 1971.

Amnesty International. *When the State Kills: The Death Penalty v. Human Rights*. London: Amnesty International Publications, 1989.

Anievas, Alexander, and Kerem Nişancıoğlu. *How the West Came to Rule: The Geopolitical Origins of Capitalism*. London: Pluto, 2015.

Arendt, Hannah. *The Human Condition*. Chicago: University of Chicago Press, 1998.

———. *Life of the Mind*. New York: Harcourt, 1978.

———. *On Revolution*. New York: Penguin, 1963.

———. "What Is Authority." In *Between Past and Future*. New York: Viking, 1961.

Austern, Matt. "What Is the Mass of a Photon?" https://www.desy.de/user/projects/Physics/ParticleAndNuclear/photon_mass.html.

Badiou, Alain. *Being and Event*. Translated by Oliver Feltham. New York: Continuum, 2005.

———. *The Communist Hypothesis*. Translated by David Macey and Steve Corcoran. London: Verso, 2010.

———. *Logic of Worlds*. Translated by Alberto Toscano. New York: Continuum, 2009.

———. *Metapolitics*. Translated by Jason Barker. New York: Verso, 2005.

———. *Philosophy for Militants*. Translated by Bruno Bosteels. New York: Verso, 2012.

Bakunin, Mikhail. "The Organization of the International." In *Writings*, 6–8. Indore: Modern, 1947.

Barad, Karen. *Meeting the Universe Halfway: Quantum Physics and the Entanglement of Matter and Meaning*. Durham, NC: Duke University Press, 2007.

Barlow, David H., and Matthew K. Nock. "Why Can't We Be More Idiographic in Our Research?" *Perspectives on Psychological Science* 4, no. 1 (2009): 19–21.

Bar-Yam, Yaneer. *Dynamics of Complex Systems*. Reading, MA: Addison-Wesley, 1997.

Bayo, Alberto. "One Hundred Fifty Questions to a Guerrilla." In *Strategy for Conquest: Communist Documents on Guerrilla Warfare*, edited by Jay Mallin, 315–62. Coral Gables, FL: University of Miami Press, 1970.

Bearbeau, Aimee. *Theorizing the Nation: The French Revolution and the Social Contract*. PhD diss., Georgetown University, 2014.

"Benjamin Franklin's Testimony to Parliament (1766)." Alpha History. https://alphahistory.com/americanrevolution/benjamin-franklins-testimony-parliament-1766/.

Bloor, David. *Knowledge and Social Imagery*. London: Routledge, 1976.

Boer, Roland. *The Criticism of Heaven and Earth*. Boston: Brill, 2007.

Bosteels, Bruno. *Badiou and Politics*. Durham, NC: Duke University Press, 2011.

Branfman, Fred. "Presidential War in Laos, 1964–1970." In *Laos: War and Revolution*, edited by Nina Adams and Alfred McCoy, 213–80. New York: Harper and Row, 1970.

Brown, Howard G. *Ending the French Revolution: Violence, Justice, and Repression from the Terror to Napoleon*. Charlottesville: University of Virginia Press, 2006.

Brown, Wendy. "Resisting Left Melancholy." *Boundary 2* 26, no. 3 (1999): 19–27.

Bukharin, Nikolai, and Evgenii Preobrazhensk, *The ABC of Communism*. Harmondsworth, UK: Penguin, 1969. https://www.marxists.org/archive/bukharin/works/1920/abc/11.htm.

Bullock, Stephen C. *The American Revolution: A History in Documents.* Oxford: Oxford University Press, 2003.

Burg, David. *The American Revolution: An Eyewitness History.* New York: Facts on File, 2007.

Burke, Edmund. *Reflections on the Revolution in France.* New York: Dutton, 1951.

Butler, Judith. *Gender Trouble.* New York: Routledge, 1990.

Butler, Judith, Ernesto Laclau, and Savoj Žižek. *Contingency, Hegemony, Universality.* New York: Verso, 2000.

Calista, Sonia. "Religion and the Russian Revolution." Hampton Institute, February 26, 2016. https://www.hamptonthink.org/read/religion-and-the-russian-revolution.

Carmichael, Stokely, and Charles Hamilton. *Black Power: The Politics of Liberation in America.* New York: Vintage, 1967.

Cassirer, Ernst. *The Philosophy of Enlightenment.* Princeton, NJ: Princeton University Press, 2009.

CERN. "Dark Matter." https://home.cern/science/physics/dark-matter.

Cigainero, Jake. "Who Are France's Yellow Vest Protesters, and What Do They Want?" *NPR*, December 3, 2018. https://www.npr.org/2018/12/03/672862353/who-are-frances-yellow-vest-protesters-and-what-do-they-want.

Collins, Jeffrey R. *The Allegiance of Thomas Hobbes.* Oxford: Oxford University Press, 2005.

Coquand, Thierry. "Type Theory." In *Stanford Encyclopedia of Philosophy*, Fall 2018 ed. Edited by Edward N. Zalta. https://plato.stanford.edu/archives/fall2018/entries/type-theory/.

Cranston, Maurice. Introduction to *The Social Contract*, by Jean-Jacques Rousseau. Translated by Maurice Cranston. London: Penguin, 1968.

Critchley, Simon. *The Faith of the Faithless: Experiments in Political Theology.* New York: Verso, 2012.

Croce, Benedetto. *Logic as Science of Pure Concept.* London: Macmillan, 1917.

Davis, Angela. "Coalition Building among People of Color." In *The Angela Y. Davis Reader*, edited by Joy James, 297–306. Malden, MA: Blackwell, 1998.

———. "Meditations on the Legacy of Malcolm X." In *The Angela Y. Davis Reader*, edited by Joy James, 279–88. Malden, MA: Blackwell, 1998.

———. "Reflections on the Black Woman's Role in the Community of Slaves." In *The Angela Y. Davis Reader*, edited by Joy James, 111–28. Malden, MA: Blackwell, 1998.

Deleuze, Gilles. *Difference and Repetition.* Translated by Paul Patton. New York: Columbia University Press, 1994.

Deleuze, Gilles, and Félix Guattari. *A Thousand Plateaus.* Translated by Brian Massumi. Minneapolis: University of Minnesota Press, 1987.

———. *What Is Philosophy.* Translated by Hugh Tomlinson and Graham Burchell. New York: Columbia University Press, 1994.

Der Matossian, Bedross. *Shattered Dreams of Revolution: From Liberty to Violence in the Late Ottoman Empire*. Palo Alto, CA: Stanford University Press, 2014.

Derrida, Jacques. "Différance." In *Margins of Philosophy*, translated by Alan Bass, 1–28. Brighton, UK: Harvester, 1982.

———. *Of Grammatology*. Translated by Gayatari Spivak. Baltimore: Johns Hopkins University Press, 1974.

———. "Signature Event Context." In *Limited Inc*, 1–24. Evanston, IL: Northwestern University Press, 1977.

———. *Specters of Marx*. Translated by Peggy Kamuf. New York: Routledge, 1994.

———. "Structure, Sign, and Play in the Discourse of the Human Sciences." In *Writing and Difference*, translated by Alan Bass, 351–70. London: Routledge, 1978.

———. *Writing and Difference*. Translated by Alan Bass. London: Routledge, 1978.

Deutsche, Rosalyn. "Hiroshima after Iraq: A Study in Art and War." *October*, no. 131 (2010): 3–22.

Douglass, Frederick. "West India Emancipation, speech delivered at Canadaigua, New York, August 3, 1857." In *Frederick Douglass: Selected Speeches and Writings*, edited by Phillip Foner, 358–68. New York: Lawrence Hill, 1999.

Drinnon, Richard. *Rebel in Paradise: A Biography of Emma Goldman*. New York: Harper Collins, 1976.

Du Bois, W. E. B. "My Evolving Program for Negro Freedom." In *What the Negro Wants*, edited by Rayford Whittingham Logan, 31–70. New York: Agathon, 1944.

Dworkin, Ronald. *Taking Rights Seriously*. Cambridge, MA: Harvard University Press, 1977.

Eagleton, Terry. "Introduction, Part 1." In *Marxist Literary Theory: A Reader*, edited by Terry Eagleton and Drew Milne, 1–15. Cambridge, MA: Blackwell, 1996.

Echols, Alice. *Daring to Be Bad: Radical Feminism in America, 1967–1975*. Minneapolis: University of Minnesota Press, 1989.

Engels, Friedrich. "Socialism: Utopian and Scientific." In Tucker, *The Marx-Engels Reader*, 683–717.

———. "The Tactics of Social Democracy." In Tucker, *Marx-Engels Reader*, 556–76.

Epstein, Joshua M. *Agent Zero: Toward Neurocognitive Foundations for Generative Social Science*. Princeton, NJ: Princeton University Press, 2014.

Evans, Fred. *The Multivoiced Body*. New York: Columbia University Press, 2008.

Fanon, Frantz. *Black Skins, White Masks*. Translated by Charles Markmann. New York: Grove, 2008.

———. "Letter to the Youth of Africa." In *Toward the African Revolution*, translated by Haakon Chevalie, 113–19. New York: Monthly Review Press, 1967.

Finlayson, Andrew R. "A Retrospective on Counterinsurgency Operations." https://www.cia.gov/static/df2d35f5993e5d6c2bd43922f308952d/tay-ninh-provincial-reconnaissance.pdf.

First Congress of the American Colonies. Declaration of Rights and Grievances. http://en.wikisource.org/wiki/Declaration_of_Rights_and_Grievances.

Fitzpatrick, Sheila. *The Russian Revolution*. Oxford: Oxford University Press, 1994.

Foner, Eric. *Tom Paine and Revolutionary America*. New York: Oxford University Press, 1976.

Forrester, Jay. *Principles of Systems*. Cambridge, MA: Wright-Allen, 1968.

Foucault, Michel. *Archaeology of Knowledge*. Translated by Sheridan Smith. New York: Routledge, 2002.

———. *Courage of Truth (Government of the Self and Others II)*. Translated by Graham Burchell. Lectures at the Collège de France, 1983–1984. New York: Palgrave Macmillan, 2011.

———. *Discipline and Punish*. Translated by Alan Sheridan. New York: Vintage, 1995.

———. "The Discourse on Language." In *Archaeology of Knowledge and The Discourse on Language*, 215–37. New York: Pantheon, 1972.

———. *History of Madness*. Translated by Jonathan Murphy and Jean Khalfa. London: Routledge, 2006.

———. *The History of Sexuality*. Vol. 1, *An Introduction*. Translated by Robert Hurley. New York: Vintage, 1978.

———. "Interview with Michel Foucault." In *Power*, edited by James Faubion, 239–97. Vol. 3 of *Essential Works*. New York: New Press, 1998.

———. "The Inventors of the State." In *Foucault and the Iranian Revolution: Gender and the Seductions of Islam*, by Janet Afary and Kevin Anderson, 208–9. Chicago: University of Chicago Press, 2005.

———. "Nietzsche, Genealogy, History." In *Aesthetics, Method, and Epistemology*, edited by James Faubion, 369–92. Vol. 2 of *Essential Works*. New York: Pantheon, 1998.

———. "On Popular Justice: A Discussion with Maoists." In *Power/Knowledge: Selected Interviews and Other Writings, 1972–1977*, edited by Colin Gordon, 1–36. New York: Pantheon, 1980.

———. *"Society Must Be Defended."* Edited by Mauro Bertani and Allesandro Fontana. Translated by David Macey. Lectures at the Collège de France, 1975–76. New York: Picador, 1997.

———. "So Is It Important to Think?" In *Power*, edited by James Faubion, 454–58. Vol. 3 of *Essential Works*. New York: New Press, 2001.

———. "The Subject and Power." In *Power*, edited by James Faubion, 326–48. Vol. 3 of *Essential Works*. New York: New Press, 2000.

———. "Theatricum Philosophicum." In *Aesthetics, Method, Epistemology*, edited by James Faubion, 343–68. Vol. 2 of *Essential Works*. New York: New Press, 1998.

———. "Thought of the Outside." In *Aesthetics, Method, Epistemology*, edited by James Faubion, 147–70. Vol. 2 of *Essential Works*. New York: New Press, 1998.

———. "Useless to Revolt?" In *Power*, edited by James Faubion, 449–53. Vol. 3 of *Essential Works*. New York: New Press, 2001.

———. "What Are the Iranians Dreaming About." In *Foucault and the Iranian Revolution: Gender and the Seductions of Islam*, by Janet Afary and Kevin Anderson, 203–8. Chicago: University of Chicago Press, 2005.

Foucault, Michel, and Noam Chomsky. *The Foucault-Chomsky Debate*. New York: New Press, 2006.

France 24. "Venezuelans Take to the Streets Again in Anti-Maduro Protests." January 30, 2019. https://www.france24.com/en/20190130-venezuela-anti-maduro-protests-guaido-us-sanctions.

Frazer, Elizabeth, and Kimberly Hutchings. "Politics, Violence, and Revolutionary Virtue: Reflections on Locke and Sorel." *Thesis Eleven* 97, no. 1 (2009): 46–63.

French, A. P. *Newtonian Mechanics*. London: Nelson, 1975.

Fromm, Erich. *Marx's Concept of Man*. Translated by T. Bottomore. New York: Continuum, 2004.

Fuller, Buckminster. *Synergetics: Explorations in the Geometry of Thinking*. New York: Macmillan, 1975.

Furet, François. *Interpreting the French Revolution*. Cambridge: Cambridge University Press, 1981.

Gaffney, Jennifer. "Memories of Exclusion: Hannah Arendt and the Haitian Revolution." *Philosophy and Social Criticism* 44, no. 6 (2018): 701–21.

Galbraith, John Kenneth. *The Age of Uncertainty*. New York: Houghton-Mifflin, 1977.

Garvey, Marcus. "Address to the Second UNIA Convention, New York, August 31, 1921." In *African American Political Thought*, edited by Cary Wintz, 218–23. New York: Sharpe, 1996.

———. "Motive of the NAACP Exposed." In *African American Political Thought*, edited by Cary Wintz, 224–28. New York: Sharpe, 1996.

———. "What We Believe." In *African American Political Thought*, edited by Cary Wintz, 234. New York: Sharpe, 1996.

———. "The Wonders of the White Man in Building America." In *African American Political Thought*, edited by Cary Wintz, 229–33. New York: Sharpe, 1996.

Gentile, Giovanni. *The Theory of Mind as Pure Act*. London: Macmillan, 1922.

Giap, Vo Nguyen. "The Big Victory; the Great Task." In *Strategy for Conquest: Communist Documents on Guerrilla Warfare*. Coral Gables, FL: University of Miami Press, 1970.

Goldman, Emma. "Anarchism: What It Really Stands For." In *Anarchism, and Other Essays*, 20–27. New York: Morther Earth, 1911.

Goodwin, Jeff, and Theda Skocpol. "Explaining Revolutions in the Contemporary Third World." In *Social Revolutions in the Modern World*, by Theda Skocpol, 259–78. Cambridge: Cambridge University Press, 1994.

Gough, Hugh. *The Terror in the French Revolution*. Basingstoke, UK: Palgrave Macmillan, 2010.

Gramsci, Antonio. "The Soviet Union on the Path to Communism." In *Pre-prison Writings*, translated by Virginia Cox, 301–5. Cambridge: Cambridge University Press, 1994.

Greer, Germaine. *The Female Eunuch*. New York: Harper Perennial, 1970.

Grotius, Hugo. *The Rights of War and Peace*. 3 vols. Edited by Richard Tuck. Indianapolis: Liberty Fund, 2005.

Guérin, Daniel. *Anarchism*. New York: Monthly Review Press, 1989.

Guevara, Che. *Guerrilla Warfare*. Translated by Brian Loveman and Thomas M. Davies, Jr. Wilmington, DE: SR Books, 1997.

Habermas, Jürgen. *Between Facts and Norms*. Cambridge, MA: MIT Press, 1996.

———. *Theory of Communicative Action*. Vol. 2, *Lifeworld and System: A Critique of Functionalist Reason*. Boston: Beacon, 1981.

Hacking, Ian. "Working in a New World." In *World Changes: Thomas Kuhn and the Nature of Science*, edited by Paul Horwich, 275–310. Cambridge, MA: MIT Press, 1993.

Haley, Alex. Epilogue to *The Autobiography of Malcolm X*, 441–523. New York: Ballantine, 1999.

Hallward, Peter. "Order and Event." *New Left Review*, no. 53 (2008): 97–122.

Hampton, Fred. "You Can Kill a Revolutionary, but You Can Never Kill the Revolution." *Power to the People: The Black Panther Speeches*. Fred Hampton, 2012. MP3 from Amazon Music.

Hardt, Michael, and Antonio Negri. *Commonwealth*. Cambridge, MA: Harvard University Press, 2009.

———. *Empire*. Cambridge, MA: Harvard University Press, 2000.

Harman, Graham. *Quentin Meillassoux: Philosophy in the Making*. Edinburgh: Edinburgh University Press, 2011.

Hartman, Mark. "Hobbes's Concept of Political Revolution." *Journal of the History of Ideas* 47, no. 3 (1986): 487–95.

Hartnett, Kevin. "Will Computers Redefine the Roots of Math?" *Quanta Magazine*, May 19, 2015. https://www.quantamagazine.org/univalent-foundations-redefines-mathematics-20150519/.

———. "With Category Theory, Mathematics Escapes from Equality." *Quanta Magazine*, October 10, 2019. https://www.quantamagazine.org/with-category-theory-mathematics-escapes-from-equality-20191010/.

Haven, Kendall F. *Voices of the American Revolution: Stories of Men, Women, and Children Who Forged Our Nation*. Englewood, CO: Libraries Unlimited, 2000.

Hegel, Georg Wilhelm Friedrich. *Elements of the Philosophy of Right*. Edited by Allen W. Wood. Translated by H. B. Nisbet. Cambridge: Cambridge University Press, 1991.

———. *Phenomenology of Spirit.* Translated by Arnold V. Miller. Oxford: Oxford University Press, 1976.

———. *Political Writings.* Edited by Laurence Dickey and H. B. Nisbet. Tranlsated by H. B. Nisbet. Cambridge: Cambridge University Press, 2004.

Heilbrunn, Jacob. "Interview with Konstantin Remchukov: Moscow Election Protests Reflect a 'Stark' Generational Shift." *National Interest*, July 29, 2019. https://nationalinterest.org/feature/interview-konstantin-remchukov-moscow-election-protests-reflect-%E2%80%9Cstark%E2%80%9D-generational-shift.

Hickey, Michael. "July–October 1917." In *Competing Voices from the Russian Revolution*, edited by Michael Hickey, 263–76. Santa Barbara, CA: Greenwood, 2011.

———. "Provincial White Collar Employees and Educated Professionals in March 1917." In *Competing Voices from the Russian Revolution*, edited by Michael Hickey, 133–35. Santa Barbara, CA: Greenwood, 2011.

Hoang, Van Thai. "Some Aspects of Guerrilla Warfare in Vietnam." In *Strategy for Conquest: Communist Documents on Guerrilla Warfare*, edited by Jay Mallin, 237–62. Coral Gables, FL: University of Miami Press, 1970.

Hobbes, Thomas. *Leviathan*. Harmondsworth, UK: Penguin, 1968.

Hobsbawm, Eric. *Primitive Rebels*. New York: Norton, 1959.

Holland, John H. *Adaptation in Natural and Artificial Systems*. Cambridge, MA: MIT Press, 1992.

———. *Emergence*. Cambridge, MA: Perseus, 1998.

———. *Hidden Order*. Reading, MA: Helix, 1995.

Hoock, Holger. *Scars of Independence: America's Violent Birth*. New York: Crown, 2017.

Horkheimer, Max. "Materialism and Metaphysics." In *Critical Theory: Selected Essays*, translated by Matthew O'Connell, 10–46. New York: Continuum, 2002.

———. "Means and Ends." In *Critical Theory: The Essential Readings*, edited by David Ingram and Julia Simon-Ingram, 36–48. St. Paul, MN: Paragon House, 1992.

———. "Traditional and Critical Theory." In *Critical Theory: The Essential Readings*, edited by David Ingram and Julia Simon-Ingram. 239–54. St. Paul, MN: Paragon House, 1992.

Horne, Alistair. *A Savage War of Peace: Algeria, 1952–1962.* New York: New York Review of Books, 1977.

Hoyningen-Huene, Paul. *Reconstructing Scientific Revolutions: Thomas S. Kuhn's Philosophy of Science*. Translated by Alexander T. Levine. Chicago: University of Chicago Press, 1993.

Huang, Yiju. "On Transference: Badiou and the Chinese Cultural Revolution," *Comparative Literature Studies* 52, no. 1 (2015): 29–46.

Hughes, Thomas P. *American Genesis: A Century of Invention and Technological Enthusiasm*. Chicago: University of Chicago Press, 1989.

Human Rights Watch. *Cuba's Repressive Machinery*. New York: Human Rights Watch, 1999.

Hume, David. *Moral Philosophy*. Indianapolis: Hackett, 2006.

———. *Political Essays*. Cambridge: Cambridge University Press, 1994.

Israel, Jonathan. *Revolution of the Mind: Radical Enlightenment and the Intellectual Origins of Modern Democracy*. Princeton, NJ: Princeton University Press, 2010.

Jay, Martin. *The Dialectical Imagination*. Berkeley: University of California Press, 1973.

———. *Marxism and Totality: The Adventures of a Concept from Lucács to Habermas*. Berkeley: University of California Press, 1984.

Jefferson, Thomas. Declaration of Independence. In *Sources and Documents Illustrating the American Revolution, 1764–1788, and the Formation of the Federal Constitution*, edited by Samuel Eliot Morison. Oxford: Clarendon Press, 1961.

John Brown Society. *An Introduction to the Black Panther Party*. http://archive.lib.msu.edu/DMC/AmRad/introblackpanther.pdf.

Johnston, Adrian. *Badiou, Žižek, and Political Transformation*. Evanston, IL: Northwestern University Press, 2009.

Jones, LeRoi. "The Last Days of the American Empire." In *Home: Social Essays*, 214–35. New York: Morrow, 1966.

———. "What Does Nonviolence Mean?" In *Home: Social Essays*, 155–78. New York: Morrow, 1966.

Kaiman, Jonathan. "Hong Kong's Umbrella Revolution." *Guardian*, September 30, 2014. https://www.theguardian.com/world/2014/sep/30/-sp-hong-kong-umbrella-revolution-pro-democracy-protests.

Kay, Jane Holtz. *Asphalt Nation*. Oakland: University of California Press, 1997.

Knudsen, J. M., and P. G. Hjorth. *Elements of Newtonian Mechanics: Including Nonlinear Dynamics*. Heidelberg: Springer, 1995.

Koellner, Peter. "The Continuum Hypothesis." In *Stanford Encyclopedia of Philosophy*, Spring 2019 ed. Edited by Edward N. Zalta. https://plato.stanford.edu/archives/spr2019/entries/continuum-hypothesis/.

Kojève, Alexandre. *Introduction to the Reading of Hegel*. Ithaca, NY: Cornell University Press, 1969.

Kołakowski, Leszek. *The Founders*. Vol. 1 of *Main Currents of Marxism: Its Rise, Growth, and Dissolution*, translated by P. S. Falla. Oxford: Clarendon Press, 1978.

Kuhn, Thomas. *The Structure of Scientific Revolutions*. Chicago: University of Chicago Press, 1962.

La Caze, Marguerite. "At the Intersection: Kant, Derrida, and the Relation between Ethics and Politics." *Political Theory* 35, no. 6 (2007): 781–805.

Ladyman, James, James Lambert, and Karoline Wiesner. "What Is a Complex System?" *European Journal for Philosophy of Science* 3, no. 1 (2013): 33–67.

Large, William. "Spinoza for Our Time: Politics and Modernity" *Contemporary Political Theory* 16 (2017): 161–64.

Lefebvre, Georges. *The French Revolution*. Translated by Elizabeth Moss Evanson. London: Routledge, 1962.

Lenin, Vladimir Ilyich. "Appeal to Party by Delegates to Unity Congress." In *Collected Works*, 10:310–16. Moscow: Progress Publishers, 1962.

———. "Decree on Separation of Church and State." February 5, 1918. https://www.marxists.org/history/ussr/events/revolution/documents/1918/02/5.htm.

———. "Karl Marx." In *Collected Works*, 21:43–91. Moscow: Progress Publishers, 1960. https://www.marxists.org/archive/lenin/works/cw/volume21.htm.

———. "Socialism and Religion." In *Collected Works*, 10:83–87. Moscow: Progress Publishers, 2010. https://www.marxists.org/archive/lenin/works/1905/dec/03.htm.

———. *State and Revolution*. New York: International Publishers, 1932.

———. *State and Revolution*. Peking: Foreign Language Press, 1970.

———. "The Taylor System: Man's Enslavement by the Machine." Translated by Bernard Isaacs and Joe Fineberg. In *Collected Works*, 20:152–54 Moscow: Progress, 1972. https://www.marxists.org/archive/lenin/works/cw/volume20.htm.

———. *What Is to Be Done?* New York: International Publishers, 1929.

Levy, "Yank" Bert. *Guerrilla Warfare*, Boulder: Paladin Press, 1964.

Lewis, Peter J. *Quantum Ontology: A Guide to the Metaphysics of Quantum Mechanics*. Oxford: Oxford University Press, 2016.

Lock, F. P. *Edmund Burke*. Vol. 1, *1730–1784*. Oxford: Clarendon Press, 1998.

Locke, John. *Second Treatise of Government*. Edited by C. B. Macpherson. Indianapolis: Hackett, 1980.

Lorenz, Edward N. "Deterministic Nonperiodic Flow." *Journal of the Atmospheric Sciences* 20, no. 2 (1963): 130–41.

Lukács, Georg. "Critical Observations on Rosa Luxembourg's 'Critique of the Russian revolution.'" In *History and Class Consciousness*. London: Merlin, 1971.

Lynch, Michael. *The Chinese Civil War, 1945–49*. Oxford: Osprey, 2010.

MacFarquhar, Roderick, and Michael Schoenhals. *Mao's Last Revolution*. Cambridge, MA: Harvard University Press, 2005.

Mandela, Nelson. *Long Walk to Freedom*. Boston: Little, Brown, 1994.

Mao, Zedong [Tse-tung]. "Be a True Revolutionary." In *Selected Works of Mao Tse-tung*, 5:37–40. Peking: Foreign Language Press, 1965.

———. "On Contradiction." In *Selected Works of Mao Tse-tung*, 1:311–46. Peking: Foreign Language Press, 1965.

———. *On New Democracy*. Peking: Foreign Language Press, 1940.

———. "On Practice." In *Selected Works of Mao Tse-tung*, 1:295–310. Peking: Foreign Language Press, 1965.

———. "On Guerrilla Warfare." https://www.marxists.org/reference/archive/mao/works/1937/guerrilla-warfare/.

———. "Win the Masses in Their Millions for the Anti-Japanese National United Front." In *Selected Works of Mao Tse-tung*, 1:285–94. Peking: Foreign Language Press, 1965.

Marable, Manning. *Black Liberation in Conservative America*. Boston: South End Press, 1997.

———. *Malcolm X: A Life of Reinvention*. New York: Viking, 2011.

———. "The Paradox of Black Reform." In *Speaking Truth to Power: Essays on Race, Resistance, and Radicalism*, 38–48. Boulder, CO: Westview Press, 1996.

———. "Remaking American Marxism." In *Speaking Truth to Power: Essays on Race, Resistance, and Radicalism*, 459–68. Boulder, CO: Westview Press, 1996.

Marchart, Oliver. *Post-foundational Political Thought: Political Difference in Nancy, Lefort, Badiou, and Laclau*. Edinburgh: Edinburgh University Press, 2007.

Marighella, Carlos. "From the 'Minimanual.'" In *The Guerrilla Reader*. Philadelphia: Temple University Press, 1977.

———. "How the Urban Guerrilla Lives." http://www.marxists.org/archive/marighella-carlos/1969/06/minimanual-urban-guerrilla/ch03.htm.

Markoff, John. *The Abolition of Feudalism: Peasants, Lords, and Legislators in the French Revolution*. University Park: Pennsylvania State University Press, 1996.

Martel, James R. *The One and Only Law: Walter Benjamin and the Second Commandment*. Ann Arbor: University of Michigan Press, 2014.

Marx, Karl. "After the Revolution: Marx Debates Bakunin." In Tucker, *The Marx-Engels Reader*, 542–48.

———. *Capital*. Vol. 1. London: Penguin, 1976.

———. "*Capital*, Volume Three." In Tucker, *The Marx-Engels Reader*, 439–42.

———. "The Civil War in France." In Tucker, *The Marx-Engels Reader*, 617–52.

———. "The Coming Upheaval." In Tucker, *The Marx-Engels Reader*, 218–19.

———. "Critique of the Gotha Program." In *Karl Marx: Selected Writings*, edited by David McLellan, 525–41. Oxford: Oxford University Press, 1977.

———. *Economic and Philosophic Manuscripts of 1844*. Translated by Martin Milligan. New York: Prometheus, 1988.

———. "Eighteenth Brumaire of Louis Bonaparte." In Tucker, *The Marx-Engels Reader*, 594–617.

———. "German Ideology." In Tucker, *The Marx-Engels Reader*, 146–202.

———. *The German Ideology*. New York: Prometheus, 1998.

———. *Grundrisse: Foundations of the Critique of Political Economy*. Translated by Martin Nicolaus. New York: Vintage, 1973.

———. *The Letters of Karl Marx*. Translated by Saul K. Padover. Engewood Cliffs, NJ: Prentice Hall, 1979.

———. "On the Jewish Question." In Tucker, *The Marx-Engels Reader*, 26–52.

———. "The Possibility of Non-violent Revolution." In Tucker, *The Marx-Engels Reader*, 522–24.

———. "Society and Economy in History." In Tucker, *The Marx-Engels Reader*, 136–42.

———. "Speech at the Anniversary of the *People's Paper*." In Tucker, *The Marx-Engels Reader*, 577–78.

———. "Theses on Feuerbach." In *The German Ideology*, 569–71. New York: Prometheus, 1998.

Marx, Karl, and Friedrich Engels. *Manifesto of the Communist Party*. In *Economic and Philosophic Manuscripts of 1844*, by Karl Marx, 203–43. New York: Prometheus, 1988.

"Massachusetts' Assembly Protests the Stamp Act (1765)." Alpha History. https://alphahistory.com/americanrevolution/massachusetts-assembly-protests-stamp-act-1765/.

May, Todd. "Is Post-structuralist Political Theory Anarchist?" *Philosophy and Social Criticism* 15, no. 2 (1989): 167–82.

McCoy, Alfred. *The Politics of Heroin in Southeast Asia*. New York: Harper and Row, 1972.

McDade, Jesse. "The Ethicality of Revolution." *Social Praxis* 1, no. 3 (1973): 291–98.

McKay, Robert. "Many Body Quantum Mechanics." In *Nonlinear Dynamics and Chaos: Where Do We Go from Here?*, edited by John Hogan, Alan Champneys, Bernd Krauskopf, Mario di Bernardo, Eddie Wilson, Hinke Osinga, and Martin Homer. Bristol: Institute of Physics Publishing, 2003.

McKibben, Bill, ed. *The Global Warming Reader*. New York: Penguin, 2012.

McLellan, David. *Marxism after Marx*. New York: Harper and Row, 1979.

McLoughlin, Barry. "Mass Operations of the NKVD, 1937–1938: A Survey." In *Stalin's Terror: High Politics and Mass Repression in the Soviet Union*, edited by Barry McLoughlin and Kevin McDermott,118–52. Basingstoke, UK: Palgrave Macmillan, 2002.

McPhee, Peter. *The French Revolution, 1789–1799*. Oxford: Oxford University Press, 2002.

Meillassoux, Quentin, *After Finitude: An Essay on the Necessity of Contingency*. London: Continuum, 2009.

Merleau-Ponty, Maurice. *Adventures of the Dialectic*. Translated by Joseph Bien. Evanston, IL: Northwestern University Press, 1973.

———. "Indirect Language and the Voices of Silence." In *Signs*, translated by Richard C. McCleary, 39–82. Evanston, IL: Northwestern University Press, 1964.

———. *Phenomenology of Perception*. New York: Routledge, 1968.

———. *The Visible and the Invisible*. Translated by Alphonso Lingis. Evanston, IL: Northwestern University Press, 1968.

Me Too. "#MeToo Masculinity, Male Privilege and Consent Toolkit." Accessed February 2020. https://metoomvmt.org/wp-content/uploads/2020/05/1.5.3_Masculinity-Male-Privilege-Consent-Toolkit_TOOLKIT_V2.pdf /.

Miller, Mary Ashburn. *A Natural History of Revolution: Violence and Nature in the French Revolutionary Imagination, 1789–1794*. Ithaca, NY: Cornell University Press, 2011.

Mills, Charles. *The Racial Contract*. Ithaca, NY: Cornell University Press, 1997.

Mintz, Samuel I. *The Hunting of Leviathan: Seventeenth Century Reactions to the Materialism and Moral Philosophy of Thomas Hobbes*. Cambridge: Cambridge University Press, 1962.

Mitchell, Melanie. *Complexity: A Guided Tour*. Oxford: Oxford University Press, 2009.

Montesquieu, Charles de Secondat, Baron de. *The Spirit of the Laws*. Translated and edited by Anne M. Cohler, Basia Carolyn Miller, and Harold Samuel Stone. Cambridge: Cambridge University Press, 1989.

Moots, Glenn A., and Phillip Hamilton, eds. *Justifying Revolution: Law, Virtue, and Violence in the American War of Independence*. Norman: University of Oklahoma Press, 2018.

Moran, Stacey. "Quantum Decoherence." *Philosophy Today* 63, no. 4 (2019): 1051–68.

Nail, Thomas. "Deleuze, Occupy, and the Actuality of Revolution." *Theory and Event* 16, no. 1 (2013): 20–35.

Newman, C. M., and D. L. Stein. "The Metastate Approach to Thermodynamic Chaos." *Physical Review E* 55, no. 5 (1997): 5194.

———. "Spatial Inhomogeneity and Thermodynamic Chaos." *Physical Review Letters* 76, no. 25 (1996): 4821–24.

Newton, Huey. "In Defense of Self-Defense." In *The Modern African American Political Thought Reader*. Edited by Angela Jones. New York: Routledge, 2013.

Newton, Isaac. *Principia Mathematica*. New York, 1846.

Nietzsche, Friedrich. *Beyond Good and Evil: Prelude to a Philosophy of the Future*. Cambridge: Cambridge University Press, 2002.

———. *Twilight of the Idols*. Edited by Aaron Ridley and Judith Norman. Cambridge: Cambridge University Press, 2005.

———. *Writings from the Late Notebooks*. Cambridge: Cambridge University Press, 2003.

Nirenberg, Ricardo L., and David Nirenberg. "Badiou's Number: A Critique of Mathematics as Ontology." *Critical Inquiry* 37, no. 4 (2011): 583–614.

Nozick, Robert. *Anarchy, State, and Utopia*. Oxford: Blackwell, 1974.

Nuyen, A. T. "Adorno and the French Post-structuralists on the Other of Reason." *Journal of Speculative Philosophy*, n.s., 4, no. 4 (1990): 310–22.

O'Gorman, Frank. *Edmund Burke*. Vol. 2 of *Political Thinkers*. London: Routledge, 1973.

Osborne, Peter. *How to Read Marx*. New York: Norton, 2005.

Osinsky, Pavel. "Modernization Interrupted? Total War, State Breakdown, and the Communist Conquest of China." *Sociological Quarterly* 51, no. 4 (2010): 576–99.

Page, Scott E. *Diversity and Complexity*. Princeton, NJ: Princeton University Press, 2011.

Paine, Thomas. *Common Sense*. In *Collected Writings*, edited by Eric Foner, 5–59. New York: Library of America, 1955.

———. *The Rights of Man*. In *Collected Writings*, edited by Eric Foner, 435–687. New York: Library of America, 1955.

———. *Rights of Man*. In *The Complete Writings of Thomas Paine*, edited by Eric Foner, 243–344. New York: Citadel, 1945.

Pateman, Carole. *The Disorder of Women*. Stanford, CA: Stanford University Press, 1989.

———. *The Sexual Contract*. Stanford, CA: Stanford University Press, 1988.

Peraeus, David. "The American Military and the Lessons of Vietnam: A Study of Military Influence and the Use of Force in the Post-Vietnam Era." PhD diss., Princeton University, 1987.

Pluth, Ed. *Alain Badiou*. Cambridge, UK: Polity, 2010.

Poincaré, Henri. *Science and Hypothesis*. London: Cosimo, 1914.

———. *The Value of Science*. New York: Dover, 1958.

Poulantzas, Nicos. "Is There a Crisis in Marxism." In *The Poulantzas Reader*, 377–86. London: Verso, 2008.

Pustay, John. *Counterinsurgency Warfare*. New York: Free Press, 1965.

Rabe, Stephen G. *Eisenhower and Latin America: The Foreign Policy of Anticommunism*. Chapel Hill: University of North Carolina Press, 1988.

Rancière, Jacques. *Dissensus: Politics and Aesthetics*. Edited and translated by Steven Corcoran. New York: Continuum, 2010.

Rawls, John. *Political Liberalism*. New York: Columbia University Press, 1993.

———. *A Theory of Justice*. Cambridge, MA: Harvard University Press, 1971.

"Recommendations of the Findings and Recommendations Committee." Youth Leadership Conference, Shaw College, Raleigh, NC, April 1960. http://www.crmvet.org/docs/6004_shaw_recommendations.pdf.

Reid, Herbert G. "Critical Phenomenology and the Dialectical Foundations of Social Change." *Dialectical Anthropology* 2, no. 2 (1977): 107–30.

Reports Branch of the Central Phoenix Directorate in Saigon. "Phoenix Fact Sheet." https://nsarchive.files.wordpress.com/2010/11/phoenix.pdf.

Reynolds, Larry J. *Righteous Violence: Revolution, Slavery, and the American Renaissance*. Athens: University of Georgia Press, 2011.

Robespierre, Maximilien. "An Idealized View of the *Journee* of 10 August: Robespierre's Account in *Le Defenseur du Peuple*." In *The French Revolution Sourcebook*, edited by John Hardman, 147–50. London: Arnold, 1981.

———. "Undated Memorandum of Robespierre, June 1793." In *The French Revolution Sourcebook*, edited by John Hardman, 163. London: Arnold, 1981.

Robinson, James. "The Cahiers of 1789." In *Readings in European History*, edited by James Robinson, 2:379–400. Boston: Ginn, 1906.

———. "The Decree Abolishing the Feudal System." In *Readings in European History*, edited by James Robinson, 2:405–9. Boston: Ginn and Company, 1906.

Rousseau, Jean-Jacques. *The Social Contract*. Translated by Maurice Cranston. London: Penguin, 1968.

Rowan, Carl. "Martin Luther King's Tragic Decision." *Reader's Digest* 91, no. 545 (1967): 37–42.

Rustin, Bayard. "The Negro and Nonviolence." In *The Modern African American Political Thought Reader*, edited by Angela Jones, 158–60. New York: Routledge, 2013.

Said, Edward. *Orientalism*. New York: Vintage, 1978.

Sartre, Jean-Paul. *Being and Nothingness*. Translated by Hazel Barnes. New York: Washington Square Press, 1956.

———. *Critique of Dialectical Reason*. Translated by Alan Sheridan-Smith. New York: Verso, 2004.

Schopenhauer, Arthur. *World as Will and Representation*. Vol. 1. Cambridge: Cambridge University Press, 2010.

Schram, Stuart. "Mao Tse-tung and Secret Societies." In *Mao Zedong and the Chinese Revolution*, vol. 1, edited by Gregor Benton, 1–13. London: Routledge, 2008.

———. *The Thought of Mao Tse-tung*. Cambridge: University of Cambridge, 1989.

Shabazz, Attallah. Forward to *The Autobiography of Malcolm X*. New York: Ballantine, 1999.

Shapiro, Gilbert, and John Markoff. *Revolutionary Demands: A Content Analysis of the Cahiers de Doléances*. Stanford, CA: Stanford University Press, 1998.

Singer, Brian. "Montesquieu on Power: Beyond Checks and Balances." In *Montesquieu and His Legacy*, edited by Rebecca Kingston, 97–114. Albany: State University of New York Press, 2009.

Smith, Adam. *An Inquiry into the Nature and Causes of the Wealth of Nations*. Indianapolis: Liberty Classics, 1976.

Solnit, David. "The Battle of the Story of the Battle of Seattle." In *The Battle of the Story of the Battle of Seattle*, 5–56. Edinburgh: AK Press, 2009.

Southern Christian Leadership Conference. *Constitution and Bylaws of the Southern Christian Leadership Conference*. http://www.crmvet.org/docs/sclc_const.pdf.

Spinoza, Baruch. *Theological-Political Treatise*. Edited by Jonathan Israel. Cambridge: Cambridge University Press, 2007.

Stalin, Joseph V. *History of the Communist Party of the Soviet Union*. Translated by Salil Sen and Brian Reid. New York: International Publishers, 2008. https://www.marxists.org/reference/archive/stalin/works/1939/x01/index.htm.

———. "Results of the First Five-Year Plan." In *Works*, vol. 13. Moscow: Foreign Languages Publishing House, 1954. https://www.marxists.org/reference/archive/stalin/works/1933/01/07.htm.

Stone, Meighan. "Five Questions with Denise Ho: From the Front Lines of the Hong Kong Protests." Blog post, Council on Foreign Relations, June 13, 2019. https://www.cfr.org/blog/five-questions-denise-ho-front-lines-hong-kong-protests.

Strogatz, Steven H. *Nonlinear Dynamics and Chaos*. Reading, MA: Perseus, 1994.

Swamy, Subramanian. "Rural Communes in China." *Indian Economic Review* 3, no 1 (1968): 49–55.

Tsoukas, Haridimos. "The Validity of Idiographic Research Explanations." *Academy of Management Review* 14, no. 4 (1989): 551–61.

Tuck, Richard. "Grotius and Selden." In *Cambridge History of Political Thought, 1450–1700*, edited by J. H. Burns, 499–529. Cambridge: University of Cambridge Press, 1991.

Tucker, Robert C., ed. *The Marx-Engels Reader*. New York: Norton, 1978.

Tully, James. "Locke." In *Cambridge History of Political Thought, 1450–1700*, edited by J. H. Burns, 616–52. Cambridge: University of Cambridge Press, 1991.

Volkov, S. "On the Samara Provincial Peasant Congress (Regarding the Land Question)." In *Competing Voices from the Russian Revolution*, edited by Michael Hickey, 153–55. Santa Barbara: Greenwood, 2011.

Washington, Booker T. "Letter to President Theodore Roosevelt, December 26, 1904." In *African American Political Thought, 1890–1930*, edited by Cary Wintz, 40–41. New York: Sharpe, 1996.

———. "Letter to William Howard Taft. June 4, 1908." In *African American Political Thought, 1890–1930*, edited by Cary Wintz, 64–66. New York: Sharpe, 1996.

———. "The Negro and the Signs of Civilization." In *African American Political Thought, 1890–1930*, edited by Cary Wintz, 41–43. New York: Sharpe, 1996.

———. "A Protest against Lynching." In *African American Political Thought, 1890–1930*, edited by Cary Wintz, 52–53. New York: Sharpe, 1996.

Weeks, Theodore R. *Across the Revolutionary Divide: Russia and the USSR, 1861–1945*. Chichester, UK: Wiley-Blackwell, 2011.

Weisstein, Eric. "Indeterminate." In *MathWorld: A Wolfram Web Resource*. https://mathworld.wolfram.com/Indeterminate.html.

Wheen, Francis. *Marx: A Life*. New York: Norton, 1999.

Wise, Tim. "F.A.Q.s." Accessed January 2014. timwise.org.

Wollstonecraft, Mary. *Vindication of the Rights of Men*. Oxford: Oxford University Press, 1993.

Wood, Gordon S. *The American Revolution: A History*. New York: Modern Library, 2002.

Wren, Daniel A., and Arthur G. Bedeian. "The Taylorization of Lenin: Rhetoric or Reality?" *International Journal of Social Economics* 31, no. 3 (2004): 287–99.

X, Malcolm. *By Any Means Necessary*. New York: Pathfinder, 1970.

———. *The End of White World Supremacy*. New York: Arcade, 1971.

———. *Malcolm X Speaks*. New York: Grove, 1965.

Yack, Bernard. *The Longing for Total Revolution*. Princeton, NJ: Princeton University Press, 1986.

Yancy, George. *Black Bodies, White Gazes*. Lanham, MD: Rowman and Littlefield, 2008.

Ypi, Lea. "On Revolution in Kant and Marx." *Political Theory* 42, no. 3 (2014): 262–87.

Zamyatin, Yevgeny. "On Literature, Revolution, Entropy, and Other Matters." In *A Soviet Heretic: Essays*, translated by Mirra Ginsburg, 107–113. Chicago: University of Chicago Press, 1974.

Zinn, Howard. *SNCC: The New Abolitionists*. Boston: Beacon, 1964.

———. "The Spirit of Rebellion." In *The Zinn Reader.* New York: Seven Stories, 1997.

Žižek, Slavoj. *In Defense of Lost Causes*. New York: Verso, 2008.

———. *The Indivisible Remainder*. London: Verso, 1998.

———. *Less than Nothing*. London: Verso, 2012.

———. *The Parallax View*. Cambridge, MA: MIT Press, 2005.

Zolli, Andrew, and Ann Marie Healy. *Resilience: Why Things Bounce Back*. New York: Simon and Schuster, 2012.

Index

www.ingramcontent.com/pod-product-compliance
Lightning Source LLC
LaVergne TN
LVHW040159080826
844660LV00001B/34